CHICAGO HEIST

John O'Brien
and
Edward Baumann

and books

South Bend, Indiana

CHICAGO HEIST

and books
702 South Michigan, South Bend, Indiana 46618

ISBN 0-89708-053-X

First Edition

Printed in the United States of America

Additional copies available:
    the distributors
    702 South Michigan
    South Bend, IN 46618

To Ray Stratton
and Charlie Marzano

Acknowledgments

The authors express their gratitude and appreciation to Russell Hardt and Robert Husted, former Purolator executives, for their notes and recollections of the big heist; to the Chicago Police Department, Illinois Legislative Investigating Commission, and to the Federal Bureau of Investigation, for making their records of the Purolator case available; and to *The Chicago Tribune* for the use of its reference files.

Contents

The CHICAGO HEIST is....

The true story of $4,374,398.96, and:

Ralph Ronald Marrera	Born June 17, 1945
Pasquale Charles Marzano	Born October 4, 1934
Peter James Gushi	Born July 15, 1927
James Andrew Maniatis	Born March 28, 1916
William Anthony Marzano	Born January 20, 1943
Luigi Michael DiFonzo	Born December 19, 1947

Supporting Cast:

Ramon (Ray) Stratton	Special Agent, F.B.I.
Joseph I. Woods	The Purolator Man
Charles Siragusa	Illinois Legislative Investigative Commission
Martin Pollakov	Siragusa's Stoolie
George Doyle	Undercover Agent
Wayne Kerstetter	Illinois Bureau of Investigation
Derrick Tricker	British West Indies Detective
Karen Tricker	His Blonde Wife
Angela Hughes	Alarm Board Monitor
Bernard Carey	Cook County State's Attorney
James R. Thompson	United States District Attorney
Michael King James Breen Gordon Nash	The Prosecutors
Julius Lucius Echeles	Defense Attorney
Joseph Oteri Thomas Troy Martin Weinberg	The Boston Lawyers
Judge William J. Bauer	Trial Judge

CHAPTER 1

Something big's about to happen.

Arcing into its half-way phase, the Sunday night moon of October 20, 1974, glowed in the Chicago sky as clear as a freshly-cleaned window pane. Here and there, flickering across the heavens like tiny moving stars, were the strobing lights of giant jetliners with their cargoes of anonymous passengers, gliding silently in and out of O'Hare International, the "world's busiest airport."

Far below the pulsing night lights of shooting-star traffic, down amid the concrete and steel structures of the lusty city, a drama was about to unfold which, by early morning, would command newspaper headlines and television bulletins throughout the world. The event would earn a place in the annals of organized crime as one of the most imaginative, lucrative, and incredibly bungled cash thefts ever executed in American history.

From within the plush, comfortable, glass-enclosed observation deck of the John Hancock Center, towering nearly one quarter mile above Michigan Avenue, sightseers could look out over an awkward box-like structure on the southeast corner of LaSalle and Huron Streets, only several blocks across the Chicago River from the Loop. It was a squat, yellow-brick building imbedded in a neighborhood etched deep with the city's stormy crime history. This was the Purolator Security building on the near North Side, within shouting distance of Holy Name Cathedral, which still bore bullet scars from the Roaring Twenties. Across from the Cathedral once stood Dion O'Bannion's Flower Shop, where on the morning of November 10, 1924, three swarthy men pumped five bullets into the altar boy turned rum-runner. Also nearby, stood the residence of John Cardinal Cody, Roman Catholic Archbishop of Chicago, who had recently become a holdup victim in his own neighborhood.

A short block west of the Purolator warehouse stretched the bustling Old Town nightlife strip on Wells Street, while a bit to the east shimmered the glitter-gulch of Rush Street. From the front of the Purolator building, the parking lot of Chicago's 18th District Police Station was visible, with its array of blue-and-white squad cars neatly asleep behind the station.

Few would imagine that millions of dollars flowed virtually unnoticed to and from the two-story structure in the rather seedy neighborhood of cheap hotels, antique shops and cut-rate saloons.

The Purolator Security Building had two single-story garages with wide overhead doors, through which rolled the familiar red, white and blue armored trucks, hauling their treasure cargoes in and out of the interior vault area. Within the vault room were two large and separate concrete money caves, each the size of a two-car garage and respectively known as the "East" and "West" vaults because of their locations from the center of the money warehouse.

Each vault had five separate alarm systems, including alarms for fire and sound. Furthermore, the systems were connected to a Purolator competitor, Wells Fargo, four blocks away. Thus the two firms constantly cross-monitored one another for added security.

Purolator, like other armored car services, carried vast amounts of cash from one client to another. This money was frequently held overnight within the vaults during the transfer process to a customer's home bank. Unlike many other businesses, every day was a working day at Purolator — the money kept rolling in and out.

Several large Chicago banks, including the Federal Reserve System, received cash daily from other banks and businesses in the area. The armored truck runs were made throughout the day, shuttling funds back to the Purolator warehouse where they were checked into the vault room and then sorted by package for the money's ultimate destination. Coins were generally held in the West Vault, while all paper money was stashed in the East Vault. All of it was placed in large "tankers," or hand propelled carts, some four feet high with hinged tops. These carts resembled old-time miners' tram cars except they ran without tracks.

All money received during a working day which was destined for the Federal Reserve, for example, was placed in a labeled tanker after being received in the vault room. The tanker was locked and sealed once the day's funds had been accumulated.

On the following bank working day the tanker was wheeled into an armored truck and transported from Purolator to the Fed, where it was unsealed and its contents distributed. This procedure was the same for the various large commercial downtown banks. Thus, at any given time, Purolator held millions of someone else's cash within its concrete vault rooms.

Naturally the money pile grew on weekends, when banks and most businesses are normally closed. Currency and coins delivered on a Friday, Saturday, or Sunday from stores, service stations and the local race track were kept in the warehouse vaults until the following Monday morning when the banks reopened.

It was business as usual for the Purolator staff on that cool October weekend, with the exception of the annual employees bash Saturday night at Johnny Weigelt's on Damen Avenue. The night before, Friday, October 18, three significant tankers marked Central National Bank, Exchange National Bank and Jewel Food Company were literally packed with millions of dollars. The Central and Exchange tankers were placed in the rear of the East Vault and sealed to await delivery. The routine was somewhat different with the Jewel tanker, since Purolator handled the Jewel Food account as the agent for Merchandise National Bank of Chicago. Its armored trucks visited each of the city's 40 Jewel stores daily to pick-up grocery money in sealed canvas bags.

These "deposits" were brought to the Purolator warehouse, counted, and tabulated. After recording the totals for the Merchandise National Bank, the money was bundled into the Jewel Food Company tanker where it *remained* in the Purolator vault, although it was on record as a deposit in Jewel's account at the bank. Each Jewel store would advise Purolator of the denominations needed to transact the next day's business. Purolator counted, dispensed and delivered these to the appropriate stores. Again, the bank was informed so the "withdrawal" would be registered on the Jewel account.

Another large Purolator customer at this time was the Hawthorne Race Course in nearby Cicero. At the end of each day, after the last horse had crossed the finish line, Hawthorne employees completed a count of monies taken in. Track officials placed the funds in sealed footlockers and sealed money bags which were then picked up by the Purolator armored car crew and taken to the warehouse for delivery to the bank on the next working day. The sealed footlockers were delivered intact, while the loose, sealed money bags were placed into the First National tanker along with other bags destined for that bank.

Hawthorne's 1974 season ended that Saturday night, and, as always, Charles McCann, the track's money manager, placed the largest bills in a silver footlocker which he secured with his personal padlock. This footlocker was always kept in the East Vault until the following Monday when McCann would personally open the lock after delivery to the First National Bank.

The horse race receipts of that night totalled over $1.7 million. It was stashed into the silver footlocker and two red tankers which were rolled into the Purolator truck at 8 o'clock. Fourteen minutes later, the seven mile run back to the warehouse was completed, with the truck clocking in at 8:24.

There were 24 Purolator employees on duty that evening, working efficiently in order to make the company dance. After the race track take was securely stowed within the East Vault, employee Luther West placed it under combination and set all alarms "on" at 9:26 p.m. With the entire operation under the watchful eye of Purolator's vault coordinator, Phillip Layne, the money was considered "as good as in the bank" according to the company's carefully planned logistics.

The party-minded crew which pitched in and helped load the vault that previous evening was in sharp contrast to Purolator's skeleton Sunday evening staff, when indeed very little business was transacted.

Earlier that evening, clocking-in 40 minutes before he was due, Ralph Marrera came to work his Sunday night guard shift at 5:50 p.m.

Ralph Ronald Marrera at 29, was a boyishly handsome, stylish, olive-skinned dude from one of Chicago's western suburbs. He was a classic nobody — a $4.30-an-hour night watchman for one of the biggest money-handling outfits in the country. Before the night was over, however, he would become the key figure in a $4.3 million mystery that would become international in scope.

Already on duty when he arrived was Angela Hughes, an attractive South Sider whose job involved monitoring the Purolator nerve center alarm board. Angela was due in at 4 p.m. that day, but punched in 45 minutes late. She was scheduled to work until midnight.

The only other Purolator employee working before midnight that evening was a "runner" positioned outside the warehouse, and in radio contact with the alarm board monitor.

The staff of three, plus the back-up security of Wells Fargo monitoring, made the Purolator money warehouse a seemingly secure bastion from any outside meddling.

Company policy dictated that Purolator's armored truck guards wear snappy blue uniforms to compliment their smart red, white and blue vans. However, the policy did not apply to employees not in customer contact. And as an unseen inside man, Marrera was privileged to work in casual civilian attire. This night he showed up toting a portable television set, so he wouldn't miss his favorite Sunday program, "McMillan and Wife," a popular detective drama series starring Rock Hudson. His early arrival surprised Robert Woolsey, the guard whom Marrera was scheduled to relieve at half-past six.

"Hey, Ralphie!" chuckled Woolsey, "What's the matter? How come you're so early — your old lady kick you out or something?"

"Naw, I just came in early cause I had nothin' else to do. What's it to you?" Marrera answered matter-of-factly.

Ralphie set up his TV set, paced about impatiently, and at 6 p.m. turned to Woolsey and asked: "What the hell are you still hanging around for, Bob? Why don't you split for home?" Then, as the astonished Woolsey asked, " What the hell are you doing?" Marrera unexpectedly grabbed his fellow guard's time card and punched him out at 6 o'clock.

"Go on. Get your ass out of here," Marrera said, jerking his thumb toward the door. Then, as Woolsey shrugged his shoulders and headed for the exit, Marrera gave him a boyish grin and yelled, "Take the rest of the night off, Bob!"

Woolsey gone, and his television show not yet scheduled, Marrera made small talk with Angela, a slim, attractive, five-feet six-inch tall, 118-pound woman with jet-black hair cut short and curled. In addition to being attractive, Angela was athletic and Ralph liked that. She'd been a star sprinter in her days at Chicago's Wendell Phillips High School, and in 1967 she won first place in a track event sponsored by Mayor Richard J. Daley's Youth Organization.

The feeling of admiration between Angela and Ralph was mutual. She once told him, "You're real fun Ralphie. You're the kind of person who can turn a lonely job into one that doesn't make you want to watch the clock."

Since Angela was involved in conversation with Ralphie, she asked that night's runner, James Smola, who was cleaning the West garage, if he would mind taking over her duties on the alarm board for a few hours. Smola declined and told Marrera, the senior member of that shift, "I think I'd like to take a walk."

"Sure, why not?" Marrera encouraged. "Go ahead. There's nothing going on here. Take the rest of the night off, what the hell. We can always call you on the walkie-talkie if we need you." And off ran the runner, making a bee-line for an X-rated movie. It wasn't the first time Smola had gone AWOL and Ralph — good fellow that he was — always covered for him.

The runner's primary job was to monitor the security board which was linked to burglar or fire alarms at the various locations of Purolator customers. When an alarm sounded, the runner's assignment was to drive a Purolator car to the scene and investigate. While away from the premises, the runner remained in contact via a two-way radio.

With Marrera's blessing the runner hopped into the company car and headed down State Street, crossing the Chicago River at Marina Towers. He easily found a parking spot just across the bridge near the Shangri-La, an X-rated movie house featuring "Behind the Green Door," with Marilyn Chambers, the Ivory Soap girl.

At about 7:30 p.m. Angela laid her head into her arms, folded across the top of the typewriter at her monitoring station, and closed her eyes.

"Hey, what's wrong, Angie? Don't you feel well?" asked Ralph, putting a comforting hand on her shoulder.

"I'm really tired, Ralphie," she sighed. "Think I could leave early, maybe 8 o'clock? We've got these friends, come in from out of town, and they're staying at our place. You care?"

"Naw, what the hell," laughed Ralph, as though just relieved of something that had been preying on his mind. "It's O.K. with me, really. Call your old man to come down and get you. Just make sure you type up your log sheet before you go. I can watch the board, and I'll punch out for you at midnight, like before."

"Baby, you are a sweet man," cooed Angela.

"All us honkies aren't bad guys," laughed Ralph.

Angela put her log sheets in order, and telephoned her husband, Grover, who said he'd be down to pick her up at 8:15. She knew it would be cool, because she'd done the same thing before — on at least five other occasions. And Ralph always clocked her out so no one was ever the wiser.

"Hey, I was just thinking," mused Ralph, as they passed the next few minutes in idle chatter. "I mean, what if your old man doesn't come for you? Could you possibly take a cab home, or the El?"

"Aw, you tryin' to get rid of me, Baby?" Angela teased. "I wouldn't take *no* cab or *no* El," she added, emphasizing the "no."

"Yeah, but what if he doesn't get here?"

"I'll just wait, Ralphie. I'll have to stay here with you."

There was a familiar horn beep outside. Grover had arrived and as Angela left she smiled over her shoulder to let Ralph know she appreciated what he'd done for her. Then she clicked the door shut behind her.

It was ghostly quiet on that Sunday night. Purolator's security monitor had cut out and the runner was sitting at an X-rated movie house watching the famous trapeze scene while holding the walkie-talkie to one ear. He was on call, if needed, but no one called. Back at the warehouse, Ralph Marrera was all alone with $40 million.

CHAPTER 2
"Where's the Fire!"

Ralph Marrera, security guard at Purolator, was faithfully on duty every third Sunday night. The company had set-up a rotation system so that its money guards would have regular weekends at home with their families. At times, Ralphie volunteered to take the Sunday night shift, but in this case, it was his regularly scheduled weekend on vault guard duty. In fact, he was also on duty the previous night (October 19) and missed the employees annual dinner dance.

With Ralph that evening, deep behind the impenetrable concrete East Vault, was more than $25 million in unrecorded cash tucked snugly away for the night. Several paces away, in the West Vault, sat another $15 million — a comfortable $40 million sitting alone with only one security guard to protect the business, treasure and reputation of the Purolator Company.

Meanwhile, after the porno flick, the runner hopped back into the company car and drove to the home of a relative. From there he made for a North Side massage parlor where he relaxed awaiting a message, if any, on his two-way radio.

In fact, there was little to fear with the apparent lack of guard-power, for at 11 p.m. an armored crew was due to take out a truck on a late run. Marrera was also backed-up by one of the most sophisticated alarm systems ever devised. Each walk-in vault, with its combination doors tightly locked, was alarmed by Wells Fargo.

The five security systems were so super-sensitive they could detect the flicker of a match, or the drop of a pencil which would alert the nearby Wells Fargo monitoring board on Ohio Street. For added protection, the fire alarms tied in with the Chicago Fire Department's Engine Company No. 42, just a few blocks south on Illinois Street. Furthermore, the armed guard on duty could see the entrance of both main vaults while locked safely inside the vault room which housed a TV monitoring system rivaling that of Fort Knox. Its twenty-four scanners peeked into every corner of the building.

When the armored car crew arrived for the midnight run, Ralph ushered the ponderous vehicle out by raising the overhead garage door at the building's west end. As the van rolled off into the night, the darkened John Hancock building loomed over the neighborhood like a towering shadow, the illuminated observation deck encircling its crown like a halo.

At the stroke of midnight, Mildred Blivens arrived to relieve Angela Hughes on the alarm board, only to find that Angela had taken an early powder leaving the board unattended. She mildly rebuked Ralph, who explained that "Angie was feeling a little punk, and I gave her the okay to duck early." The runner, he advised her, was "on the air."

The initial hint that anything was amiss at Purolator came at 1:11 a.m. Monday, October 21 when a flashing light on the Wells Fargo monitoring board indicated a noise had sounded in the East Vault. This was the first signal to eminate from the vault all night.

On duty for Wells Fargo was watchman Ashok A. Patel, a native of India. He attached no particular significance to this early morning signal since there had been a series of "false alarms" in recent weeks. The first few times Patel dutifully dispatched his runner to investigate, but as the alarms became more frequent, he simply made telephone checks to confirm that all was secure.

On each occasion, the Purolator guard who assured Patel that everything was fine was none other than Ralph Marrera. Earlier that same evening, a light on the board indicated that someone had entered the money warehouse, but a check with Marrera found the situation "all clear."

Monitoring board wages do not pay people to be smart. It never struck the Indian as unusual that Marrera was always the guard on duty when the false alarms were sounded.

Only three minutes after the noise alarm, the smoke sensor alarm in the East Vault went off, and all circuits were immediately broken! Patel did dispatch his runner now — just in case.

At that same moment Mildred Bivens heard a hissing sound and the acrid aroma of smoke penetrated her nostrils. She immediately left the alarm board in the Purolator building and ran to the west garage for fresh air. When she returned, Marrera told her he'd just been notified by the Wells Fargo monitor that the East Vault intrusion alarm had sounded, and it had been followed by a fire alarm.

Five blocks away the men of Engine Company 42, asleep in one of Chicago's newest and most modern fire-protection facilities, swung into action, roused by an electronic alarm in Chief Edwin H. Nelson's office showing intense heat at Purolator. The initial signal sounded an ordinary still alarm, but Nelson and his firefighters would later recall this post midnight run as anything but that.

The engines kicked on with a roar, and the red, white and green lights flashed as the door rolled up to release the fire fighting vehicles. Two black-over-red pumpers, a ladder truck, and a rescue squad screeched out of the station on Illinois Street, their sirens shattering the quiet of the night.

The run from the firehouse to the Purolator building took less than a minute. Marrera, a holstered pistol at his side, stood in the doorway of the money warehouse as the Second Fire Battalion arrived — 23 men, led by Chief Nelson, a 14-year firefighting veteran.

The 41-year-old chief could smell smoke before he was out of his buggy. He instinctively noted that there was a fire hydrant directly in front of the Purolator building, on the corner of Huron and LaSalle, and another on the opposite end of the block, in front of the Hotel Wacker.

The chief moved quickly toward the security guard, crisply shouting orders to his men as he went, and Marrera made his first move. He stepped squarely into Nelson's path, planted his legs firmly apart, and placed his right hand over his holster.

"Stop!" he commanded.

Incredulous, Nelson reined up and gawked at Marrera in disbelief. For a moment he considered sidestepping the guard and obeying his fireman's instinct. The pungent aroma of smoke filled the air, but the improbable sight of this man blocking his way, hand on holster, puzzled him.

"What the hell is this?"

"I'm not supposed to let even the police in here," Marrera shouted officiously. "Nobody gets in! Those are orders."

"Wait a minute," Nelson gasped. "Nobody gets in?"

"You got it," said Marrera. "Not even the cops."

Nelson took a deep breath, and shouted in exasperation, "Look! Do you want us to help, or not? My men here have just been jangled out of the goddam sack and they aren't about to be playing midnight games. If there's a fire here, we're going in — and those are MY orders. We're not taking any chances with that hotel full of sleeping people sitting there on the corner. Now move your ass!"

Marrera hesitated a moment, then nodded affirmatively. "Okay, Okay," he told the fire chief. "But not all of them can come in." Nelson beckoned to a handful of his men, and Marrera reluctantly stepped aside to allow the firefighters to enter the building. If there was a fire, it had been burning throughout the strange confrontation.

"I can't see any fire, and I can't see any smoke, but I can sure as hell smell it," Nelson commented aloud. "Any of you guys see anything?"

"No, chief, but I sure as hell smell the same smoke you do," the nearest man answered.

Turning quickly to the armed guard, Nelson demanded, "Where the hell is the fire?"

Marrera boyishly shrugged his broad shoulders and replied, "I don't know of any fukkin' fire. Maybe there's something wrong with the air-conditioning system. Or it might be something down the basement, or out in the goddam garage." At no time did he mention the nearby East Vault, although the monitor board indicated heat sensors had gone off inside.

Nelson and his men, some of them carrying portable fire extinguishers, fanned out through the building. They combed the basement, checking every corner, eyeing the rafters, and poking the beams of their flashlights into the air-conditioning system. And sniffing. Always sniffing. As each location was checked out one of the men would call, "Nothing here, Chief."

Then Nelson found the panel — the monitoring board adjacent to the East Vault — and it showed a fire in the vault. He and his men had been in the building for ten minutes, examining every nook and cranny, yet they had not thought of checking the locked vaults. They got no information from Marrera, who stood aloof from the proceedings, appearing totally unconcerned.

"Over here, guys," Nelson called, as he ran to the vault and placed the palm of his hand gingerly on the steel door. It was warm! Not too hot to touch, but warm enough to tell Nelson he had found his fire.

"Come on, give it a pull," he ordered his huskiest fireman, pointing to the door handle. But it wouldn't budge. It was securely locked.

Only then, did Marrera step forward to help. "The branch manager's got the combination," he volunteered. "I could call him at home."

"Get him down here," ordered Nelson. "Fast!"

Marrera looked up a number, and telephoned the suburban home of Russell E. Hardt, regional vice president and branch manager of Purolator in Chicago. Hardt, however, was already on his way. Minutes earlier he'd been jolted from a sound sleep by the Wells Fargo monitor, informing him of a fire on Alarm No. F-62, the Purolator East Vault. The monitor reported that the Wells Fargo runner, as well as firemen, were being barred from the building.

Hardt phoned Mildred Bivens to make sure there was someone on duty to permit firemen access to the building. He then pulled on some clothes and jumped into his car. Along the way in from suburban Summit he called Purolator on his car radio and asked Mrs. Bivens to notify Pat Hopkins, the vault supervisor. She advised him that Hopkins was already on his way down.

When Hardt arrived on the scene 45 minutes later, the firemen were still crowded about the locked vault, while Hopkins struggled unsuccessfully to open it. Police from the nearby 18th District were also standing by, and news reporters were congregating in front of the building.

Hardt pushed his way to Hopkins' side and commanded, "Here, Pat. Let me do that." As the firemen stood back with their extinguishers aimed, he worked the combination — several times before getting it right — while Hopkins flipped the handles, which had been jammed, and swung open the East Vault door.

Clouds of dense, gray smoke billowed into the room and Chief Nelson distinctly detected the odor of gasoline as he and his men coughed and gasped for fresh air. The vault was so tightly packed with tankers and money pouches it was impossible to enter. Hardt, Hopkins, and other Purolator employees, newly arrived for the late-night shift, cleared the opening to make way for the firefighters.

Chief Nelson and Hopkins went in first, and quickly established that there were no visible flames. They could only stay a moment, though, because of the dense smoke. Nelson and five hand-picked men then pulled on their gas masks and blindly entered the vault carrying hand pumps. The smoke was so heavy they could see nothing but whiteness, so they just sprayed ahead as they inched their way in.

Actually there was no fire! Lack of air in the tightly locked vault had almost immediately smothered whatever blaze there was.

Robert E. Husted, Purolator's electronics security manager, arrived and brought in fans, as well as emergency lighting, since the vault's wiring had been burned away.

Husted, a rugged, ex-police officer from Kenosha, Wisconsin, called in additional security personnel to help monitor the gathering crowd. Hardt, meanwhile, telephoned the head of Purolator security in Dallas, Texas, to advise that "we've got a problem here." He asked Dallas to take the necessary steps to inform the insurance holder in New York.

With the smoke beginning to clear Nelson spotted several gasoline-filled plastic bags, intact. They were the type people use to bring home ice cubes from the liquor store. The highly combustible contents, remarkably, were kept from igniting by the almost immediate loss of oxygen. Then, as the smoke continued to rise, Nelson saw for the first time what the bags of gasoline were set upon.

"I can't believe my eyes!" he gasped. "Look at all those stacks of money!" He backed out of the vault, turned to Hardt, and asked "How much money's in there?"

"Oh, I don't know. I'm not sure," Hardt fibbed, "Maybe a million."

Nelson and his firemen were in a state of shock. None had ever been close to that kind of cash. There were "stacks and stacks of it" in the vault. Bundles on top of bundles.

"None of it's burned," Nelson said to Hardt, surprised at the sound of awe in his own voice. "Some of it's singed, but that's all."

Actually the "maybe a million" Hardt off-handedly referred to, turned out to be twenty-five times that amount, all in $5, $10, $20, $50, and $100 bills. Some, but not much, of the currency was singed around the edges by the erupting firebombs. But it was like trying to burn a big city phone book. The bills were so tightly bundled, and stacked row on row, that the fire never got a chance to take hold before consuming every inch of oxygen in the air-tight vault.

Had the money been consumed by the flames, no one would ever have been able to tell whether any of it was missing!

But an elaborate scheme had failed because whoever planned it had neglected to reckon with air, the one commodity almost everyone takes for granted. The lack of it had smothered the flames and foiled what could have been the "perfect crime."

CHAPTER 3

Purolator admits:
We've been robbed!

The onlookers who had curiously crowded around the open vault door were—with possibly one exception—totally unaware that a theft had taken place. After all, the vault had been securely locked since Saturday night, as verified by Wells Fargo records. And, no alarm had been reported to indicate otherwise. Obviously there had been a terribly intense blaze inside the vault — perhaps touched off by a short circuit in the alarm system, they figured — but fortunately smothered before it could destroy any of the millions in greenbacks.

But there was the curious presence of the gasoline-filled plastic bags. How did they get inside the vault, and how long could they have been there?

Now that the smoke had cleared, Chief Nelson and several of his men, assisted by Hopkins and Husted, re-entered the vault where they waded ankle-deep in currency, scattered about when the blast ruptured some of the money bags. Upon close inspection, they found eight of the gasoline-filled containers secreted inside Hillman's grocery bags and placed strategically about the interior. In all, about 15 gallons of the fuel had failed to ignite.

Nelson estimated from the size of the vault that the fire burned no longer than two minutes before all oxygen was consumed, and the fire was probably burning itself out when he and his men arrived.

Now the newspeople from Chicago's three major dailies,

four major television stations, and several radio stations began to gather en-force. They had learned from police radio calls of a fire in the money warehouse, and all were under pressure to get the story for their Monday morning editions and news shows.

The reporters, long accustomed to being permitted behind police lines, were miffed at being barred from the building. They clamored for details as Police Sgt. Charles Roberts stepped outside to brief them:

"We don't know for sure yet whether there's been a theft, or anything," he began. "But. . .why else would anyone set a fire in a vault? We just don't have any answers yet, but as soon as we know, you'll know. That's all I can tell you right now."

When pressed for additional information, Investigator Thomas Ryan reiterated what Roberts had explained, and added:

"We aren't going to have any way of knowing whether any money is missing until a complete inventory can be made. Period. That's all we can tell you fellows. You've gotta be patient."

Hardt, the Purolator executive routed from his night's sleep to unlock the vault, explained:

"We're still checking to see whether anyone could have even gotten in here in the first place. There were armed watchmen on duty throughout the weekend, and I had to come down personally to open the vault for the firemen. There is no way this vault could have been opened otherwise, without setting off an alarm. Believe me, fellas, we just don't know ourselves what's happened here at this time."

Further complicating the early hours of investigation were two curious bomb explosions in the general area of the Purolator warehouse.

The first blast occured at 12:20 a.m. Monday, less than an hour before the muffled gasoline explosions in the Purolator vault. It ripped off the front of a nearby nude manicure parlor, the Harem Leisure Spa, on North LaSalle Street, just one block from Purolator, and scared the hell out of Alan Fleshman, a 50-year-old salesman, who was walking his dog nearby.

from Chicago to Canberra, Honolulu to Hong Kong, would recount the event in front page headlines for days to come. Chicago reporters vied hourly for new angles, badgering anyone they could — spewing out fact and fiction for their voracious customers. One newspaper played up the other nearby explosions with a front page diagram showing the respective locations of the Purolator warehouse, George Dunne's apartment, and the Harem Leisure Spa. But another paper quickly knocked this story down, with a paragraph buried deep in its own report saying: "Police discounted theories that there was any connection between the theft and other North Side bombings this weekend. . ."

The Chicago Tribune quoted Michael O'Donnell, commander of the police Vice Control Division and an organized crime expert, as saying the bombing at the nude manicure parlor just an hour before the vault theft was discovered "resembles a crime syndicate scare tactic."

While checking other angles in the ever-mushrooming case, FBI agents began to compile a list of Purolator employees, to find out if anyone had failed to show up for work at his appointed time.

Husted, meanwhile, determined that the gasoline found in the vault was apparently Purolator's own. A pump was positioned along the wall in the garage to service the armored trucks. This internal gas supply avoided the risk of stopping at public filling stations while their trucks were loaded with money.

All in all, it was not shaping up as a very good day for Joseph I. Woods, president of Purolator's Chicago Division. The ex G-man and former Cook County sheriff was 1,000 miles away, in New Orleans on business, when he learned his employer had just been busted for untold millions of dollars while his back was turned. Woods cut his trip short and hustled back to Chicago to see what he could do, smarting like the farmer whose chicken coop had just been raided by the fox.

Adding to the irony, FBI Director Clarence Kelley was on his way from Washington, at that very moment, to deliver a speech to the prestigious Chicago Crime Commission.

Windows in a women's dormitory of the Moody Bible Institute across the street also were knocked out. Chicago is one town where nudity and religion can co-exist in the same neighborhood.

A few hours earlier, another blast bounced George Dunne, the 61-year-old Cook County Board president, out of bed in his Gold Coast home on East Chestnut Street. Dunne, a longtime political crony of Mayor Richard J. Daley, awakened to find an exploded bomb on his rear doorstep.

Police immediately surmised the explosions were planned to distract authorities while thieves emptied the Purolator vault. But they later determined that the two neighborhood bombings were unrelated. Jeffrey Weiss, manager of the Spa — one of several North Side nudie joints blasted in a mysterious wave of Chicago bombings — claimed he knew of "absolutely no reason why anyone would want to bomb me." He said he had just closed up shop for the night, and was driving two of his employees to a CTA elevated train station when his building was hit.

Dunne, who was alone on the second floor of his three-story building told police, "I can't even dream of a motive." The November election, in which he easily swamped his Republican challenger, was still two weeks away.

The first chilling hint of a major crime at the Purolator building came in a 3 a.m. phone call from Lt. Richard Dwyer, the watch commander of the 18th Police District to Chicago FBI headquarters.

Dwyer advised federal agents that a fire had swept one of the Purolator vaults, and there was, he hastened, a possibility that federally-protected funds might be involved. "When the firemen got into the vault they found evidence of at least seven, one and two-gallon, gasoline incendiary devices. Some of the damed things are still intact," Dwyer related. "The bomb and arson guys carried them out to the sidewalk, where they'd be safe. We were afraid if we left them sit in the vault, they might still go off.

"From the looks of the scorched walls inside the vault, there was one hell of an intense blaze for a little while, anyhow. Our preliminary investigation indicates that one of these gasoline bombs had been rigged up to some kind of a chemical detonating device."

The next call came at 5:40 a.m. from the detectives at the scene. They advised the FBI that a preliminary arson investigation indicated that an undetermined, but probably large, amount of money, some believed belonging to various banks, had been stolen. The chemical detonating device on one or more of the gasoline bombs appeared to have been timed to set off the explosions several hours after the actual theft.

"It's starting to look like the fire was intended to wipe out the fact that anyone had been here at all," Investigator Thomas Ryan said.

If everything in the vault had burned, so intensely as to wipe out even the traces of gasoline, who would ever know that anything had been taken? It would appear to have been a tragic and enormously expensive accident — perhaps sparked by a faulty electrical alarm wire.

Lt. Edward Nickels of the Damen Avenue General Assignment detail arrived at 6:45 a.m., quickly surveyed the situation, and called in his top detectives. He organized his men into search teams and directed them to go over every inch of the Purolator property, inside and out. Each team was accompanied by a Purolator employee, who would know if anything on the premises had been disturbed, or was missing.

In the ladies restroom, on the second floor, detectives found a number of plastic bags used by the company to store damaged currency, along with numerous brown paper bags. They also noted that plastic seals, used to tag the money tankers, were randomly lying about in the vault room area, inviting anyone to open a tanker without authorization, and then reseal it to cover up the entry.

Hardt, meanwhile, told investigators that a quick check indicated that some $635,000 belonging to the Merchandise National Bank of Chicago was unaccounted for. Nickels relayed the information to an FBI agent on the scene as an observer, and the bureau officially entered the case at 7:25 that morning.

"It was a long process to determine whether anything was unaccounted for, because we have in excess of forty million dollars on hand between the two vaults," Hardt now admitted. "Much of this money is 'bank to bank' cash, as well as money belonging to other banks, but held by Purolator." Such was the case of the Merchandise National cash, found to be missing when investigators discovered a tampered seal on the Jewel Tea Company tanker.

The FBI immediately launched a three-phase investigation: First, the time period of the theft had to be determined. Secondly, they had to narrow the 'possible' time frame into a 'probable' one. Finally, agents had to figure out how the theft occurred, and whether an employee of Purolator could have been involved.

To specify a time period, the FBI had to learn, as quickly as possible, the exact loss. Once agents knew *which* tankers and money bags had been tapped, they would know when those tankers were loaded and sealed. The theft could not have occurred before that time.

In order to calculate the losses, all remaining monies would have to first be delivered to their proper destinations. The cash could be checked against papers listing the various amounts enroute from client to client. Meanwhile, all the money held by Purolator for clients also had to be counted. A million dollars was soon discovered missing from each of three tankers marked Central National Bank, Exchange National Bank, and Jewel Tea Company. The sealed Central and Exchange tankers had been placed in the rear of the East Main Vault on Friday, October 18, with nothing to be added on Saturday. Both were found with broken seals and large amounts of their contents gone.

A 'possible' time frame was coming into focus: The theft took place sometime after business hours on Friday, and before the fire-bombs were detonated.

Now the Monday morning papers were hitting the streets. Chicagoans always go to bed on Sunday nights secure with the knowledge that they will wake up to something interesting or spectacular to devour with their morning coffee. It's always been that way. Windy City weekends seldom let you down.

This whopper exceeded all expectation! The news media

CHAPTER 4

"Christ, it's bigger than Rondout!"

At 9 a.m. on Monday, October 21, a Purolator armored truck rolled down a concrete ramp into the basement of the towering First National Bank of Chicago, in the heart of the city's bustling financial district. The vehicle supposedly contained a deposit of $1,724,084.30, representing the Hawthorne receipts held in the Purolator vault for safekeeping over the weekend.

As part of the FBI plan to follow up on all monies held in the vault over the weekend, Purolator supervisors Casey Gomorczak and Herman J. Gahn accompanied the shipment from the money warehouse to First National. They carried a deposit slip for $332,143, which represented the cash placed in the metal footlocker by Hawthorne's head cashier Saturday night, and another slip to cover $1,391,941.30 believed contained in sealed money bags on a flat-bed truck. The money was to be deposited in the estate of Thomas Carey, which was the race track's account.

After the truck was unloaded in the basement of the bank, Gomorczak and Gahn, along with the Purolator vault supervisor, Pat Hopkins, were led to the bank's Silver Vault Area, where they explained their mission to bank officials. The Hawthorne Race Course money manager, McCann, was also waiting for them to unlock the footlocker, as was his custom.

Then the surprises came in one-two-three order. First McCann used his key to open his personal lock on the three-foot long, eighteen-inch deep metal locker. As he raised the lid he, and the men surrounding him, detected the unmistakable aroma of gasoline.

"What the hell!" he exclaimed, flipping the locker lid open for all to see. Inside the container, where he had personally locked away more than $300,000 on Saturday night, was only a small amount of charred currency, and a supermarket shopping bag containing a plastic sack full of gasoline. Some of the highly flammable fluid had, by that time, leaked from the bag.

Inadvertently the bomb, one of the eight or nine remaining intact from the Sunday night blaze, had gone undetected by Purolator employees in the confusion following discovery of the theft.

Again, the lack of oxygen inside the footlocker had prevented the gasoline from igniting, despite the intense heat that had engulfed it when the other firebombs went off in the East Vault eight hours earlier.

"Get back," McCann warned. "Don't anyone light a cigaret. Phew! One spark and this whole damned thing could go sky high."

The men encircling the silver footlocker quickly backed away, and an urgent call was put in to bank security officers. Chief John Reihel and Sergeants Harry Greenholt and Eugene Sullivan responded immediately, along with former Secret Service agent Edward Tucker, the bank's security director.

While Reihel, Sullivan and Greenholt sealed off the section of the bank's vault area and money dock to protect other bank employees and customers, Tucker placed a hurried call to the police bomb squad. Gomorczak, meanwhile, was on another phone, notifying his office and detailing the hairy incident to the stunned FBI men still at the burglary scene.

Three FBI agents, Thomas J. Green, Bruce Knipp, and Thomas H. Greene were in the bank vault area within minutes, arriving just ahead of Police Officers Arthur Nolan and Donald Pike of the bomb squad. Nolan and Pike, after calmly but quickly surveying the situation, used chemicals to neutralize the gasoline bomb before removing it.

Police crime investigators arrived with their lab materials to dust the footlocker for fingerprints. The entire area was then put off-limits until the odor of gasoline cleared. The Purolator supervisors were joined by Richard Wood, Harry Fisher, George Hansen and James Swann, officials of the bank's operations, general services, law and audit divisions, as the count of Hawthorne money began.

The sealed bags, believed to contain $1,391,941.30 were found to hold only $1,609 — a loss of $1,390,332.30. And the metal locker, into which $332,243 had been placed by the Hawthorne cashier Saturday night, now held only $2,143. Between the footlocker and the money bags, the Hawthorne account was short $1,720,332.30.

The FBI men made careful note of the tabulation for their growing report, and a now relaxed Tucker warmly praised Nolan and Pike for removing the potentially explosive device from the bank without incident. He would later write a letter of commendation to Police Superintendent James M. Rochford.

At the very moment of the bomb's innocent delivery to the bank, a distinguished visitor was looking down upon the sprawling city as his jet moved into a landing pattern over O'Hare Field. It was the FBI Superchief himself, Clarence Kelley, accompanied by some of the Bureau's top brass. They were met at the airport by a delegation of Chicago FBI agents who momentarily interrupted their investigation at Purolator to roll out the red carpet for their boss.

Kelley, however, did not come to personally take over investigation of the biggest cash theft in American history. He was in town to keynote the Chicago Crime Commission's annual meeting of top civic, business, and law enforcement leaders, in the International Ballroom of the Conrad Hilton Hotel.

In fact, his message made no mention of the vault caper, perhaps because local authorities could not bear to mar his visit with the bad news, or dim the commission's annual shindig — an event of much chest-thumping to renew the city's ongoing war against crime. The FBI chief marched to the podium, amid a thunderous ovation, and deplored the rising crime rate and the lack of meaningful controls on handguns. "The odds are strong that nothing will happen to you if you are a criminal," he told his enraptured audience.

Meanwhile, parts of the Purolator loot were either being buried in a Northwest side bungalow basement or on the way out of the country to the British West Indies. And back at Purolator, FBI investigators took the news of the First National Bank bomb discovery as the best opportunity yet to determine the time period of the theft.

A check with Hawthorne Race Course quickly established that many witnesses saw the money sealed into the silver footlocker, and placed aboard the armored truck at 8 o'clock on Saturday night — with no gasoline bombs aboard. The truck was clocked out of Hawthorne at 8:10 p.m., according to both Purolator and track records, and clocked on arrival at the money warehouse at 8:24.

The armored truck driver, messenger and two guards were interviewed. All told the same story of delivering the Hawthorne receipts intact to Purolator. FBI agents agreed that the seven mile trip, negotiated in 14 minutes, hardly gave the truck crew time for a side trip to pick up bombs, much less dispose of the contents of the footlocker and money bags.

Next to be interviewed were the vault room employees who signed receipts for the Hawthorne shipment. They were in accord that the locked money containers were taken off the armored truck and placed directly into the East Main Vault without any tampering.

The FBI determined that two dozen Purolator employees were on duty when the money arrived, and a number of them pitched in to help shove the tankers and footlockers into the vault, so they could clean up their evening's work and get to the company party. Because of the confusion, nobody was certain of the exact time the money went into the vault, but all agreed it was some time between 8:50 and 9:10 p.m.

Both Purolator and Wells Fargo records confirmed that the East Main Vault was placed on combination and alarmed at 9:26 p.m. Saturday, October 19. The dual records also showed that the East Main Vault sound alarm went off at 1:11 a.m. Monday, October 21, and at 1:14 a.m., the smoke sensor alarm was activated, after which all circuits were broken. The vault clock was stopped at 1:11, its electrical wires burned through and melted from the heat of the blast.

The FBI was now satisfied, for investigative purposes, that the theft had to take place between 9:26 p.m. Saturday and 1:11 a.m. Monday, at least with respect to the Hawthorne haul, and undoubtedly the other millions as well.

The inventory of missing money was nearing completion, and auditors now suggested the loss was "close to five million dollars!"

"Christ," mused an FBI agent, letting out a long, low whistle. "This one's bigger than Rondout!"

For more than half a century the Great Rondout Train Robbery, with its more than two million dollars in loot, had gone unchallenged as the greatest cash heist in the history of America, and that happened only 32 miles away. The time was shortly before 10 o'clock on the night of June 12, 1924, when two men hidden in the baggage car of Milwaukee Road train No. 57 crawled over the tender, into the locomotive, and ordered the engineer to bring the train to a steaming halt at the Buckley Road crossing in Rondout, Illinois, just west of Lake Bluff. Four more bandits were waiting at the scene, and peppered the mail car with bullets and tear gas bombs before forcing the frightened and confused train crew to carry 63 mail pouches full of money to waiting autos. In the confusion, the gang leader fired five shots into a fellow robber, mistaking him for an intruder, and the bandits dragged the wounded man off with the loot.

William J. Fahey, a Chicago postal inspector and famed super-sleuth, headed that investigation. By tracing the wounded man, authorities eventually apprehended all six members of the gang and — to the astonishment of almost everyone — discovered Fahey had masterminded the holdup. The more than two million dollars was recovered, and all seven men were sentenced to long prison terms.

Over the next fifty years, whenever lawmen discussed great thefts in America, the Rondout Train Robbery was bound to come up. An now FBI men, from the very same district, were faced with an even bigger one. In the Rondout Robbery there was no question when or how the theft took place, or how many people authorities were looking for. In the Purolator theft, the only thing the investigators knew was that the money was gone. A lot of it.

Joe Woods arrived late on the scene and was briefed by his former FBI comrades. He crammed his hands deep into his britches and bit his lip. "If the money all burned up," said Joe, "who'd ever think any of it was taken?" There was a trace of admiration in his voice as he added, "It would have been the perfect crime."

CHAPTER 5
Some * * * * Goofed!

C harles Siragusa, blunt-spoken executive director of the Illinois Legislative Investigating Commission, took one look at his Monday morning newspaper and exploded! He slammed the paper down upon his mahogany desk, grabbed his black touch-tone and punched out the number of the Cook County State's Attorney's Office.

The receptionist's "Good Morning . . ." was cut short by Siragusa's gruff demand for Nicholas Iavarone, the head of the Special Prosecutions Unit.

"*This* is the thing, Nick!" he shouted without introduction. "They hit the goddam Purolator vault!"

Siragusa's anger was well based as he recalled that he had gotten the original tip on the big score from one of his own stool pigeons.

"Jesus Christ! I passed it all on to you guys and the IBI, and now look what the fuck happened!" he bellowed.

Siragusa, known by everyone as "Charlie Cigars," was Chicago's one-man enemy of organized crime and a brazen publicity seeker. He came to town in 1963 as the 49-year-old executive director of the respected Illinois Crime Investigating Commission. Before his appointment, the Commisssion had interviewed 56 other candidates, and unanimously selected Charlie for the job. He arrived a veteran of 28 years in federal narcotics service, an expert on the Mafia, and a crime-fighting reputation he had nurtured in the New York City drug festering grounds. His motto was simple enough: "Buy and Bust."

As a federal narcotics agent Charlie Cigars had an uncanny ability to crawl into the criminal mind and anticipate its next move. He had participated in well over 5,000 drug busts in New York, Italy, France, North Africa, Mexico, Turkey, Syria, Lebanon, Jordan and Egypt — 25 countries in all, and he won the U.S. Treasury Department's highest award for undercover work against smuggling and dope rings.

A swarthy man with a "Mustache Pete" face, he was American born of Sicilian ancestry and wore expensive suits cut to accent his muscular build. Now past 60, Siragusa was in prime health and a dynamo of action, with a vocabulary liberally laced with profanity. That morning, the day following the Purolator theft, Charlie's expletives were flowing like a mountain rill in springtime.

Prosecutor Iavarone's morning had begun as an avalanche of scolding poured forth from his receiver. He winced and held the phone at arm's length, yet the angry voice came through as if it were still held tightly against his ear.

"Listen Nick! My guys risked their fuckin' asses on this job and now some son-of-a-bitch blew it! We had Gushi and Marzano by the short hair and they didn't even know it, god-dammit! Now this score, this Purolator thing — goes down and they're gone out somewhere where Jesus lost his sandals. With millions, Nick! With fuckin' millions, swiped just two miles away!"

Siragusa slammed down the phone in utter frustration and bellowed "SHIT!" loud enough to rattle the merit certificates on his office walls. He knew Charlie Marzano and Pete Gushi almost as well as he knew himself, and he finally thought he had a real chance to nail their pelts to the same wall.

Siragusa recalled that the guy who plugged Charlie Marzano and killed his brother, Danny, in a street shootout years earlier, was Charlie's own brother-in-law, Louis Vasselli, who blasted away at them with a gun in each hand. Louie was charged with murder but a judge let him go, saying it was a family affair, and justifiable homicide. Marzano still had five holes in him, just to remind him of his wife's brother.

Marzano and his associate, the hulking Pete Gushi, were products of the "The Patch," and the pair used to steal together in the old neighborhood. Now, at 47, Gushi lived in suburban Oak Lawn. He was a convicted hijacker, an ex-narcotics peddler, a fence for stolen property, and generally a born loser when it came to crime. The rotund Gushi once described himself a genuine "master criminal," but Siragusa knew him as a pathetic "master bungler."

In 1963, while spending time at Leavenworth, Gushi tried to hang himself, but even that failed because the knots on his bedsheet broke. The home-made death noose was unable to hold his 230-pound frame. Years later, the balding Gushi's most noteworthy claim to fame would be his living next door to James "Jimmy the Bomber" Catuara, a long-time south suburban Chicago rackets chief, best known for his gold colored Cadillacs and preference for English Oval cigarets; a man of distinct style and class to the aspiring Gushi.

Earlier that year, in September, Gushi opened his contribution to free enterprise, a discount store appropriately named "The Family Bargain Center" on West 111th Street, in south suburban Worth, Illinois. The store was an ideal place from which to fence everything from prime cuts of stolen meat to cosmetics and appliances.

The word "fence" is the common underworld term that was first used in England during the end of the 17th century. The infamous Jonathan Wild was the most eminent and powerful fence in history, controlling the London underworld for more than a decade. The term is believed to have evolved then, descriptive of selling stolen goods over the back fence. It was also used to refer to the go-between, the person who accepted such goods from one side and sold them to the other.

Gushi's store did not go unnoticed by Siragusa, as the small-time Jonathan Wild began his operation almost in his back yard. Immediately Charlie Cigars set out to bust him. He assigned two of his best undercover men, Martin "Marty" Pollakov and Edward Doyle to infiltrate Gushi's operation.

Pollakov, a dour-faced man of 27 with a medium build,

fell victim to Syndicate loan sharks in the late 1960s. In fear of his life he went on the payroll as a stool pigeon for Siragusa in 1969. He had been on the state agency's payroll since with his very own Confidential Informant number, C.I. 74102.

Doyle was an ex-Marine, with a regular commission agent rating, and Siragusa instructed him to accompany Pollakov underground into the world of crime.

Together they posed as flunkie crooks. To bolster their image they approached Gushi, whom Pollakov already knew, with 200 cases of Alberto-Culver VO-5 hair conditioner — which they claimed was stolen and required fencing through Gushi's new bargain store. In making the approach, Pollakov asked Gushi, "Is this place legit or illegit?"

"We go with the hots," Gushi winked.

The introduction grew into a cautious friendship, with Pollakov showing up at Gushi's store almost daily, often pinch hitting as store manager, handyman, or errand boy, whatever Gushi needed help with. Each morning before meeting Gushi, Pollakov would report to Siragusa on the small-timers that Gushi was doing business with in fencing stolen securities or other ill-gotten goods. And Siragusa dutifully relayed the fresh information to Nick Iavarone, in the state's attorney's office.

Among the many reports given by Pollakov were those of meetings between Gushi and James Maniatis, a close friend and known police character. The white-haired Maniatis was a shuffling, slow-moving man nearing his sixties, with his 195 pounds spread thickly over his five-feet five-inch frame. He ostensibly worked as a clerk in Gushi's store.

Gushi occasionally used Pollakov to cut deals and negotiate "buys" from other local fences, or boosters, and from time to time Pollakov arranged to help Gushi dispose of goods through his own friends — actually undercover agents working for the investigative commission. In mid-September Gushi told Pollakov that they could pick up several thousand wrist watches through Maniatis. The watches had been taken in a burglary of the Douglas-Dunhill Company in nearby Oak Forest.

It was the classic fencing operation. Maniatis knew a source who would sell him the watches at $5.50 each. Gushi negotiated an arrangement to sell them to Pollakov's "friends" for a neat $9.00 apiece — leaving a tidy profit of $3.50 per watch, without ever handling the goods.

Pollakov reported the deal to Siragusa, who arranged to get the needed money for the purchase from the Travelers Insurance Company. Then, carrying $4,500 of the insurance company's cash, Pollakov went with Maniatis to a sleezy garage in Crestwood, Illinois, to meet the watchman. Pollakov gave the $4,500 to Maniatis, who handed $2,750 of it to his contact in exchange for 500 watches. The remaining $1,750 was given by Maniatis to Gushi, and Pollakov delivered the watches to Charlie "Cigars" Siragusa.

The same scene was reenacted twice more over the next few days, with Pollakov purchasing a total of 1,500 stolen watches for $13,000. Of that money, $8,250 went to Maniatis for his source, and $5,250 was pocketed by Gushi, the fence. The watches were turned over by Siragusa to the insurance company, and the evidence obtained during the transaction was passed along to Iavarone for prosecution.

Soon Pollakov was meeting daily with Gushi for breakfast, generally at the Holiday Inn at Madison and Halsted Streets, just west of the Loop, or at Mama Batt's Restaurant on Chicago's South Side. Batt's, at Michigan Avenue and Cermak Road, was next door to the New Michigan Hotel, which used to be known as the Lexington Hotel when it served as headquarters for Al Capone and his mob in the 1930s.

As the friendship between the two men developed, so did Gushi's braggadocio. One morning, over coffee, he blurted, "You know, I'm sick and tired of being poor all my life, but I won't be much longer. Now I'm either going to be a rich man or a dead man." Pollakov's ears pricked up, and he casually asked, "What's that supposed to mean?"

"One of the biggest cash scores that ever hit this country," Gushi muttered defiantly.

"No shit!" said Pollakov admiringly, "And *you're* in on it?"

"Right at the top," boasted Gushi. "And its gonna be big."

"When is all this supposed to happen?" asked Pollakov.

"It's gonna go down on Sunday night, Maybe September 29th if everything goes right — but I'm not saying where," Gushi answered the now mesmerized Pollakov. "It could be here. Could be in Florida. Who knows? You'll know when it happens. You'll read about it in the papers on Monday, and when you do, we'll be basking in the warm sunshine. Then, when the heat dies down we'll bring it all back in burlap bags. Yeah, bulging burlap bags. Ha, ha."

Pollakov anxiously fed the latest tidbit to an unbelieving Siragusa, who immediately asked, "Is that nutty blabbermouth giving us bullshit? Or, do you think this is for real?"

"I think somethin's cooking," Pollakov replied, "The old man's been having a lot of hush-hush meetings with different people lately. They're sure as hell hatching something."

Charlie Cigars would have loved to wallow in the glory of breaking up "the biggest cash score that ever hit this country," but his hands were tied. He already had several operations going, and his manpower was spread thinner than he liked. So, he did the next best thing. He notified Wayne A. Kerstetter, the superintendent of the Illinois Bureau of Investigation.

The IBI chief took no chances. After consulting with Iavarone, he ordered his Organized Crime squad to mount a non-stop around-the-clock surveillance on Gushi. This was about all Siragusa could hope for and he was satisfied. If anything would ever come of it, he could always claim credit for providing the IBI and Iavarone with the original tip.

Meanwhile Doyle, who Gushi knew only as Pollakov's pal and sidekick "Eddie," began accompanying Pollakov on his visits to the discount store. As long as he was hanging around anyway, Gushi put him to work, mopping floors, dusting shelves and arranging stolen goods on the display counters.

"Eddie-the-Mope" became a source of amusement to Gushi who continually poked fun at his sloppy dress and mannerisms. "He's so fuckin' dumb, what do you want him around for?" he once asked Pollakov suggesting a possible change.

"Oh, Eddie's a little dumb, maybe, but he's a good guy, and he does like you tell him, you know . . ."

Doyle played the dummy and kept his ears always open. His chores were extended to exercising Gushi's dog, and becoming his "gofer," running errands for the master. All the while he was soaking up bits of gab between Gushi and his mysterious underworld friends, and feeding whatever he learned back to Charlie Cigars.

On September 13th Pollakov, in thick with the boss, picked up Gushi at his home and drove him to a nearby diner for breakfast. Over ham and eggs the loquacious Gushi related how a funny thing had happened the previous afternoon while he was meeting his pal, Charlie Marzano, and several other friends.

"We was at the Southwest Inn on Cicero Avenue and the place was all steamed up. It was surrounded by IBI agents," Gushi recalled.

"How did you know that?" asked Pollakov wiping up some egg with his toast.

"Oh, Charlie figured that out," Gushi explained. "See, first I though they might be from the IRS, you know, putting on some heat. But Charlie, he's got this little police monitor, and he could listen in and tell who they were. It fucked up our meeting though, and I hadda go back last night and meet him again at Niko's on Harlem Avenue."

Ironically, the IBI agents were tailing Gushi. But Marzano who was used to being under surveillance, took it for granted they were watching him and called off the meet. Now, after Gushi had led the IBI to Marzano, both men were under surveillance.

As Pollakov and Gushi left the diner and headed toward the Holiday Inn, where Gushi had an appointment, Pollakov asked him about Marzano, whom he obviously admired.

"Oh, Charlie? I've known him since we was fifteen years old," Gushi said. "He's the strongest man in the world, you know that? I ain't shittin' ya either. He plays handball, and he works out at the 'Y' *every* day."

"Yeah? What's he do?"

"Charlie, he builds his own electronics equpment," Gushi boasted. "He even got his own library on the subject. And you know — ha, ha, this is funny — awhile back there was this big jewelry score up in Evanston, and the coppers were pretty sure Charlie was in on it."

"Yeah?"

"Yeah, so here's what happened. Get this. The Chicago ID (Intelligence Division) dicks and the 'G' both got tails on Charlie. They got three cars on him constantly, days and nights. And Charlie knows it, 'cause he's listenin' in on 'em. Ha, ha. But that ain't the best part. You know what he used to do? He'd stop his car, real fast, and jump out and walk back and talk to those creeps. Haw! That's the kinda guy Charlie is."

"Yup. Sounds like he's got balls," Pollakov said in admiration.

"More balls than a bowling alley," laughed Gushi.

They had arrived at the Holiday Inn. The appointment was with Allen Wainer, a 69-year-old ex-con who had served prison terms for conspiracy to transport stolen property and for counterfeiting postage stamps. He was Gushi's financial backer, and Pollakov had met him before.

Pollakov sat staring at his coffee cup as the two men chatted mostly about the doings at Gushi's discount store. Then Gushi mentioned that he had met Charlie Marzano the previous night. "Something's wrong with the mileage on the map," Gushi continued, "And we might have to rent a plane. We gotta go around Cuba. We gotta rent a plane, and besides Charlie's a pilot."

"So then, you should rent a plane," Wainer replied simply.

Then Gushi asked, "Do you know the guy from Boston?"

"Yeah," Wainer replied, "Louis DiFonzo."

The conversation meant nothing to Pollakov, but he relayed it to Siragusa, who directly passed it on to the IBI and Iavarone. Gushi was involved in something with Charlie Marzano and Louis DiFonzo. Both Gushi and Marzano were, at this time, under 24-hour surveillance, and tension mounted within the various law enforcement agencies as September

29th — "D-Day" (for dollars) neared. But no one knew where the action would go down.

"It could mean a big securities heist," suggested Siragusa "but we've got to keep our options open. The target could be a brokerage house loaded with negotiables, or maybe an armored car. Check out all places where gold bars are stored."

He made a list of banks, businesses and security houses, to pinpoint possible targets, but quickly found that "there's one hell of a lot of places in Chicago with that kind of money."

The state IBI agents under the direction of organized crime sleuth Lawrence Casey, broadened their non-stop watch to include dozens of lesser known thieves capable of carrying off a score the likes of which Gushi boasted. The 24-hour tail was placed on anyone Gushi regularly associated with, including Wainer and the white-haired misfit, Jimmy-the-Greek Maniatis.

They watched Gushi meeting with Charlie Marzano and his cousin, Tony Marzano, along with a handsome dark-haired man in his late 20s, at regular breakfast sessions in a suburban Berwyn restaurant. They ran a license plate check on the dark haired man, and identified him as Ralph Ronald Marrera, 29, a resident of the suburbs.

Incredibly, other than that routine license plate check, officials did no further investigation on the clean-cut Marrera. Had they done so, they would have found that he was employed as a guard at Purolator, one of the largest money warehouses around! They would have pin-pointed the "where."

Pollakov got to meet Gushi's friend, Charlie Marzano, when he visited the store in Worth on September 16. While Pollakov and "Eddie the Mope" eavesdropped, Gushi, Marzano and Al Wainer held a long meeting in the rear of the shop. They complained about the surveillance at the Southwest Inn, and decided to hold future meetings at the Holiday Inn in suburban Hillside. Doyle also heard Marzano tell the others, "I want 44 per cent."

On the morning of September 21 Doyle, in his role as "Eddie the Mope," overheard Gushi take a telephone call from Luigi DiFonzo, who gave him directions to Harvey's Restaurant in suburban Countryside. "We'll meet you there, but Charlie's late," Gushi said. A short time later Marzano arrived at the store, and he and Gushi left for Harvey's.

Three days later the trusted Pollakov was allowed to sit in on a breakfast meeting between Gushi and the Marzano cousins, Charlie and Tony.

"Pete says I can trust you, so I'm taking his word for it," Charlie told Pollakov. "Here's what I want you to do for me. I want you to buy me a van. I'll give you the dough, and a phony driver's license, so they won't know who you are."

"What kind of van?" Pollakov asked.

"I want a light-colored one, like delivery men, or the utility companies use. I'll have Pete, here, get back to you."

The following day, September 25, Doyle and Pollakov arrived at the store to find Gushi and Charlie Marzano already there, holding a whispered conversation. They overheard Gushi say he had received a telephone call from DiFonzo, who wanted to meet them at the Hickory Hills Country Club at 2 o'clock that afternoon.

That night Gushi telephoned Pollakov at home and told him they had found a used van for sale in nearby Summit for $2,000. He asked Pollakov to stop at his place to pick up they money and driver's license. "You go out and look at the van. If it looks good, you buy it," he said.

When Pollakov arrived at Gushi's, however, he was told the deal was off. "I couldn't get ahold of Charlie, and he's got the fake license," he said. "Dammit, that van is going to bring back around $2 million!"

Pollakov let out a low whistle.

"You're fuckin' right. I'm 80 per cent sure I'll be leaving town Monday for a couple of weeks," Gushi said, poking Pollakov in the ribs for emphasis.

When Pollakov arrived at the store the next morning Gushi said there d been a change of plans. They were going to opt for a new van. Pollakov accompanied Gushi and Marzano to Hawkinson Ford on West 95th Street in Oak Lawn, where Charlie had found the one he liked.

"This is the one I want you to buy," Marzano said, taking Pollakov over to a mint-green Ford Econoline van. He handed Pollakov a piece of paper containing the van's stock number: 7646. The trio then returned to the discount store, where Marzano gave Pollakov a driver's license bearing the name, Charles Russo. "Here's the license I want you to buy the truck with. And here's 500 bucks. I'll have the rest of the money tomorrow."

The next day was Friday, September 27 — two days before D Day. As Pollakov, Doyle, Gushi and Maniatis had breakfast together Gushi explained that there had been a slight change in plans. "Charlie wants Jimmy-the-Greek to buy the van in his own name. That way nobody might get suspicious."

"Wait a minute," protested Maniatis, "I don't want nuttin' to do with this. I'm havin' trouble with the IRS now."

"Nothing's gonna go wrong," Gushi assured him. "If anyone should ever ask you, you can say you sold the van to me." He then handed Pollakov $3,900 in cash and told him to drive Maniatis to the Hawkinson Ford lot to pick up the van. "You can take 'Eddie the Mope' here with ya," he laughed.

At 9 a.m. Pollakov, Doyle and Maniatis drove over to Oak Lawn and purchased the Ford Econoline. The nervous Maniatis recited the information on his driver's license for the salesman, but refused to show him the license. As he handed the dealer the full cash price, $3,887, he muttered that the van "reminds me of my old Hudson."

That afternoon an anxious Charlie Marzano drove out to Gushi's store to inspect the van, which was parked out back. He went over it carefully, almost lovingly, checking the engine oil and the Econoline's interior. He noticed some glue had been spilled near the right front door, and asked Eddie if he'd clean it off. Doyle dutifully obeyed. He cleaned the glue spot, and while he was down on his knees he secretly scratched an identifying mark under the right front wheel well.

The next day Gushi was nervous as a cat, and flew into a rage against a cash register salesman, threatening to kill him.

He had to be restrained by two friends, with whom he'd been arguing earlier. "It's either tomorrow night or three weeks from Sunday, October 20," he told Pollakov, as the two sat in the rear of the store, sipping drinks to calm Gushi down. "You'll know, if you don't see me in the store Monday. You'll read it in the papers."

Every suspect, except Marrera, was being shadowed from the time he left home in the morning until he tucked himself between the sheets at night — but September 29 came and went, and nobody read anything out of the ordinary, crime-wise in the newspapers the next day.

On Monday morning, when Pollakov found Gushi in the store, he said, "I thought you were gonna take a trip."

"We weren't ready yet," Gushi told the inquisitive snitch. "The money, it won't be there for another three weeks, but my people and me, we can wait."

Charlie Marzano, who was in the store, along with Maniatis, called Pollakov aside and said, "Here, let me tell you what that dumb son-of-a-bitch did."

In purchasing the van Maniatis applied for the license plates directly through the dealer, which can be done in Illinois, without mailing the fee to the Secretary of State's Office and waiting for the mailman. But in his nervousness he took the envelope containing the plates home with him, instead of leaving them in the van. When he opened the envelope in the security of his own home only one license plate fell out — not the two required by Illinois law for display on the vehicle.

By the time he'd worked up enough courage to explain the fluke to Gushi, who relayed the information to Marzano, the dealership had closed, and there was no time to correct the error before the weekend. So, rather than jeopardize an otherwise perfect crime by driving to and from the scene in an improperly licensed vehicle, the cautious Marzano scratched the mission.

"Now, here's what I want you to do," Marzano told Pollakov. "I want you, not that dumb Greek bastard, to go and pick up the right license plates for me. OK?"

At Marzano's bidding, Pollakov drove back to Hawkinson

Ford and picked up a new set of plates, Illinois license number 56174B. He then drove to the Worth Village Hall and purchased a vehicle sticker, number 1590. He returned to the discount store and turned them over to a grateful Marzano.

"You know," Marzano said, in thanking him, "I could have bought all those wrist-watches myself if I wanted to, and made a neat 25-grand profit. But that kind of dough ain't nothing to me with the kind of score we've got lined up, believe me."

As Marzano prepared to leave, the queasy Maniatis grumbled that he didn't like having his name connected with the van that was going to be used for anything risky. "Hey, I'm nothin but a poor flea-market prowler and odd-jobber," he whined. "What am I gonna tell the Internal Revenue Service if they ask me how I got the kind of money to buy that van, huh?"

"Don't worry, Jimmy," Marzano assured him. "We just need it to haul some furniture. When it's over, the van's yours. My gift to you. Now, what do you say?"

Before he could answer, Gushi interrupted. "Yeah, just a couple of hundred pounds," he laughed. "You'll read it in the fuckin' papers."

"I think I need a drink," Maniatis said, shrinking.

Later Pollakov learned from Gushi that the "job" was such that it had to be carried out on a Sunday night. And, not just any Sunday night. Only every third one. He said it might be October 6, but he was rather sure the big day would be October 20.

"There's a 99 per cent chance we can get away with this," Gushi boasted over drinks in the back of the store. "We're goin' in with rifles . . . carbines, and take four guys out of the way if we have to. Fuckin' right. And if any cop shows up, we'll take him out of the way, too."

The liquor, as always, was giving Gushi diarrhea of the mouth. Pollakov poured him another. The information was subsequently relayed to Siragusa, who passed it on to Iavarone and the IBI.

The 24-hour surveillance of the suspects continued until

Sunday, October 13, when, without warning, it was abruptly ended. Red-faced officials would later explain that they could no longer spare the manpower.

So, beginning October 13 — for one full week leading up to the night the Purolator vault was plundered — the subjects who had been so busily planning what they boasted would be the biggest heist in history, were free to come and go as they pleased, totally unobserved. And Siragusa had it all there, in his books — the plot, the names of the suspects, their backgrounds and police records, the van they were going to use, and even its license number. And the exact date of the hit!

Little wonder that Charlie Cigars was furious as he picked up his newspaper that black Monday morning and read that Purolator had been sacked. That was the score that Gushi had been babbling about. And the son-of-a-bitch was telling the truth!

CHAPTER 6

The Wolf in the President's pants.

One of the many mysteries in the sensational Puro-lator vault case was how Ralph Marrera managed to get a job with the international money-handling firm in the first place. He was a known associate of some of the biggest thieves in Chicago, and left his previous job under a dark, suspicious cloud.

A handsome ladies' man, the brown-eyed Marrera was a muscular 180 pounds and wore his black hair modishly over his ears.

One of the curious things about Ralph was his apparent desire to make himself appear two years older than his actual age. Records in the Bureau of Vital Statistics in Chicago list his birth date as July 17, 1945, which would have made him just 29 at the time of the October melo-drama. Yet court records show that, whenever he listed his date of birth with employers, or with the police, he put it down as July 17, 1943. Thus, throughout the long investi-gation following the Purolator theft, police and newspapers listed Marrera's age as 31.

For a man in his twenties, and with no advanced educa-tion or special skills, Marrera was doing well indeed. He and his wife, Alberta, with two youngsters just entering grade school, owned the two-flat where they lived on South Clinton Avenue in Berwyn, a western suburb of Chicago. The building was valued at $40,000. He also held a financial interest in the family-owned New Ritz Hotel, south of the

Loop — not bad on a guard's salary of $4.30 an hour, or about $9,000 a year with overtime.

Ralph joined the Purolator payroll in September, 1973, as an alarm monitor. In hiring Marrera for this responsibility, the Purolator bosses were apparently unaware of Ralph's highly questionable friends, or the fact that he'd been dismissed by Wells Fargo only a month earlier. A simple reference check could have disclosed this.

As a pre-requisite to being hired by Purolator, Ralph took and passed three polygraph tests administered by the world renowned lie-detector firm, John E. Reid & Associates, of Chicago. On his employment application, Marrera explained that he left Wells Fargo because "I was not satisfied with the pay and the attitude of my bosses."

Actually, Marrera's performance at Wells Fargo did little to inspire his bosses. They dismissed him after he failed a lie detector test involving a theft from a Wells Fargo client he was supposed to be guarding. In January of 1973 the Tiara Corporation, a jewelry manufacturing firm in north suburban Evanston, was burglarized for $800,000 worth of gold and jewelry while Marrera was on guard duty there. The ensuing investigation exposed Ralph as a likely suspect in setting up the job which involved defeating a sophisticated alarm system.

During the investigation police learned of Marrera's visits to the neighboring suburb of Cicero, where he was seen with Charlie Marzano, a Little League baseball coach and renowned burlar alarm expert. On February 11, 1973, in a search of Marzano's home, police reported confiscating a vast array of equipment capable of circumventing or deactivating alarm systems, along with manuals relating to their manufacture and use.

Although no charges were filed against Marrera or Marzano in the Tiara theft, Marrera left Wells Fargo at his employer's demand and promptly joined Purolator. He worked as an alarm board watcher only a few months before being switched to the far more responsible and trustworthy position of armed vault guard. The apparent ineptitude with which Ralph was hired at Purolator, belatedly, caused the firm to review its hiring and security procedures.

A month after Ralph went to work for Purolator, another unusual man, Joseph Ignatius Woods, joined the security firm. Woods, 57, was a lanky, smiling ex-FBI agent whose sister, Rose Mary, served as personal secretary to Richard M. Nixon, President of the United States.

Woods came to work wearing one of Mr. Nixon's old blue suits of clothes, a hand-me-down gift from the President to a fellow Republican.

Woods, a former sheriff of Cook County, liked to point out that his dimensions were precisely those of the President of the United States. And Mr. Nixon, always an impeccable dresser, did not hold onto his wardrobe selections long enough to let them go out of style. Aware that Rose Mary's brother had eleven children to support, Nixon passed on his tailor-made discards, in mint condition, to smiling Joe.

Unfortunately, however, the slimmer Woods did not have enough bottom to fill out the President's pants. "The goddam thing hangs on him like a sack," one Purolator employee snickered as Woods strutted around the office like a blue serge peacock in the the act of moulting. "Nixon's waistline must be twice as big as Joe's."

"Yeah, you can only alter a suit so much," laughed another, behind Woods' back. "You can't make a peacock out of a pelican."

Woods, who was suspected of being one of the few genuinely honest men in Chicago politics, was a native of Sebring, Ohio, and still spoke with an Ohio drawl. He initially aspired to the Roman Catholic priesthood, but dropped out of the seminary in 1941 to join the U.S. Marine Corps. He served in the Pacific during World War II, participating in the Ie Shima and Okinawa campaigns, and came marching home a first lieutenant. After the war, he worked as a salesman in Washington, D.C., until his commission as a special agent for the Federal Bureau of Investigation came through in 1951.

During the next ten years, Woods served in every phase of criminal investigation. While attached to the FBI field office in Birmingham, Ala., he received J. Edgar Hoover's personal commendation for the arrest of a nationally sought bank robber. Three years later, at the Memphis field office, he was again commended by Hoover for helping to bring about the arrest of one of the nation's "Ten Most Wanted" criminals. He was honored once more in 1960 for "very essential" work leading to the solution of the kidnap/murder of a Virginia family.

In 1961 Woods resigned from the FBI to become chief investigator for the Better Government Association of Chicago, a citizen's watchdog agency. Later he served one term as Cook County Sheriff, and then was elected to the Cook County Board of Supervisors as a Republican from suburban Oak Park.

His sister, Rose Mary, had been with Richard Nixon since he entered the United States Senate. The foul matter of Watergate had not yet hit the fan when Woods went to work for Purolator, nor had Rose Mary made nationwide headlines in connection with the celebrated erasures of the Nixon tapes.

Joe's appointment with Purolator was clearly political, with the agency's top brass banking on his clout with the right people to give them a leg up on their competitors. Decked out in his Presidential finery, he came to work every morning, continually talking about his friendship with the man in the White House. Occasionally, he even handed out "Nixon" pens to people he especially wanted to impress.

At the Purolator offices Woods was generally known as a "glad-hand, fare-thee-well, bullshitter" who was not the least bit bashful about picking up the telephone and pushing the armored car business on his cronies and political contacts. On one occasion he called Robert E. Husted, department manager of Purolator's electronics security system, into his office and grandly motioned for him to take a seat. Woods then made himself comfortable in the swivel chair behind his desk, looked up the phone number of a well-known businessman, and gave him a call.

"This is Joe Woods, present Cook County commissioner and former sheriff," he announced, letting the importance of his political connections sink in. "I'd like you to talk to my man here about your security needs." After explaining his present position with Purolator, Woods wound up the conversation saying, "Let's have lunch some time," and handed the phone to Husted to make a sales pitch.

Woods was also a licensed polygraph operator, and had a lie-box in his office, but no one had ever seen him use it. The firm brought in an outside operator, whenever testing was required.

Although it was not necessary in his position, Joe always carried a small automatic pistol in his coat pocket. He liked to appear discreet about it, but generally made sure someone was present whenerver he "checked it out." It was the subject of another office gag: "Joe's about as discreet with that gun as a five-year-old kid towing a howitzer."

Purolator, the company for which both Marrera and Woods worked, was an international operation with two basic divisions. One manufactured oil, gasoline, and air filters for combustion engines; famed for its radio and television "Purolator . . . Purolator . . . Purolator Filter" jingle. More recent was its service end of the business. The Purolator Corporation of Piscataway, New Jersey, acquired the Armored Express Corporation of Chicago in 1973 for 72,000 Purolator common shares, and assumed its assets, obligations, and clients. Annual sales at the time amounted to $7 million in the fast growing security business.

Purolator boasted the "World's Largest Armored Car," a 31-ton monster — the weight of a medium tank — capable of hauling eighteen tons of money. The service operation provided red, white and blue armored car and courier transport for banks and businesses the world over, moving and protecting such high-value items as jewelry, government food stamps, bonds, exotic animals — and millions and millions in cash.

So, on the evening of October 20, 1974, the stage had been set for the biggest cash burglary in America's history. Between the $40 million in cash and the thieves were the absent supersleuth in baggy Presidential pants, and the wolf in sheep's clothing who, incredibly, was being paid by Purolator to watch the money.

CHAPTER 7

"I think we've got our Mister Inside Man."

The inventory was finally completed, and the loss was set at exactly $4,374,398.96. It was, indeed, the biggest cash burglary, ever, in the history of America — more than twice as large as the ex-champ, Rondout. Other big cash thefts, standouts in their time, but suddenly dimmed by Purolator, included the $1,551,277 robbery of a United States postal truck near Plymouth, Massachusetts, in 1962 by a gang posing as police; and the famous 1950 Brinks Express garage holdup in Boston, where 11 men wearing Halloween masks got $1,219,218.

But Purolator was now the undisputed king, and the FBI moved into the next phase of its inquiry — to establish the "How?".

Chicago FBI Chief Richard G. Held took personal charge of the case. "The Federal Bureau of Investigation is in this case because of the apparent involvement of the Chicago Crime Syndicate," he said, "both in masterminding and executing the theft, and in disposing of or hiding the loot through mob operatives throughout the world. In addition, the vault contained monies belonging in part to the Federal Reserve Bank."

Chief Held appointed a 27-year FBI veteran, Ramon "Ray" Stratton — one of the first government men on the scene — to coordinate all activities of the various law enforcement agencies involved in the investigation. Stratton was the highest-paid FBI street agent at the time and preferred street work to shuffling papers. Because he was so good at it, the bureau made a rare exception in his case. It paid him supervisory wages and gave him a loose rein.

Stratton hardly resembled the Hollywood version of the G-man. Instead, he could have been easily mistaken for the typical uneasy husband in a lingerie department at Christmas time. He was 46 years old, the scoutmaster of Boy Scout Troop 159 in his suburban home of Arlington Heights. He had to struggle to hit a bull's eye on the pistol range. He was a Chicago Bears football fan, enjoyed reading paperback westerns, grew roses in the garden behind his home, and spent much of his job time chasing bank robbers.

A native of Astoria, Oregon, Stratton joined the FBI as a clerk when he was only 16. He served three years with the Army, and graduated from Northwest College of Law in Portland. He rejoined the FBI as a full-fledged special agent.

James Fioramonti could tell people a lot about Ray Stratton. As an agent assigned to the Bureau's C-3 bank robbery squad in Chicago, Stratton once spent three years carefully piecing together a case of mistaken identity, proving that Fioramonti had been wrongfully arrested by police and convicted of a 1966 holdup of a North Side savings and loan association. Stratton's determination resulted in a full pardon for the innocent man.

He was that kind of gumshoe. A human bloodhound. And when Held assigned him to the Purolator caper, Stratton's fellow agents laid odds that, for whoever pulled off the heist, it would be only a matter of time before the bloodhound closed in.

The Federal Bureau of Investigation was not alone in unravelling the massive case, of course. While the loss was being determined, and a probable time frame for the burglary established, scores of Chicago police officers and detectives joined with the FBI agents in questioning Purolator employees, and establishing the firm's operating procedures.

The case represented, from the moment the firebombs were detonated in the East Vault, a model of cooperation between the Chicago Police Department and the FBI. There was no hot-dogging, grand-standing, or juggling of clues in order to hog the credit. All agencies were moving toward a united goal — to find out who did it, and to nail them.

By now, it was known how much money was taken and roughly when the score went down. Still to be resolved was the "How?"

Investigators requested the time cards of every Purolator employee who had access to the vault room, plus the guards' logs which recorded all who entered and left the vault room. Authorities then began the task of interviewing every person known to have entered the building between Saturday night and Monday morning, when the firebombs erupted. A review of operating procedure at the warehouse disclosed that the outer perimeter doors were kept locked at all times. No one could have entered without being admitted by a guard.

Access to the vault room could only be gained through the second floor office area of the building, there to be admitted by a receptionist, through an electronically controlled door. The employee must then proceed through the general office area, and down a stairway to the entrance of the vault room.

On either side of this entrance were several bin areas, described by one investigator as "short hallways with electronic doors on either end." The doors were controlled from inside the vault room. Armored truck messengers, bringing their collections into the bin area on a normal working day, had to be admitted through the first door by a vaultman.

Once in the bin area, the messenger checked the money he had delivered, in sealed bags or footlockers, into the vault room through the second doorway. This entrance consisted of two half doors, one above the other. The top half was normally opened to form a teller entrance. The bottom half was opened only to permit the shoving of footlockers into the vault room. No one but the vaultman himself was permitted to perform the latter function.

An armed guard was always stationed inside the entrance door, with a clear view of the bins on either side of him and of both entrances to the East and West Vaults. At the west end of the vault room, there was another electronically controlled door. Only a few paces from the alarm board, this door was controlled by a dispatcher at the entrance desk.

This was the door through which tankers, too large to move through the bin areas, were admitted to the vault room. The dispatcher, a managment employee of the money firm, was the only person who had authority to admit anyone into this area.

Could this be the "How?"

At any given time there were supposed to be at least two employees in the locked vault room — the armed guard and the alarm board monitor. But on a normal working day, there were some forty employees with access to the room, with as many as twenty-five working in the area at once.

Would it be possible, because of the number of employees in the vault room, and the general confusion in handling large amounts of money, for a vaultman to surreptitiously shove a footlocker full of cash into the bin area, out of sight? He could trigger the outside bin area door and leave it slightly ajar. Then, after checking out of the vault room, he could return during the quiet evening hours, pull open the bin door and remove the footlocker. Although unlikely, Stratton admitted that this approach "Isn't outside the realm of possibility."

Investigators estimated that it would have taken three footlockers, crammed full, to remove the amount of missing money from the East Vault — a task certainly requiring more than one person to accomplish.

The introduction of the gasoline bombs was also puzzling. Since sealed footlockers come into the vault room throughout the normal business day, bringing the firebombs in with money shipments would take the cooperation of at least one messenger and probably an entire crew of an armored truck, plus the assistance of the inside vaultman. This possibility was quickly ruled out as employees were questioned and their time patterns over the weekend became established.

For purposes of investigation, then, it was assumed that several tankers were opened, including those from which no money was removed — some time after they were placed into the vault — and the gasoline incendiary devices were placed among them.

Lt. Edward Neville, veteran commander of the Chicago

Police Bomb and Arson Unit, determined that a chemical time fuse was used to ignite the gasoline in at least two of the white plastic bags. "This was done for the sole purpose of causing a rapid, very hot fire," he explained to Stratton.

"I guess we can thank our lucky stars they didn't know beans about physics," Stratton commented.

"If they did, you can tell your Purolator friends their insurance company would have been paying off on twenty-five million smackers," Neville answered. "Instead of four."

"Four point three-seven-four," replied the meticulous. Stratton.

The vexing question of how anyone could enter the locked vault became less and less of a mystery as more and more Purolator employees were questioned. Only four officials of the money firm had been given the combination to the vault: 30-60-80-50-93. However, investigators soon established that virtually every vault man was aware of the combination. One of them, Phillip Layne — the man who supervised the tucking away of the Hawthorne Race Course money — even had the *secret* combination *taped to the inside of his locker door* because he could not remember it! Investigators further determined that the trusting Layne seldom bothered to lock his locker door. The unflappable Joe Woods saw nothing wrong with this practice, however. When slack-jawed investigators questioned Layne's carelessness, Woods explained:

"The combination is changed regularly to throw off thieves. It doesn't do much good to memorize it, because it soon gets changed."

Woods was blissfully unaware that a Purolator Securities policy calling for the vault combination to be changed every six months had been ignored for over a year. The last time the combination was changed was March 8, 1973. According to policy, it should have been changed in September of 1973, again in March of 1974, and once more in September of 1974 — a month before the burglary.

When asked about the apparent breach of company rules, Hardt could not explain why the combination had not been changed in the September of the previous year, or in March.

He said, however, that "definite plans were made" to have the combination changed in September of 1974. The man charged with that responsibility, Robert Murphy, left the company on August 31 for a higher paying job and the combination change was never accomplished.

It was quickly changed, however, on October 21, 1974, following the discovery of the awesome theft.

Police and FBI agents also discovered a curious practice at Purolator: Anyone entering the vault was told to "check" his wallet outside. This was done as a precaution against anyone taking "free samples" while inside the money room. A number of persons authorized to have the vault lock combination were known to have kept it in their billfolds.

Investigators now knew that almost anyone at Purolator, including the janitor, could have had the secret combination. It could have been picked up anytime over the last year and a half, either by peeping into an authorized holder's billfold while he was inside the vault, or by copying it from Phil Layne's unlocked locker door.

In fact, when Chicago detective John Whalen accompanied Layne to his locker to see where he had the combination taped, they opened the locker door and discovered that the piece of paper on which the combination had been written was gone. The list of suspects, at this point, was appalling!

There was also the fact that the vault had no time locking device — something that would have prevented it from being opened over the weekend, even by someone who knew the combination. The man in Mr. Nixon's old blue suit once again leaped in to explain. "That's because of the frequency we have to get into and out of it at various times. We are not like a bank, which uses time locks. We are a service organization. We've got to get the money in and out at irregular times, when our customers require service. That's the kind of business this is."

Robert Husted, the electronics security system manager, had another, more earthy explanation:

"Bullshit! The time locks had been out of commission for years."

The questioning of employees was intensified. "Whoever

did this had to have a knowledge of Armored Express operations," said Investigator John Terretta, of the police department's General Assignment Unit. "But everyone who was
supposed to have reported for work today has shown up as
scheduled. They've all agreed to take polygraph tests, and we
are going to have to take some of them up on it."

In all, fifteen employees, including security guards and
others who worked inside the building over the weekend,
or had any connection with the vault, were given lie detector
tests after questioning by the FBI. Some of the tests were
administered by a portable polygraph in the Purolator office,
and the subjects quickly dismissed. Others were taken to
Chicago Police Headquarters on South State Street for testing.

Police found that two Purolator employees responsible
for vault security on Saturday were not those normally
assigned to the task. This appeared significant at the moment,
but was later attributed to trading off shifts so certain people
could attend the annual Purolator employees party at Johnnie
Weigelt's.

Interviews were also conducted with those Wells Fargo
employees who were assigned to watch the alarm board
covering the Purolator plant. From these interviews, authorities developed other curious and nagging particles of information. On several occasions during the past few weeks, "false
alarms" were received at Wells Fargo indicating the East
Main Vault door at Purolator had been opened. Whenever
any such thing happened, the Wells Fargo employee on duty
at the monitoring board was instructed to notify an official
of Purolator. Instead, all the Wells Fargo employee did, in
each instance, was telephone the duty guard at Purolator to
inquire whether everything was all right, and each time the
guard assured the Wells Fargo monitor that all was well.

A back-check of records of both companies, on nights the
alarms were sounded, showed that the Purolator guard on
duty who gave the all-clear signal in each and every case was
Ralph Marrera!

The Wells Fargo monitor board watchman on duty Sunday
night was grilled extensively by FBI agents, but they got nowhere. Ashok Patel, the Indian, had a language difficulty.

He was unable to give a clear story as to whether the vault alarm light flashed during the evening, but said he thought it didn't.

From a review of Purolator time cards and logs, the FBI determined that only three guards were on duty during the period from Saturday night to early Monday, when the firebombs exploded.

The first two, including Robert Woolsey, who Ralph Marrera punched out early Sunday night, became the subjects of intense questioning. Woolsey and his fellow guard, their stories cleanly collaborated by other employees, were finally released as having "no logical information" regarding the theft.

The third, of course, was the cocky Marrera, who had presumably gone home to rest up, having stayed on duty longer than usual to do what he could "to help." Stratton suspected Marrera from the moment he entered the case, after being told of Ralph's unusual action when firemen arrived, and was anxious to question him in detail. He also wanted to talk to Angela Hughes, the alarm board employee, who was the only other person on duty in the building with Marrera throughout that evening.

Other employees had to be interviewed first, however. There was James Smola, the elusive alarm runner who had arrived at the burglary scene with his replacement, Michael Mormino, shortly after the firebombs exploded. Smola had been scheduled to work 5 p.m. to 1 a.m. on the night of the theft, and Mormino was the 1 a.m. to 9 a.m. man. Smola related how he had been performing "miscellaneous duties" in the Purolator garage when Mrs. Hughes asked him to watch the alarm board for her, but he refused. He said he was out of the building most of the evening, and went to Mormino's home at 11:20 p.m. to wake up his relief.

From Mormino's they drove to the Anchor Club, a North Clark Street bar near Purolator, where they had a few drinks and engaged in small talk. Smola said the two men were on the way to the money warehouse when they received a radio call from Mrs. Bivens that there was an emergency. Smola's story was confirmed by Mormino, who arrived to put in the most exciting work night of his life. Investigators then called

Mildred Bivens, the alarm board monitor who came on duty at midnight Sunday to work the early Monday morning shift, and who was with Marrera when the alarm went off. She told the agents:

"I heard this hissing sound. Then it got louder, like a big gust of wind came up. It blew paper and dust around on the vault area floor. Then the noise got louder."

Firemen were on the scene before the dust could settle, she said. Mrs. Bivens reiterated how Marrera at first tried to keep them out. Then she disclosed something that would help Stratton immensely in piecing his mystery puzzle together.

"Who, besides Ralph Marrera, was present when you came on duty at midnight?" she was asked.

"Only Ralph. He was the only one there."

"The time cards and the log indicates you relieved Angela Hughes."

"Oh, no. I normally do, but I didn't last night. She had gone home early. And, when I got there, Ralph was the *only one* in the building."

Advised of Mrs. Bivens' statement, Stratton clasped his hands across his stomach in a gesture of utter satisfaction, smiled broadly, and remarked, "Well, I think we've got our Mister Inside Man."

CHAPTER 8
Surprise in the Feds' own files!

Two more bombshells that made the eccentric case all the more unbelievable were uncovered by agents making a routine check of Chicago FBI records for up-to-date information on Ralph Marrera.

First, they learned that in January of 1973 Chicago police considered Marrera as the suspected inside man of the massive Tiara Jewelry burglary in Evanston. Subsequent investigation revealed his close association with Pasquale Charles Marzano.

At 40, Charlie, as he was known to his circle of friends, could pass as a nice guy from the suburbs. Police, however, knew him as Charles Michael, alias Patsy Marzano, alias Charles Rossa, alias Charles Marks.

He was a self-taught electronics and burglar alarm expert, strong as an elephant, and a survivor of street corner gun battles and burglary investigations. He grew up, like Gushi, in "The Patch," a rough and tough neighborhood just southwest of Chicago's Chinatown, known as a breeding place of cartage thieves, cat burglars and pushers. In 1959 he took five bullets in a street-corner shooting at 31st Street and Normal Avenue, where his brother, Danny Marzano, 26, was slain. Charlie, rushed to Michael Reese Hospital in critical condition, was back on the streets in no time.

He was a prime suspect in the Tiara caper from the beginning. The burglars had apparently been supplied with detailed building plans which enabled them to cut through a three-and-a-half inch thick concrete wall in the only spot where such drilling could be accomplished without meeting the steel cross-beams. After slipping into the building through the hole, the burglars climbed atop a jeweler's workbench and pulled out the ceiling tiles to expose the telephone lines to the alarm circuit on the outside door.

Once locating the proper wires, they attached a highly-sophisticated control box to the line and circumvented the alarm system, described by police as "one of the best in the country." Wires to the building's alarm equipment were cut and tripped from the control box which the burglars had installed to other parts of the building. All this was done by removing additional ceiling tiles and tracing the important telephone line. The burglars then climbed into a false ceiling to a connecting building, and thwarted yet another door alarm with their equipment, deactivating a second alarm circuit and an electric eye.

They were thus able to enter the section of the building containing the precious metals and gems. After scooping up everything of value, they quickly removed their control devices from the security system and fled as the alarm sounded.

The operation was so smooth that they were well out of sight by the time the first Evanston squad car arrived from the station only a block away!

Fascinated FBI agents, who had stored the file away almost two years earlier for future reference, now studied it with great excitement. The similarities to the Purolator case were remarkable. And there was Ralph Marrera, in both incidents!

Suspicion immediately fell upon Marzano, the unemployed electronics expert with a record of five arrests and no convictions. He had lived on South Parnell Avenue in Chicago, but was then residing in Cicero under the name of John Roberts. His home, driver's license and even the utility bills were under the phony name.

Marzano was placed under close surveillance following the Tiara theft. It was then that police discovered his close association with Marrera, as well as a number of gangland figures, convicted burglars and known robbers.

Three weeks after Tiara, in mid-February, 1973, Chicago police officially entered the case in cooperation with Evanston authorities and arrested the 38-year-old Marzano. They gained entry to his Cicero home by obtaining a search warrant. There they found evidence which quickly brought the FBI into the case. Captain William Hanhardt, commander of the Chicago Police Burglary Section, explained that his men found electronic equipment capable of deactivating and circumventing the most sophisticated burglar alarms ever manufactured to protect banks, jewelry stores, and places where large quantities of money and other valuables were kept.

"We found dozens of highly restricted manufacturers' manuals and handbooks describing the workings of locks, safes, and burglar alarm systems, along with professional drawings of the secret systesm," he said. "There was also a huge store of cutting torches, power tools, drills, saws, lock picks, key codes, and other equipment that only an expert would know how to use."

Marzano was charged with possession of burglar tools, and receiving stolen property. But authorities were unable to link him to the Tiara case. The $800,000 in loot was never recovered, despite rewards of up to $53,000 offered by the company.

Marrera's connection to the Tiara incident and his known association with Marzano were two more nails in the case that Stratton was piecing together. The connection with Marzano, a known burglar alarm expert, gave Stratton his Number Two Suspect.

If, as the Indian who monitored the Wells Fargo alarm board indicated, the alarm actually did not sound when the the vault was opened — then the intricate alarm system had to have been compromised by an expert. The FBI already had established that almost anyone working in the money warehouse could have had the combination, but it would have taken a man of Marzano's expertise to keep the alarm from going off.

The FBI ordered an extensive examination of the system

to see if it had, in fact, been compromised. It was first studied by technical employees of Purolator, followed by technicians from Illinois Bell Telephone and the manager of Wells Fargo Alarms Systems, who originally installed it. The FBI then called in technicians from the Chicago Police Department as well as specially trained FBI agents. Finally, engineers from the FBI laboratory in Washington were flown in for their opinion.

The electronic components within the vault could not be examined for possible circumvention, since they had been severely fire-damaged. Someone would have had to have gotten inside the vault to get at them. Wells Fargo personnel, in replacing the damaged system with a new one, discovered an open circuit. The system was thoroughly rechecked, and it was learned that the installers had used the same wires that had beeen a part of the damaged system. A further check of the line revealed that when the original system was installed, the workers never used the ground wire provided by Illinois Bell Telephone Company for that purpose. Instead they used a "common ground," which was nothing more than a wire imbedded in the concrete under the vault.

Aside from questionable workmanship, the results of the exhaustive tests were frustrating. There was absolutely nothing to indicate that the East Vault security systems, elaborate as they were, had been compromised or sabotaged. The examination yielded no clamp marks, as might have been made by diverting the electric current. There was no evidence of short circuiting. There were no fingerprints or smudges. And, a microscopic examination showed that even the dust on the system was still uniformly in place.

"Well, boys, I'll tell you something," Stratton speculated, jamming his hands into his rear trouser pockets. "We are either dealing with the greatest electronics experts of all time — or else those birds just said 'alarms be damned' and let 'em go off. And found some way to cover up. That just has to be the answer."

The agents agreed. The inside man — and they were now positive of his identity — got rid of the witnesses and opened the store to his accomplices. "Then he unlocked the safe with the combination he'd probably filched from Layne's locker, and let the alarm lights flash," Stratton continued. "Then, when the monitor guy at Wells Fargo made what had become almost a routine phone check, Mister Inside told him everything at Purolator was hunky-dory. That's the way I see it."

Still unanswered were the questions: Why, with $25 million in the vault they broke into, were the thieves content to take only a small part of it, leaving nearly $21 million behind? And, why was Ralph Marrera left behind to face the music?

"My guess is they were working on a time schedule, and the dough they got was all they had time to handle," suggested Stratton. "Or, could be something scared them off.

"And, maybe the bombs went off prematurely. Maybe they were set to detonate some time after 1:30, after Marrera would have gone off duty. That seems plausible, since Marrera's replacement would then be the guy who looked bad, if anyone. Maybe the fuses, or chemical activating device, or whatever they used, just burned down quicker than they figured."

Meanwhile, FBI agents came up with a second blockbuster of their own. There was one other brief entry in the Marrera file.

It advised that early in September the Illinois Bureau of Investigation (IBI) learned from an informant that a "big cash score" was about to go down, and among those reportedly involved were Pasquale Charles Marzano and Peter James Gushi, the known underworld character and mover of stolen goods.

Furthermore, the IBI had set up a net of surveillance, observing Marzano and Marrera meeting several times, and once spied on a three-way meeting between Marrera, Marzano and Gushi. Incredibly, although the IBI agents had established Marrera's identity and reported his activities to state authorities, they had failed to determine that he was then working as a security guard for one of the biggest money movers in the business.

Finally, after four full weeks of painstaking observation, they unexplainedly withdrew their surveillance — just seven days before the record-breaking assault on the Purolator millions!

CHAPTER 9

Ralph goes on the lie box.

By late afternoon on Monday, the day the big score was discovered, the burgeoning investigation was jumping off in so many directions that Ray Stratton announced to his staff, "I'm thinking of getting myself a scorecard.' Law enforcement agencies already involved in the case, in addition to the FBI, included Siragusa's Illinois Legislative Investigating Commission; the Illinois Bureau of Investigation, or so-called "little FBI"; the State's Attorney's Special Investigations Unit; and the Chicago Police Department.

The number of special agents, detectives, crime lab tech-technicians, and prosecutors directly involved surpassed 300. Iavarone's staff, like the IBI, had been kept informed by Siragusa of Gushi's boasts, and suddenly everyone was out looking for Ralph Marrera, who wasn't home to callers.

The FBI moved in fast, scooping up the IBI files on the Gushi surveillance, plus those of the Marzano cousins and Marrera. The files contained vast amounts of information here-to-fore not furnished to either federal authorities or Chicago police, because the state agency — fearful of a leak — had figured to work the case exclusively.

It is not uncommon for law enforcement agencies to withhold information from each other. For one thing, they don't want to appear to be alarmists. Tips of all sorts of criminal activity, real or imagined, from well-meaning sources, are rampant. If such exchanges were more common, lawmen would be buried in each other's gossip and intelligence — criss-crossing one another's tracks chasing stories. Furthermore, it is a well known fact in Chicago that the Mafia, or local crime syndicate, has always had its own men in key places — in the police department, in the prosecutor's office, and even on the judicial bench. Judges have been known to show up as pall bearers at gangster funerals, and entire files on certain criminal activities have disappeared from locked cabinets at police headquarters. Thus, the fewer people in on an operation like the Gushi surveillance, the less chance there was of a leak.

Poring over the information now being made available to them for the first time, FBI agents repeatedly came across the names of Pasquale Charles Marzano, Peter James Gushi, James Andrew Maniatis, Allen Morton Wainer, Luigi Michael DiFonzo, and William Anthony "Tony" Marzano.

Information provided by Pollakov, the undercover informant, indicated Charlie Marzano was probably the mastermind, assisted by his cousin, Tony, and Peter James Gushi. DiFonzo, a roving financial wizard who had been in trouble with the law before, and presumably was to take the money to Grand Cayman Island in the Caribbean and launder it in secret bank accounts.

Also popping up in the Pollakov reports was mention of an obscure charter boat skipper out of Miami, a sailor named Redmond, who was supposed to ferry DiFonzo and the booty to George Town, the Island's capital, 500 miles away.

Wainer's role was questionable. According to Siragusa's stoolies, he provided the "up front" money for Maniatis to buy the Ford van and arranged for Charlie Marzano to meet DiFonzo. Whether Wainer even knew what the money was to be used for, however, was never established. The lowly Maniatis, it appeared, was brought into the caper simply to obtain the van — so it could not be traced to any member of the gang. Charlie Marzano had taken great care in choosing the vehicle he wanted. His first choice of color was off-white, so it would resemble the Ford vans used by Purolator. A van that color would attract little suspicion around the money warehouse neighborhood. But none was available, so he settled for mint green, which would give the appearance of a utility vehicle.

After reviewing the IBI files based on data from Pollakov and Doyle, the FBI agents went over the surveillance logs. They quickly established that, during September and early October, organized crime investigators had observed repeated meetings between the Marzanos, Luigi DiFonzo, and Ralph Marrera. At least one meeting was observed between Charlie Marzano, Marrera, and Gushi. Agents then pulled Marrera's Purolator file and began checking his time cards backward, from the day of the burglary.

They already knew, of course, that he was the regularly scheduled guard on duty for Sunday night, October 20. The last Sunday before that on which he was regularly scheduled was September 29. It was also learned that, with some difficulty, he had changed shifts with other guards so he would be on duty Sunday night, October 6.

That explained the confusion over the October 6 date. The gang did not know, until too late to move, whether Ralph would be on duty that night. Investigators now figured the boasting Gushi deliberately miss-spoke himself when he told Pollakov "the money won't be there for three more weeks," after the September 29th date came and went without event. It wasn't the money that had to "be there." It was Marrera.

Stratton picked up the file, bit the side of his lip and frowned. "Bring in Ralph Ronald Marrera," he ordered crisply. "Find him, and invite him to our office for an interview. If he declines, you are to arrest him on charges of bank larceny, and use of explosives and incendiary devices during the commission of a federal felony. Tell him just that!"

FBI agent Joseph Burke and another agent drove out to Marrera's duplex on Clinton Avenue in Berwyn, but were told he was not home. "We'll wait," Burke told Marrera's brunette wife, Alberta. Within an hour Marrera arrived, and did not seem at all surprised to find two FBI men waiting for him.

"Ralph Marrera, we would like you to accompany us to the Dirksen Federal Building where the agent in charge would like to discuss the investigation into the Purolator burglary with you," Burke said.

"Sure, I'll be glad to go downtown," Marrera said placidly. "I figured you guys would be wanting to take a statement from me, or something. Hell, I want to do all I can to help. This whole thing is really something, isn't it?"

At bureau headquarters in the federal building Stratton introduced himself, and informed Marrera of his rights. Then, after establishing that Marrera knew his rights, Stratton asked whether he would be willing to submit to a polygraph examination. "You bet," said Marrera. He agreed so readily that Stratton wondered how long he had rehearsed the scenario that was unfolding.

The lie test was administered in the FBI office by Leonard Harrelson of Leonarde Keeler, Inc., one of the most highly-respected polygraph experts in the business. Stratton had prepared the questions. After it was over Harrelson advised Stratton that Marrera had failed the test badly.

"Just look at these lines, Ray," he said, spreading the lie-test graph across Stratton's desk. "See here, he constantly lied during the examination regarding knowledge and participation of the crime. The test shows he is clearly implicated and knows the identities of all the offenders."

Stratton walked over to Marrera, still connected to the lie box, and held up the strip of greenish graph paper, curled at the edges.

"Tsk, tsk, tsk," Stratton began, shaking his head from side to side. "Do you know what this says, Ralph? This tells me you've been a little loose with the truth. In fact, the graph here indicates you've been lying like a rug."

Marrera stared Stratton right in the eye, a look of puckish innocence on his face.

"We've got you, Ralph, and you know it," Stratton said. "We know you've been in on this from the start. We know that you know who else was in on it, and we know that you know where the dough is. Don't you think it would be in your own best interest if you started cooperating? Save your ass, Ralph."

Marrera responded by pulling off the polygraph wires that were affixed to his body and cursing, "Fuck the lie box! It doesn't prove anything." He was then questioned at length by Stratton. And despite being confronted with his zero score on the polygraph, he steadfastly denied any conection with the Purolator caper. He said he had no idea how the firebombs got into the vault, and insisted that Angela Hughes would back up his story.

"Well I think we can clear this all up right here and now," Stratton reasoned. "We'll just set you down on the polygraph again here and give you a wide open chance to clear yourself. Now, what more could we do for you than that, huh?"

Before taking Stratton up on the offer, Marrera received permission to call his lawyer, Gerald Nussbaum, who advised, "Don't you do it, Ralph."

"Well then, I guess we're through with you for the time being," Stratton said evenly. "We're going to see you again, you can be sure of that. But for now, the Chicago P.D. is waiting outside. They have a few questions they want to ask you, Ralph. This happened in their jurisdiction, too, you know."

"No, no! Wait Don't do that, please," Marrera begged, suddenly losing his cockiness. "I don't want to talk to no cops. They'll beat the shit out of me. I know they will."

"Nobody is going to beat the shit out of you, I guarantee that," assured Stratton. "You have my word on it. Now, if you want to cooperate with us in this, the government will put you in protective custody and see that your family is taken care of. Otherwise, Ralph, we'll have to let you go, and several of Chicago's finest are anxiously awaiting your presence."

A less than happy Marrera was then turned over to Chicago detectives Stanley Golucki and John Whalen. They had been on duty in the Purolator garage at 6:30 p.m. questioning employees, when FBI agent Thomas Greene advised Lt. Nickels that Marrera had been taken into custody. Nickels told Whalen and Golucki, "Get over there, and grab him when the 'G' gets through talking to him."

On arriving at the federal building, Golucki and Whalen found two men they recognized as IBI agents waiting in Stratton's outer office.

"What are you guys doing here?" Whalen asked.

"We want Marrera, too," he was told. "We were down here on something else, and we saw the feds bringing the guy in. We had him and several other mopes under surveillance for over a month in a cartage theft investigation." They then briefed the police investigators on Marrera's association with the Marzano cousins and Gushi.

"O.K., might as well get in line," Whalen laughed. "You can have him soon as we get done talking to him."

Whalen and Golucki then read Marrera his rights under the Miranda decision, and he agreed to cooperate with them, but refused to accompany them to police headquarters. "Right here," Marrera insisted. "I'll be glad to answer all your questions. But you gotta talk to me right here." A smiling Stratton then offered the two detectives space in his office to carry out their questioning. Marrera talked freely.

"You know, I don't know anything about what happened there. Honest, I don't. The FBI claims I flunked the lie box, but I can't explain that. Maybe I'm just nervous or something. Actually, I think I should be considered a hero! I was the guard on duty, and I'm the guy who discovered the fire. It was me who called the company brass. You know, I stayed down until 7:20 a.m. this morning, just to do what I could do to help out."

"Where'd you go then? We checked your house, and you didn't go home." Whalen asked.

"I know. I went over to the New Ritz Hotel on South State. My family owns it and I manage the place," Ralph explained. "I spent the rest of the day there, doing maintenance work, odd jobs — crap like that."

"Where did you go after that?"

"Then I went home. When I got there around 4:30 the FBI was waiting for me, and I came back here with them."

"Look,' Golucki said. "Everybody who works for Purolator is being interviewed over in the building. It's a lot more convenient that way, with everyone under one roof. Then, if you need somebody to back up your story, that person is there. Come on over there with us, huh? It'll make this whole thing a hell of a lot easier for all of us."

"I don't know," Marrera said, looking at Stratton for moral support.

"It's O.K. Ralph, I give you my word," Stratton responded. "Nobody's going to knock you around. That just happens in the old movies."

Marrera reluctantly agreed to return to the Purolator warehouse with the two policemen, and Whalen advised the two IBI agents where they were going.

There Marrera was confronted with log records indicating he had previously switched days off so he could work the same Sunday night shift with Angela Hughes, and had apparently established a pattern of letting her go home early. Robert Cummins, a polygraph examiner for John Reid & Associates was in the building, testing other Purolator employees, and the two detectives asked Marrera if he, too, would be willing to submit to a lie test. Ralph's cockiness suddenly returned.

"Say, if you've got enough evidence, charge me. Then convict me. This is the biggest score ever, so I'll take my 20 or 30 years, write a book in the joint, and make a million on the book!" he challenged.

The detectives stared at him incredulously. "I guess this interview is over, for the time being," Whalen said. "You're free to go."

As Marrera stormed from the building he was confronted by the two IBI agents who had spotted him earlier in the federal building. They handed him a subpoena, issued by Iavarone, to appear before the Cook County Grand Jury in the Criminal Courts building the following day. Marrera reluctantly accepted the official summons. The sunshine seemed to be draining from his handsome Mediterranean face now as the late afternoon slowly drifted into night.

CHAPTER 10
The snitch is snatched.

A strange but effective investigator arrived at the Purolator building on Tuesday, October 22, representing Commercial Union Insurance Company of New York City, the money handler's insurer. He looked like a senior citizen basketball player — six and a half feet tall, bean-pole thin, in his early 60s, with short gray hair. He wore steel-rim spectacles, a baggy, brown suit, and carried a small notebook and several stubby pencils everywhere he went. He also bore the unmistakable aroma of someone who had not recently been near a bathtub or shower.

The Purolator employees immediately dubbed him "B.O. Plenty," and the name fit. He was a complete non-entity, who seemed to have the ability to walk over to a wall and completely disappear. He liked to hang around in the shadows, eavesdropping. But his locker room bouquet always gave him away. B.O. made it a point to interview each and every Purolator employee, making notations with his tiny pencil stubs as he talked. Purolator provided him with office space for this purpose, in an effort to keep him from prowling around the warehouse.

Among the first to undergo B.O.'s interrogation ordeal was Robert Husted, the firm's electronic's security systems manager. B.O. sat behind a desk in the small office and Husted sat in a chair opposite him, leaning back as far as he could in an effort to breathe air from the doorway. As they talked B.O. nonchanlantly propped one leg up on the desk to make himself more comfortable. In doing so, his skinny leg was exposed, and the sharp-eyed Husted, a former police-man, spotted a tiny microphone taped to it.

"You sneaky son-of-a-bitch," Husted laughed uproarious-ly. "You're wired for sound. Well I'll be gawd-damned!"

A curious co-worker, poking his head into the office to see what the laughter was about, discovered the impish Husted crouched forward in his chair shouting up B.O.'s baggy pantsleg, "Testing. One... two... three... four.... Testing! Testing!"

The FBI, meanwhile, was talking to Angela Hughes. Chicago police had already interviewed her, and confirmed that she had not worked a full shift Sunday night. Now it was Ray Stratton's turn. He pointed out that her time card and the guard's log sheet agreed that she had worked her full shift. However, Mrs. Bivens, who was her relief, insisted that when she came on duty at midnight she found Marrera alone.

Confronted with this, Angela took a deep breath, bit her lips, and sighed, "Okay, so I wasn't really there." She then furnished the FBI with a written statement confirming that she left her station at the alarm board at 8:15 p.m., leaving only Marrera on duty. Not just in the vault room, but in the entire building.

"But I wasn't there when it happened, and I don't know anything. I'm glad I left early. You don't know the feeling I have, of just escaping from something horrible," she said. "The way I look at it, my life wouldn't have been worth two cents if I'd been there when the action started. They would have killed me to shut me up, whoever they are. For all that money, wouldn't you?"

As for leaving her post unattended, Angela felt no particu-lar pangs of conscience.

"Look, that monitor board was never really unattended. Ralph was there. He knew the procedure."

Did anything at all unusual happen up to the time she ducked out early and headed for home with her husband?

"No, I wouldn't say so. I didn't notice anything unusual

about the vault area. Ralph got two or three phone calls, but I have no idea who they were from. Each time it rang, Ralph, he jumped up and said, 'I'll get it I'll get it.' Otherwise, I can't say anything strange happened. At least while I was there, you know?"

What about after she left? Did she think Marrera could have had anything to do with the theft?

"To me, Ralph might have had something to do with it, the way things went down, and all. Then again, you know, I just don't know. They couldn't get in unless Ralph, uh, let them in . . ."

Angela did not return to work that night, or ever again. Both she and Marrera were suspended — permanently — "for violation of company rules."

FBI agents, led by Stratton, now walked over to the office of U.S. Attorney James Thompson, which is in the same building as bureau headquarters, to go over the case in detail. Stratton wanted authorization to charge Marrera, so he could lock him up before somebody else got to him.

"Look, Jim," Stratton told the tall blond prosecutor. "This dude, Marrera, knows where more than four million bucks is stashed. A lot of people would dearly love to know just where that money is. If the Mob gets hold of Marrera they'll hang him up on a meat hook and put a blow torch to his balls until he tells them everything they want to know. Then we'll find him in the trunk of a car. You know how these boys play. All I want to do is keep him alive. He's so scared now he's liable to take a powder and we'll never find him."

"I know what you re saying, Ray, but there isn't anything we can do right now," Thompson said. "I'm going to have to turn you down. All your evidence, up to this point, is purely circumstantial. What's more, there hasn't been any decision yet as to whether prosecution will be in Federal Court or at the local level by Cook County."

Marrera, meanwhile, was taken before the County Grand Jury, and questioned under oath about the heist. He was before the panel for a full half hour, and steadfastly denied any involvement. And, at the moment, nobody could prove otherwise.

While Marrera was making his denials, "so help me, God," IBI agents picked up the informant, Martin Pollakov, and put him under wraps in their North Michigan Avenue head-quarters. Pollakov, the other side's "inside man," was far too valuable to leave unprotected. Chicago, after all, was a city where curious "accidents" had been known to happen.

When word leaked out that Pollakov was in cold storage Charlie Siragusa went into a boil. Already unhappy with the results of his liaison with the IBI, this development was more than he intended to sit still for. Grabbing the phone off his desk he punched out Supt. Kerstetter's unlisted number.

"Wayne! What the hell do you guys think you're doing? Why was my stool kidnapped? Why the hell is he being held prisoner? Why wasn't I even notified, for chrissakes? God-dammit, Wayne, you gumshoes just can't kidnap people. Not my stool, you can't. Don't pull that kind of shit on me!"

Kerstetter reluctantly agreed to give Siragusa his pigeon back, if only to stem the flow of invective and restore har-mony. But Pollakov was not free for long. He indeed *was* far too valuable to leave out on the streets, and the FBI promptly grabbed him. That didn't make Siragusa happy, either, but he knew he couldn't fight Uncle Sam, having once been on that team himself. What really galled him though was that someone else had "my stool." Traditionally, law en-forcement agencies do not share their informants with one another, especially if they are reliable. One reason is the fear they might lose their snitch to another agency that might pay him more.

Pollakov, the high school dropout who fell victim to the juicemen, and started selling tidbits of information to the law to get even, suddenly found himself playing in the big leagues.

After questioning Pollakov extensively, and tieing together every part of his story to their own satisfaction, the FBI issued a nationwide alert for Charlie Marzano, Peter Gushi, and the 1974 green Ford Econoline 200 van, assumed to have been used to haul away the money. "These men are believed to have left Chicago. We are alerting all local police agencies, and advising anyone who spots the suspects to grab them, and the van, and to contact the FBI," Stratton announced.

The balding, bespectacled Gushi was described as having an arrest record that included busts for hijacking and receiving stolen property. In 1968 he was indicted, with three others, in a mob scheme to get money from a Chicago bank for making high interest juice loans. But the case was dropped after the government's star witness was killed in a plane crash. Marzano, although he had been a suspect in illicit activities, was not known to have spent time in jail.

The final development on this busy day was a news conference called by Joe Woods, the ex-FBI man, and senior vice president of Purolator. Woods announced a reward of $195,000 for information leading to the recovery of the missing money, or the arrest and conviction of the thieves.

"We are asking anyone who has any information in this case to contact either Richard G. Held, agent in charge of the Chicago office of the Federal Bureau of Investigation; or Lt. Edward Nickels, commander of the Damen Avenue General Assignment Unit of the Chicago Police Department," he said. "And, oh, yeah. I'll take calls, too."

Appropriately, the bounty offered in the largest cash heist in America was also the biggest reward ever offered for information in a criminal case anywhere in the country.

CHAPTER 11
Ralphie takes on the lam.

If Monday and Tuesday had been bad days for Ralph Marrera, Wednesday was bleaker yet. Before Ralph had a chance to drink his breakfast coffee, FBI agents were at his door with a Federal Grand Jury subpoena ordering him to: "...lay aside all business... and appear forthwith."

Now jobless, Ralph had no immediate business to lay aside. "No problem," he smiled confidently. "Haven't you guys heard? I've been fired. My time is yours."

The jaunty Marrera was taken downtown to the ninth floor of the Dirksen Federal Building, where FBI headquarters is located. From there, Marrera called his lawyer and was then left to cool his heels. Eventually, he was greeted by Ray Stratton who stuck his head in the door and beckoned, "Come along with us."

The next stop was the U.S. Attorney's Office where Ralph's lawyer, Nussbaum, was waiting. There, with Nussbaum's consent, arrangements were made for the FBI to "interview" his client again — a task which consumed the entire day.

While Stratton and other agents grilled Marrera, IBI investigators drove out to the Maniatis apartment in suburban Worth, Illinois. To their amazement, the green Ford Econoline van was parked in front! A search warrant was immediately obtained and the impounded vehicle was turned over to Chicago Police Department evidence technicians for processing in a local police garage.

James Maniatis was taken into custody and, after two hours of interrogation, he was hailed before the Cook County Grand Jury that listened to Marrera's denials the day before. Without hesitation, the jittery Maniatis answered all questions put to him. He was then cautioned not to leave town and released.

The long absent Pete Gushi finally showed up at his Oak Lawn home. He was also apprehended and questioned extensively by the FBI. However, instead of appearing before the grand jury, Gushi was released seven hours later, without charge.

Meanwhile, evidence technicians working extensively on the Ford Econoline van had struck paydirt. A discarded scrap of paper in the vehicle was dusted for latent fingerprints, and one appeared. The print, checked against those of the known suspects in the case, positively matched the fingerprints of the missing Charlie Marzano.

After carefully going over every inch of the van with a vacuum cleaner, police technicians found several tiny flecks of red paint which forensic experts matched to the red paint of the money tankers in the Purolator vault. Police knew they had possession of the vehicle used to haul away the loot.

The suspects were known, and the evidence was good, but every cent of the money remained missing. Police Commander Victor Vrdolyak acknowledged the money would be "very difficult to trace" since the denominations were not exactly known, and no one had information of the serial numbers. Even so, the commander added, the thieves would have a hard time disposing of the cash. The sheer size of the haul was a major obstacle to its disposal. The missing cash weighed at least one thousand pounds, and the mere logistics of moving it around would pose a problem for whoever had it.

"You don t carry that amount of money around in your wallet," deadpanned Joe Woods. "And if they start to spend it in large amounts, it will certainly attract someone's suspicions. We have our sources watching the race tracks and dice tables from here to Las Vegas."

What, then, would thieves do with a thousand pounds of hot United States currency? The headaches of crime. Police advanced various theories. A favorite proposal was that whoever pulled off the job was working with Crime Syndicate mobsters, whose many outlets were ready to swallow up the cash in advance of the theft. The money could be quickly divided and distributed to mob emissaries throughout the country, and carefully filtered through their "legit" business operations, such as taverns, nightclubs, and any of a dozen other fronts.

"It is certainly a possibility," admitted an underworld intelligence analyst. "But the thieves would have to have had good mob connections, because it would not be an easy thing to pull off. For one thing, the Syndicate's cut in something like this would be anywhere from half to two-thirds of the take."

Woods was hoping that the $195,000 reward would smoke the money out, no matter who had it. "The amount of the reward might even lead someone connected with the Crime Syndicate itself to tip us off to the money's location, or tell us who committed the theft," he smiled, wistfully. Woods was grasping at invisible straws. Such things simply do not happen in Chicago. At any rate, the reward announcement had activated the public and false reports were already filtering in.

A woman said she saw a man resembling Gushi enter a vacant factory building on South Damen Avenue, in the South Side Englewood Police District, on Monday night. Watch Commander George Keller ordered the structure put under surveillance, and the watch continued for nearly 12 hours until the woman viewed a photo of Gushi and decided he wasn't the person she had seen after all.

By now, so many agencies were participating in the investigation that State's Attorney Bernard Carey called for a law enforcement "summit meeting" for the following day to coordinate, review, and exchange information. This meeting was the first such gathering of top local, state and federal sleuths in Chicago since the 1966 murder rampage of Richard Speck, convicted slayer of eight student nurses.

Ralph Marrera, meanwhile, had been questioned throughout the day by federal agents. Confronted with evidence of the IBI surveillance, he admitted having a daily meeting schedule with Charlie Marzano, and also one meeting with Gushi. He further admitted that Angela Hughes had indeed left the Purolator plant at 8:15 Sunday night, leaving him alone in the building until midnight, when Mildred Bivens arrived. He steadfastly denied any knowledge of the burglary. Despite being pointedly advised that he was the "key" to the theft, and could be the target of a gangland assassination to seal his lips, Marrera emphatically refused an offer of government protection. Then, with his lawyer's permission, he was fingerprinted and phtographed for federal records.

Stratton asked Marrera a final time. "Will you, or will you not, accept federal protection?" And again Marrera rejected the offer. "Okay, then, I guess you might as well go," Stratton told him. "If you want to be a dummy there's nothing we can do. I feel sorry for you, Ralphie."

The time was exactly 6 p.m. It had been a long day for all of them. As Marrera ducked out the door Stratton nodded to three other agents. "Better keep an eye on that dude." Whether Marrera anticipated the move, or did not know who might be after him, he bolted from the federal building on the run, zig-zagging his way through the sidewalk crowds of evening home-goers on Dearborn Street like a demon pursued by Beelzebub. The FBI agents, trailing him for his own protection, followed Marrera at a trot into a nearby store building, down the aisles between the cosmetic counters, and out the back door. Ralph sprinted down the back alley and into the next side street, where he held up an arm frantically and hailed a cab. As the agents flagged down a taxi to continue the chase, Marrera's hack suddenly lurched to a stop a half block down the street. Ralph tossed a dollar bill on the front seat, jumped out, and disappeared into another store.

Marrera dashed through the store, out the back way, into another cab on the next street, and was gone before his hapless protectors could catch up with him. But the getaway cab was still in view. The chase now wended its way north on Michigan Avenue opposite Grant Park. At Randolph Street the lead cab screeched to the left and stopped alongside the massive Chicago Public Library building.

Marrera tossed the fare behind him and scooted into the Illinois Central commuter tunnel that passed beneath Michigan Avenue. There he was swallowed up by the crowd, surging like lemmings toward their out-bound rush hour trains.

CHAPTER 12

The airport theory takes off.

The Summit Meeting of law enforcement agencies was convened on Thursday morning, October 24, in the West Side office of State's Attorney Bernard Carey. The state's attorney of Cook County has two offices in Chicago, one in the gray columned Egyptianesque Criminal Courts Building; the other in the towering rust-colored steel and glass Civic Center, across from City Hall in the Loop.

This gathering was held in the Criminal Courts Building at 26th Street and California Avenue. Present at the meeting were a representative of the U.S. Attorney's office; Ray Stratton and another agent from the FBI; five key members of the Chicago Police Department; five agents from the IBI; and five members of the state's attorney's prosecuting staff, including Nick Iavarone. Ralph Berkowitz, Carey's first assistant and political adviser, presided.

"The purpose of our meeting here today is to work out a plan of the responsibilities of each agency, so we don't duplicate efforts and work at cross purposes," began the gray-haired Berkowitz, popping a gum ball into his mouth — his way of kicking tobacco.

"It's high time. I'm damned concerned that we've never done anything like this before," Police Commander Victor Vrdolyak, commented. "We get these reports that some other agencies were aware weeks in advance that Purolator was in the works, but Chicago Police got no warning whatsoever."

"Hell, if these reports are true, it would have been in the best interest to share the information," added Deputy Chief Walter Karlblom. "The Chicago Police Department is the most talented, best equipped of any police department in the country."

Nobody disagreed with him at that point. The matter was not discussed further, since what had happened could not be revoked. Withdrawing of the surveillance just one week before the burglary was a sore point with several people in the room, and a matter of acute embarrassment to the IBI.

Some harsh words were exchanged between Stratton and the abrasive Berkowitz at several points, as the G-man attempted to brief his associates on what was known so far, but the assistant state's attorney interrupted with suggestions of his own.

Frustrated, Stratton finally pointed a warning finger at Berkowitz and admonished, "Ralph, I want you to shut up until I'm done talking. Just shut up! After I've made my presentation, you can talk all you want. Understood?" The red faced Berkowitz did not reply.

From the meeting came an agreement by all present that the FBI would prepare the results of all interrogations, and coordinate all aspects of the case under Stratton. Prosecution, as the case developed, would be handled by both Federal and State levels.

Still baffled over the whereabouts of the thousand pounds of cash, investigators traded theories on where it could have gone after the green van pulled away from the Purolator plant that Sunday night.

One idea was that all the money was flown out of town, possibly to Mexico, from where it could be transferred to a numbered Swiss bank account. It was known that a number of top Chicago hoodlums either had access to or owned modern aircraft. The plane theory appeared credible, especially since the van, when recovered, had only 186 miles on the odometer. With this in mind, flight records from O'Hare International Airport, Midway Airport, Meigs Field, and a number of smaller flying fields in the city and suburbs were ordered checked for the day after the theft.

Another stated possibility was that the money was sorted and placed into specially-marked bundles, and dropped into the night deposit boxes of Chicago banks with crime syndicate connections immediately after the burglary. The mobsters could have recovered the money when the banks opened for business Monday, and deposited it into various masked accounts.

In reconstructing the crime, investigators figured the entire operation took less than a half hour, even though the thieves apparently were aware they had a full three hours to work before anyone was scheduled to show up for Purolator's midnight shift.

Investigators then reviewed the list of suspects as they were now known — Marrera, Maniatis, Gushi, and Charlie Marzano — and then discussed plans to provide protective custody for any of them who might be inclined to help solve the mystery.

The meeting ended with an agreement of mutual cooperation to assure a successful conclusion to the investigation. It was also agreed that, in order to effect some control over the news media, all future press releases would be disseminated through Berkowitz, of the state's attorney's office and Assistant U.S. Attorney Michael King, for the federal prosecutors.

After leaving the Criminal Courts Building the group went downtown to the Federal Building for a follow-up session, in which Stratton asked FBI agent Michael Balgley to sit in. At this meeting the IBI distributed copies of all information it had uncovered on James Maniatis, Peter Gushi, Charlie Marzano and Ralph Marrera. The agency also turned over 11 pages of surveillance reports detailing the activity of the undercover operators, Michael Doyle and Marty Pollakov, of the Illinois Legislative Investigation Commission.

Meanwhile, Joe Woods' rich reward offer and his plea for help from the public was beginning to get results. Or so it seemed.

Detective Richard Stevens, working in the Damen Avenue headquarters, received an anonymous phone call from someone asking to speak to "Mr. Nickels," about the Purolator case. Stevens got Lt. Edward Nickels on the line. "If you wanna know where Ralph Marrera is, be on the corner of North Avenue and Ashland Avenue at 8 o'clock," the male caller said. Marrera's whereabouts had been a mystery since he gave FBI agents the slip the night before.

Nickels arrived at the appointed location with fifteen minutes to spare. He was wired up with a microphone and recording device, to tape the conversation with the informant, and was also under surveillance by his own men and FBI agents, in case anything backfired. Nothing happened, however, and Nickels waited on the corner in vain — his recorder picking up nothing but the sounds of city traffic. After an hour the stake-out was called off.

Next the FBI received a phone call from a woman identifying herself as Terry Icwaiticowski, a reporter for the *Economist* newspaper on the city's Southwest Side. She said she'd received an anonymous call from a man who claimed to have been in on the Purolator job. The money, he said, was hidden in the basement of the Larry German home in suburban Burbank. The caller said German and his wife were both involved.

Coincidentally, the FBI received a call from Jack Casey, operations manager of a South Side cartage firm. Casey had also gotten an anonymous call from a man who claimed involvement in Purolator. The caller said he'd received only $15,000 for his share of the loot, and was angry after learning the actual loss from the newspapers. The caller named one of Casey's drivers, Larry German, as one of the bandits, and said German had used one of the firm's trucks to haul away the loot.

Chicago police, assigned to follow up the twin tips, went to the German home in Burbank, and were admitted by German's wife, Marge. When they asked for her husband, she directed them to the front room, where German was lying on the floor, recovering from a broken leg. He was in a cast from his ankle to his hip, and had been so for several weeks.

The astonished Germans denied any knowledge of the

theft, and signed a consent form permitting the detectives to search their home. A thorough search of the premises was conducted, and police found "nothing of evidentiary value." They apologized to the amused Germans and went on their way.

Another tip did bear fruit, however. Shortly before noon Thursday, Lt. Nickels was contacted by Larry Buchman, a television news reporter for Channel 7, the ABC outlet in Chicago.

"I think I might have something pertinent to the investigation," he told Nickels.

"We're taking all calls," Nickels quipped. "What have you got, Larry?"

"I was having dinner last night with John Coleman, and we were discussing how these guys might have gotten all that money out of Chicago," Buchman related. "Well, while we were talking, John suddenly remembered an incident that happened about a month ago, when he was out at one of the airports...."

"Hold it, Larry," Nickles interrupted. "I'm going to send somebody over to talk to you in person. Will Coleman be there?"

"Yes, Ed. He'll be here."

Investigators John Whalen, Stanley Golucki and George Berndt were dispatched to the television studios at State and Lake Streets. Buchman was waiting, and introduced them to Coleman, the station's flamboyant weatherman.

Coleman, was known as the "Channel 7 Weather Clown" by his detractors, including the city's TV columnists, because of the slapstick manner in which he did his weather forecasts. The newscast on which he performed had the number one viewer rating in Chicago, however, and he was not about to change his act, which included throwing furniture at off-camera technicians during the show.

Coleman, dead serious now, and a little embarassed, told his story. He did not want to be mistaken for another kook, but what he had to say just might help when pieced in with other information collected by the police.

"Well, first off, I'm a licensed pilot, but I don't have my

own plane. Whenever I want to go up, I rent one from T. & G. Aviation at Midway," he explained. "I was out there about a month ago — on the 27th or 28th of September — when these three guys came into the office and told Tom Gold- thorpe — he's the owner — that they were from out of state and were interested in buying an airplane.

"I, ah, couldn't help notice how nervous they appeared, and my presence seemed to agitate them. They were — all three — 'hoodlum types,' and had that crumpled Las Vegas look, if you know what I mean. Well, I had a short conver- sation with Tom about the plane I wanted to rent, and he said that particular one wasn't in service, so I left."

Coleman was asked if he felt he could identify the trio if he ever saw them again, and he answered, "Hmm. Yeah, I think I could."

The weatherman was then shown fifteen police mug shots. Included in the batch are those of Marrera, Gushi, and Charlie Marzano. From the fifteen, Coleman selected the photos of Marzano and Gushi as resembling two of the three men he had seen at Midway.

"This fellow here resembles the guy who was supposed to be the pilot," he said, placing his finger on the photo of Marzano. "And this other one," he said, pointing to the pic- ture of Gushi, "looks like one of the two guys who was with him. I can't be positive from the photos, now, but I think I would recognize them if I saw them again."

Walen, Golucki and Berndt headed for T. & G. Aviation Activities, Inc., on the edge of Midway Airport, where they talked to the operators, Tom and Gail Goldthorpe.

The Goldthorpes remembered the incident related by Coleman. The trio said they were from "around Miami," and were looking for an airplane they could fly down there and resell. They discussed several planes, but left because they did not feel the price was right.

The Goldthorpes could not identify the men from photo- graphs, however they were able to pinpoint the date as September 27 — two days before the big score was origin- ally scheduled, until Maniatis blew the deal with the license plate mixup.

Authorities downtown were notified, and the investigation of airport facilities in an ever-widening circle from Chicago was intensified. The airport theory was beginning to take off!

CHAPTER 13

Gushi kisses $300 grand good-bye.

While Chicago police were interviewing Coleman, the TV weatherman, Peter Gushi had a visitor in his Family Bargain Center that would make Thursday, October 24, a day that would stick in his mind for the rest of his life, and make his blood run cold whenever he thought about it.

It had already been one hell of a week, these past three days, beginning at 5:30 Monday morning when the telephone in his home jangled him out of bed and he heard Charlie Marzano's voice growl, "Let's have breakfast."

That was the signal. Actually Gushi had nowhere near the starring role in the drama that his babbling mouth once had led Pollakov to believe. He hadn't gone anywhere with his rifle at the ready, prepared to blast his way to glory in the morning headlines if necessary. He was, in fact, safe at home, nervously pacing the floor, when the big score went down. He didn't even know for sure if it was coming off. He would not know, either, until he got the "let's have breakfast" phone call. That was his signal to meet Charlie Marzano in the parking lot at Denny's Restaurant in Hickory Hills.

Gushi shook his wife, Mary Jane, and said, "C'mon. We gotta get goin'."

"Goin' where?" she protested. "It's 5 o'clock in the morning. It ain't even light out yet."

"Shake your ass and do what I say. I can't tell you nothin'."

The one thing that the women who live in the shadow world soon learn is, don't ask questions. The woman is the boss of the house, she raises the kids, but never questions her husband's outside activities or his source of income. Mrs. Gushi, her hair in curlers, rolled grumbling out of bed and stuffed her feet into bedroom slippers. She sleepily flipped a scarf over her head, tied it under her chin to hold down the curlers, and slipped a light coat over her nightgown.

The Gushis got into their car, Pete behind the wheel, and headed west on 95th Street. A few moments later he eased his Buick into the far end of Denny's parking lot near the entrance to the Illinois Tollway. They had not long to wait before the green Ford van pulled in, Charlie Marzano behind the wheel, and rolled to a stop some distance away. Seconds later Lou DiFonzo rolled up in his flashy blue-black Lincoln Continental Mark IV, followed by Marzano's sleepy-eyed cousin, Tony, driving his white Ford sedan.

DiFonzo got jauntily out of his Lincoln, strolled over to Gushi's car, and draped himself over the open window. He was just about to say something when an angry Charlie Marzano shouted, "Get the hell back into your car. What d'ya think this is, a fuckin' convention?"

Charlie then pulled the van alongside Gushi's car, slid the side door open, and pulled out a suitcase. "There's 400 grand in here. Hold it for me," he said. "Tell her to take it home and put it away." Gushi got out of the Buick and went around to the rear to unlock the trunk and raise the lid. He quickly pulled out his two-suiter traveling bag and tossed the Marzano suitcase into the luggage compartment in its place. Mrs. Gushi, her nightgown blowing in the early-morning wind, got out of the car from the passenger side and surveyed the operation.

"What am I supposed to do with that, stick it in the cookie jar?" she complained.

"Stick it in your ass!" Gushi roared, not wanting to appear henpecked in front of his friends. "You heard the man. Take it home and hide it." He slammed the trunk lid down and handed his wife the keys. "Take off. I'm goin' fishing. See you in a couple of days."

As Mrs. Gushi pulled out of the restaurant lot and headed unhappily back to Oak Lawn, Charlie waved the men to their cars and ordered, "Let's get the fuck outa here."

"Wait a minute," the dapper DiFonzo called, standing beside his Lincoln. "I, uh, locked the goddam car with the keys inside and the motor running."

"You dumb fuck!" Charlie exploded. "You're supposed to have an 180 I.Q. Jeezus Christ!"

DiFonzo ran into the all-night restaurant and emerged with a wire coat hanger, straightening it as he hustled back to the car. "Gimme that," Charlie demanded, whipping it out of his hand and twisting the end into a little horseshoe shape. As the others watched apprehensively, Marzano deftly shoved the wire down between the window glass and the rubber molding, hooked the door handle, and jerked it open. "Now can we get the hell out of here?" he asked sarcastically, slamming the bent coathanger to the pavement. "All we need is for some fuckin' cop to drive up and see me breaking into Louie's car, with all this dough."

The cops, at that very moment, were converging on the Purolator building, miles to the north, where it had just now dawned on the security company officials that they'd been robbed.

"Pete, you ride with Tony," Marzano commanded. "Louie, you stay right behind me, and Tony, you follow Louie." The unlikely caravan — the new green van, the spit-shined Lincoln Continental, and Tony's battered Ford, headed for Gushi's family discount store in nearby Worth. Needless to mention, they were super-careful, along the way, not to break any traffic laws.

At the Family Bargain Center they quickly unloaded the van, and deposited the loot in some traveling luggage in the two cars for a fast trip to Florida. The van was left behind at the store, with the keys in the ash tray, for Maniatis to claim as his reward. Then, with Gushi and DiFonzo taking the lead in the Lincoln, and the two Marzanos "riding shotgun" a short distance behind in the Ford, they returned to the tollway.

It was a strange quartet — the slovenly Gushi, hawking and

spitting his morning phlegm into a handkerchief; the dapper DiFonzo with his pompadour hairdo and expensive French-cuff shirts, and the two swarthy Marzanos, bleary-eyed from lack of sleep. They swung south on the Tri-State and headed for Indiana as fast as the law would allow, then they rolled off the interchange at Gary and onto Interstate 65, bound for Indianapolis.

About halfway down in Hoosier country, Gushi, who kept looking over his shoulder to make sure the other auto was there to act as a "crash car" in case a roadblock should be set up, noticed Marzano's Ford weaving from side to side. "Pull over," he told DiFonzo. "We got trouble." Tony, who was driving the Ford, and Charlie, sitting alongside, were having all they could do to stay awake after their long night's work.

"We're gonna stop for coffee," Gushi suggested, making it appear that he and DiFonzo were the ones who needed a break. He spoke into his radio and heard Charlie's crackled approval. Both cars were equipped with mobile radios. The two cars swung off the road at the next exit ramp and drove a short distance west to Lafayette, Indiana, where they pulled into the Rose Haven Diner.

As Tony rested his head on the restaurant table and closed his eyes, Gushi made a telephone call to his contact who was supposed to provide the boat ride out of Florida. "The guy says he can't take us," he said, returning to the group. "There's a storm, or somethin'. He won't go."

Charlie lifted his head and glared at him red-eyed. "A deal's a deal," he said. That was Marzano's code of honor.

"The guy says no," Gushi protested. "I can't do nuttin' about it."

"You were supposed to have this whole fuckin' thing set up. Now, here we are, on the way to Florida and nobody to pick us up. What the hell do you think we cut you in on this for? You're supposed to have the contacts."

Gushi shrugged his shoulders and said, "Can I have a drink? I usually have a drink for breakfast."

"You'll drink orange juice," Marzano ordered.

"I've got an idea," DiFonzo said. "We're all a little tired, and we'll still be driving by this time tomorrow, for crissakes.

Why don't we hop a plane and fly down? We'll be there in time for dinner."

"And leave the cars behind?" Charlie asked incredulously.

"We've got to leave them behind some time," DiFonzo said. "Why not here, instead of down there?"

"What have you got in mind?"

"There's a private jet service over in Ohio. We charter a plane and we're down to the sunshine in no time. Let me give them a call."

"Okay with me," Charlie said, with a weak wave of his had.

DiFonzo got some change from the waitress and went to the phone. He returned to the table a short time later to announce, "It's all set."

After breakfast they all felt better, and headed back on the road to Indianapolis, where they looped around the city and picked up Interstate 70, heading eastward to Columbus, Ohio. Several hours later they found the airport road, with a sign to Executive Jet Service.

There, identifying his group as fishermen on a vacation, and himself as James Morini, DiFonzo chartered a Lear jet to take the quartet with their heavily-laden suitcases to Grand Cayman Island for $4,600. DiFonzo paid for the flight with 46 $100 bills. After two hours in the air the co-pilot came back and advised his passengers that there would be a re-fueling stop in Miami, where the group would have to pass through customs.

"Just a fuckin' minute," Charlie protested. No way was he going to open those suitcases for anyone.

"Let me handle this," DiFonzo said, putting his hand on Marzano's arm. "We were talking about that just before you came back here," he told the co-pilot. "We've got some business to transact in Miami before we go down to the islands, so that'll be fine with us. We'll get off there and catch a later flight."

Tony Marzano tipped the pilot and co-pilot each a C-note as the quartet got off the plane and grabbed a cab to a nearby motel. There Gushi was again put to work — unsuccessfully — attempting to line up a charter boat to Grand

Cayman. The seas were rough, and no one would risk their boat or life for any kind of money.

Charlie was disgusted with Gushi for failing to carry out his assignment. Gushi went out and bought a newspaper, and almost fell over. The Purolator theft was the headline story in the *Miami Herald*, with the loss initially estimated at $3.8 million. The story told of the FBI's knowledge of the identity of the suspects, and that a nationwide search for them was in progress.

Gushi's gills turned green. He threw down the paper and made his way to the motel bar, where he proceeded to get knee-walking drunk.

Meanwile, back in Chicago that Monday night after the heist, the FBI and police were still soaking up the IBI surveillance reports on Gushi. On the outside chance that he might still be around, Lt. Nickels dispatched Sgt. Ed Wodnicki and two of his detectives out to the Gushi home in Oak Lawn to look around.

On arriving, the first thing they saw when they drove up to the Gushi home on Laramie Avenue at 9:45 p.m. was a Miller Locksmith truck parked in front of the house. Curious that a locksmith would be out working at that late hour, police waited and questioned him when he emerged from the house.

"All I know is, I got a call from this customer who wants me to come out tonight and change the front and rear locks on the house. She says it can't wait until morning. So, I did the job, and she pays me cash," he said.

"Was there anyone else in the house with the woman?" Wodnicki asked.

"Yeah, some guy in his 50s, I'd say. He was just sitting there, not saying anything."

Posting one of his men at the back door, Wodnicki and the other policeman went to the front door, and rang the bell. They identified themselves to Mrs. Gushi and asked if they could speak to her husband.

"He's not here," she responded. "I haven't seen him in a couple of days."

"Would you mind if we came in and took a look around

for ourselves?" the sergeant asked.

"You can't come in," Mrs. Gushi said, slamming the door.

Oak Lawn police were called for assistance, but Mrs. Gushi, now communicating by shouting from a second story window, refused to let anyone in and refused to answer the door.

The man inside the house was the hapless Jimmy-the-Greek Maniatis. He had come over to find out where to pick up his new van, and she invited him to stay for supper. As the nervous Maniatis wondered how he was going to get out of this pickle, Mrs. Gushi telephoned her husband's lawyer, Gerald Werksman, and told him what was happening.

"I'll be right out, Mrs. Gushi," he advised. "Don't you let anyone in the house until I get there."

Turning to the confused Maniatis, Mrs. Gushi commanded, "Come on, Jimmy. You've got to help me with something." She bounded up the stairs to her bedroom, and returned with two bags, one a valise and the other a small suitcase.

"Over there," Mary Jane Gushi said, motioning to a planter in the front hallway. "Lift those flower pots out of there carefully." As the bewildered Maniatis complied, she dumped the contents of the bags — bundles of U.S. currency wrapped in rubber bands, into the planter. "Don't stand there gawking!" she told Maniatis. "Help me put the plants back." And they did, completely concealing the money.

Werksman arrived on the scene within the hour, and after a twenty-minute talk with Mrs. Gushi, emerged from the house to advise police, "My client's wife has consented to a search of the premise on two conditions: One, that only two investigators be allowed inside the house, accompanied by me; and two, that the search be limited to locations where a man the size of Peter Gushi could be concealed. Drawers, shelves, et cetera, are not to be searched. Is that agreeable?" The police agreed. After all, they had no search warrant.

And so, while Gushi was getting bombed at a Miami airport motel bar, Sgt. Wodnicki and one of his men conducted a room by room search of his home, looking for him. On several occasions, when they got down on their knees to peep under beds, or on their toes to peer atop closet sheves, they were blocked by Werksman, who reminded them of the terms of the search.

The uneasy white-haired man, now sitting on the front room sofa, identified himself as James Maniatis, but on advice of Werksman he and Mrs. Gushi refused to answer any questions. The unsuccessful search ended, the police headed back downtown and Maniatis made a bee-line for home to spend a sleepless night.

Gushi awoke with a $3.8 million hangover the next morning and decided he'd had enough of the operation. It wasn't at all like he had imagined it, lolling on the beach in the Caribbean, watching the bathing beauties go by as he sipped rum cocktails in the tropical sun. He put on his thick eye-glasses, wiped a bead of sweat off his nose, dressed and told Charlie he wanted to go gome.

"You wanna go home?" Charlie asked.

"Yeah, yeah, I think I better," Gushi sniffled.

"The asshole misses his wife," Tony volunteered.

"Okay, I'm sending you home," Charlie said. "But you don't go from here. We don't want anybody checking your airline ticket from Miami. You hop a plane for New York, get the fuck off, and then buy a ticket from New York to Chicago. That's where you been if anyone asks any questions. In New York on business."

"What about you guys?" Gushi asked.

"Louie's gonna fly ahead with the dough. He knows all about handling money," Charlie explained. "Tony and me will follow him on another plane."

"You gonna trust him with all that dough?" Gushi asked.

"Don't you trust him? You brought him into the fuckin' deal," Marzano said. "Fine time to be talking about trust now."

They checked out of the motel, got into a cab, and headed for the airport.

Back in Chicago before the end of the day, Gushi took a taxi from O'Hare International to his suburban home. He was in and out of the house in minutes, after Mary Jane told him the cops had turned the joint upside-down looking for him. He jumped into his car and headed straight for the Loop, and

Werksman's office on LaSalle Street. He was carrying two packages containing nearly $37,000.

"Jerry, I want you to set this aside for bond money. I can't tell you nothin' more, so don't ask. Just set this aside in case it's needed," he said. When Werksman balked at accepting the large sum of money, Gushi put his arm on the lawyer's shoulder and assured him, "Don't worry, Jerry. It's from the store. What d'you think — I'd stick you with something hot? Ha, ha. This is from the store." Everything from the store was hot, but Gushi didn't mention that.

On Wednesday, the FBI nailed him and hauled him in for questioning. They knew something, too. Gushi could tell by the way the creeps talked and by the questions they asked. To his surprise they didn't take him before the grand jury, which meant that he was probably a "target," and not a prospective witness. The sons of bitches would be back too, Gushi also knew that. What if they came with a search warrant? He'd be caught with the goods, while his pals were out of the country, living it up with their share. Maybe coming back to Chicago hadn't been so smart after all.

From the dough Marzano tossed in his car trunk at Denny's parking lot, there was still a good 300 thou stashed under the artificial flowers in the planter box in his living room. Even after the thirty-seven grand he took out to leave with Werksman. Gushi reflected on his wife: Dippy broad — the planter box was the first place anyone would look. Besides, that Greek, Maniatis, knew where it was and it wouldn't take much to squeeze it's location out of him.

Gushi sat in his plywood office at the discount store that Thursday morning pondering the week's events so far. Small wonder he was jumpy as a trampoline. He couldn't believe all that had happened in just three lousy days — from the time of Charlie's "breakfast" call he'd been to Columbus, Miami, New York, back to Chicago, and in the hands of the FBI. He'd been hitting the bottle heavier than usual since Monday, but the booze did little to calm his fractured nerves.

Where was Pollakov and his asshole sidekick, Eddie the Mope? Why hadn't they shown up so he'd have someone to go to breakfast with? He was still sitting there at 10 in the morning, trying to sort it all out, when a young boy, maybe 12, wandered into the store.

"Whadya want, kid? Gushi barked, annoyed that the little smart-ass had parked his bicycle right near the door, where a customer might stumble over the goddamn thing."

"Where's the owner?"

"Me, kid. I asked ya what ya wanted."

Without another word the boy handed him a matchbook cover. Gushi opened it, and noted a pencil-scrawled telephone number. The prefix was 448, meaning it was a local number, somewhere in the neighborhood. Under the number it said "10 min."

"Hey, who give ya this?"

The youngster pointed to a white sedan parked across the street. Shadows hid the faces of the two men sitting inside.

"They gimme a dollar to give that to you." he explained.

Gushi pushed past the boy toward the door, squinting through his thick eyeglasses, but the sedan pulled quickly from the curb, cut into traffic, and disappeared into the confusion of vehicles on 111th Street.

The guy who grew up in "The Patch" immediately recognized a message when he got one. He broke out in a sweat, and wiped his bald head with a handkerchief as he told himself to get on the phone and dial that number. But not the store phone. The lines were probably bugged. So he hurried to his car and drove nervously to a nearby liquor store. He dialed the number on a pay phone, and let it ring, maybe twenty times. No response. He hung up, and his dime clunked down into the return box. He fished it out, dropped it into the slot again, and dialed the number once more. A man's voice answered "Yeah!" on the first ring, and from the background noise Gushi could tell he was talking to someone in a phone booth near a highway.

"Where's he at, Pete?" the voice demanded. "Where's Charlie?" The only "Charlie" Gushi knew was Marzano.

"Who am I talking to?"

"You're talking to two partners who got left out. There's

gonna be blood. Charlie's ass and yours. We want our share. We got two million dollars coming — our half," the voice continued. "What do you want to do, Pete? Do you want to do it the hard way, or the easy way?"

"I dunno what the hell you're talkin' about," Gushi stammered. "What the hell is this? I don't know what you're talkin' about."

"There's gonna be a lot of blood, Pete," the voice threatened. "Is that how you want it? Look — how much money you got, Pete?"

Gushi paused, drew a breath of resignation, and said, almost automatically, "Maybe a couple hundred thousand dollars."

"We'll take that for openers," the voice advised. "But, if you don't deliver the green stuff, we'll get you. We don't care who you run to. We'll get you."

"No. No," Gushi sputtered, his knees so wobbly he feared he'd fall down with the phone in his hand. "Just tell me what I gotta do. I ain't gonna try to pull nothin'. Honest to God!"

The voice now gave Gushi his do-or-die instructions: Tomorrow, at 4 a.m., he was to be waiting with the money in the alley behind his home. A car would enter the alley, and flash its lights three times. It would then proceed through the alley without stopping. The car would then make a second pass, to make doubly sure nothing was amiss. On the third pass it would stop behind the house, and Gushi would present himself — *with the money.*

The caller had to be from The Outfit — the Crime Syndicate. Who else would know? But Peter Gushi had connections, too. Them bums didn't have him, yet. He decided to contact his Gumba — his *compare* — the man in organized crime to whom he accounted, and from whom he sought high level advice: His good neighbor, James "Jimmy the Bomber" Catuara.

Jimmy the Bomber earned his nickname in 1933 when, at age 27, he was sentenced to prison for compounding explosives. He was also known as "The Owl," and was now a high-ranking Mafiosi in the the Chicago Crime Syndicate.

If anybody could call off the dogs he would.

Gushi called Catuara's number, but got no answer. He tried repeatedly throught the day, always careful to use a pay phone. He finally got through, at 2:30 p.m., but Catuara's wife said the Bomber was not home. Gushi left an urgent message for Catuara to call him. But, by nightfall, the call still had not been returned.

Gushi, frantic now, began calling around town in a mad effort to reach his protector. He even dialed the Hawk Social and Athletic Club on Chicago's South Side, a place Catuara frequented. At last he discovered Catuara at home. He did not ask why Jimmy hadn't returned his call. He just blurted out, "Gumba, I gotta talk to you."

Catuara: "I can't meet with you."

Gushi: "But, I need your help, Gumba."

Catuara: "You're on your own."

Gushi: "I'm on my own?"

Catuara: "You are on your own."

Gushi: (Silence)

The message was now as clear as the window glass in Gushi's store. His *compare* didn't even ask what he wanted. He just told him he was on his own. As he hung up he realized that if Jimmy the Bomber couldn't help — wouldn't help — he must be dealing with some really big heat. The "Big Outfit" itself!

Gushi returned to his home in nearby Oak Lawn and mixed a stiff drink. Since Purolator he'd been putting away a quart of whiskey a day. Then he went to the front room and started scooping the packages of money out of the planter. But the hollow center was too small for his beefy arm to get all the contents. He ran to the basement and returned with a sledge, whereupon he proceeded to batter open the planter. Now the $300,000 or more tumbled out. He returned to the basement, bundles of bills in each hand, and stuffed the currency into an old suitcase. Once it was crammed full, he looked around to make sure he was alone, dipped his hand into the satchel and withdrew two bundles, containing $24,610. He carefully but quickly stuffed the two bundles into a hole in the wall behind the furnace. Who would know?

There was nothing to do now but wait, and drink. Gushi accomplished both with a minimum of enthusiasm. On one trip to refill his glass he armed himself with his large revolver.

At the appoined hour he hefted the suitcase containing the three hundred grand and walked tipsily into the cool night air. He was coatless, wearing only light slacks, and his bedroom slippers. It was brisk, and there was a frost cover on the ground as he stood beneath the weeping willow tree at the rear of his home. Yet Peter Gushi was perspiring. Beads of sweat trickled down his bald forehead, and his armpits were sopping wet. His shirt stuck to his back. Down the alley the crunch of gravel could be heard. Gushi was scared shitless!

An auto appeared, flashed its lights three times, and moved slowly toward him. Gushi pressed his body against the cold trunk of the tree. The car rolled by, and he could see the silhouettes of two men inside. At the opposite end of the alley it turned around. Its headlights blinked three times, and it proceeded through the alley as before. The car slowly turned around again and faced into the alley. The headlights flashed three more times, and it began the final pass. Like a rabbit, Gushi darted out from under the willow, leaped the low wire fence, and dropped the suitcase on the ground. Back over the fence he vaulted, hurrying toward the safety of his house like a scared mouse.

He lurched past the open door, slammed it and bolted it behind him, and retreated to the kitchen. There, from behind the drawn curtains, he watched the auto slowly approach, his heart pounding, as he caught his breath. Then he noticed there were two cars, not one, barely moving through the alley.

They eased to a silent stop behind the house — they knew exactly which one — and one man got out of the lead vehicle. He walked almost casually over to the suitcase, picked it up, and placed it in the car. He got back in, and quietly closed the door. The car moved ahead, and slowly disappeared behind a neighbor's garage.

The second car remained until the first was clear of the

alley. Then it, too, proceeded on at a deliberate pace. Gushi recognized this as the "crash car" on hand to block any pursuit, should he have been foolish enough to disclose his pre-dawn mission to anyone.

In the days to come, Gushi would tell his story repeatedly to the FBI, and three separate lie detector tests would support him on every point. But right now he was thinking only one thing. As the tail lights of the "crash car" disappeared into the night he crossed himself and said, "Thank God I'm still alive." Then he walked over to the kitchen cabinet and, without bothering to flick on the light, poured himself a good stiff belt.

Less than four years later, as Jimmy-the-Bomber Catuara, Gushi's god-father, was driving his red Cadillac along Ogden Avenue at Hubbard Street on Chicago's West Side at 7 o'clock in the morning, two men ran up and opened fire on him. Catuara was struck in the left side of the neck by two bullets fired through the window on the driver's side. As he lurched to the passenger side in an effort to escape, the second man fired a shot through the right side window, blowing a hole in the right side of his neck.

Blood spurting from both sides of his neck, the nearly decapitated Catuara hit the door handle and flopped out of the car, face down in the street. The two gunmen stood over him and fired a final shot into the 72-year-old man's back. As Jimmy the Bomber's blood flowed down the nearby sewer the two killers calmly walked away.

These were the kinds of people Peter Gushi played with. It was a winner-take-all game.

CHAPTER 14
Ralph's last day of freedom.

By Friday, October 25, enough pieces in the baffling case had fallen into place to satisfy the meticulous Ray Stratton, who asked for a meeting with U.S. Attorney Thompson. He and his chief aide in the case, special agent Michael Balgley, were ushered into the federal prosecutor's office late in the afternoon.

They spread out their thick Purolator file, and formally presented their case against Marrera. Much of it had been put together by Balgley, whom Stratton called "Bags," a 34-year-old FBI veteran of nine years from Brooklyn, clean cut, boyishly handsome, and smart. The boy next door type. His role as "coordinator for all leads" in the case was to handle the mountain of paperwork and keep track of communications between the various agencies.

Thompson was impressed with what he saw, and put in a call to State's Atty. Carey and his first assistant, Berkowitz, and asked them to come to the Dirksen building so Stratton could outline the case for their benefit.

Unlike their previous go-around, there was no antagonism between Stratton and Berkowitz this time. Several times during the presentation he turned to Carey and said, "This guy really knows what he's talking about, Bernie."

It was agreed at the conference that Thompson would file the first official charges in the case. Stratton then went before U.S. Magistrate Carl B. Sussman and signed a federal complaint charging Ralph Marrera with bank larcency, bank burglary, and use of explosives while committing a federal felony.

Sussman issued a warrant for Marrera's arrest, and set a cash bond of $500,000. Conviction on all counts carried a maximum penalty of 110 years in prison and a fine of $90,000. Considereing that, the high bond did not seem unreasonable. Marrera, who hadn't been seen since he lit out on the run from the federal building that Wednesday, after almost three days of questioning, now became the subject of the biggest manhunt in Chicago since eight student nurses were murdered by Richard Speck in a South Side townhouse some eight years earlier.

A dragnet of more than 300 Chicago policemen, led by a 40-man squad of FBI and state agents was loosed in the city and suburbs to find Ralph, and every 15 minutes the police radio was interrupted by a special broadcast, ending with the warning: "Dangerous... considered armed... approach with caution...."

"Every cop in town is looking for Marrera," declared Stratton. "It's a full-court press from here on out." It was quickly established that Marrera had not returned home since leaving the FBI office Wednesday evening on the run, and he was listed as "whereabouts unknown."

Police staking out his duplex in Berwyn learned from neighbors that nobody had been seen entering or leaving the house in two days. Other officers began questioning anyone who might have known Marrera, to determine his haunts.

Sgt. Daniel Centracchio and Investigator Carl J. Menconi of the Damen Avenue General Assignment Unit talked to Mike Mormino, 28, the Purolator runner. He told them that he had once helped Ralph carry an air conditioner home, and Marrera asked him to help install a burglar alarm in his garage, but he declined. On another occasion, he recalled, Marrera took him to a night club act in the Holiday Inn at Madison and Halsted Streets, where Marrera seemed to know the manager.

Menconi and Lt. John Terretta then interviewed Gordon Harrison, 31, a former Purolator employee, who was responsible for hiring Marrera. Harrison, who now owned a small flying school, left Purolator five months earlier, and offered to take a lie test to establish that he knew nothing about the theft. How Marrera got hired in the first place, with his background, suddenly emerged from the interview. Harrison disclosed that he knew Marrera before, and was his boss when they both worked for Wells Fargo. In fact, Harrison knew Marrera was fired from Wells Fargo for his suspected involvement in the Tiara theft in Evanston, when he got him on the Purolator payroll.

Although he knew Marrera only from work, and never socially, he recalled that Marrera liked to frequent the Holiday Inn on West Madison Street.

This was the second acquaintance of Marrera to associate him with the Holiday Inn. Menconi and Terretta drove to the Inn to check the parking lot for Marrera's car. Not finding it, they talked to Robert Cataldo, the Inn's manager. He did indeed, know Marrera. As a matter of fact, Ralph was there on Wednesday night — not long after his flight from the Federal Building. But he wasn't around at the time.

As the search for Marrera continued, police received another tip on where the missing money might be. Fire Department scuba divers climbed an abandoned water tower, not far from the factory building police had staked out a day earlier. The tipster said the money was stashed inside, in watertight canvas bags. Firemen looked, but found nothing.

In the garage behind Marrera's home police found a black and red Oldsmobile. The license plates checked to Marrera's father, Ralph Sr., in the same suburb. His home, too, was placed under surveillance. So was the New Ritz Hotel, near police headquarters.

As the day ended and Marrera seemed to have eluded the dragnet, the FBI — still playing all bases — reissued its nationwide alert for Pasquale Charles Marzano. The search for Marrera continued through the night, and all day Saturday, October 26. Going over a list of Ralph's friends, and places he was known to visit, police checked out 25 of them but all for naught. Police distributed photos of him at O'Hare, just in case he might have skipped town, but no airport employee recognized Ralphie's photo.

Marrera, as it turned out, had taken his wife and their two small children to the Oak Park home of his in-laws, Mr. and Mrs. Matthew C. Sperduto, and there proceeded to sleep away the weekend — not far from the home of Joe Woods. It was his first undisturbed sleep since the theft, and the stream of endless questioning by lawmen.

Chicago police found the Sperduto name while checking civil records to determine the addresses of Marrera's relatives in the area. Oak Park is located just north of Berwyn, where Ralphie lived, but finding the connection was an involved process, since Marrera's mother-in-law had married previously, and Sperduto was not Marrera's wife's maiden name.

Sgt. Thomas Kelley, of the Chicago Police Robbery Unit, Sgt. Edward Wodnicki of Damen Area General Assignment, and nine detectives headed for the Sperduto home on Forest Avenue, in the near west Chicago suburb. They surrounded the home, and the two sergeants approached the front door, accompanied by several detectives. The Sperdutos had sent out for a pizza a short time earlier, and when Matt answered the police knock he got the surprise of his life.

"Is that my pizza?" he asked, as he opened the door, money in hand. When Kelley and Wodnicki identified themselves, the startled Sperduto slammed the door in their faces before they could state their mission.

"We're after Ralph!" they shouted, through the closed door.

To their astonishment, a woman's voice yelled back, "He's sleeping!"

"You have to let us in, ma'am," Wodnicki shouted. "We have a warrant here for Ralph Marrera's arrest."

"Chicago cops don't have any jurisdiction in Oak Park," another voice yelled from within.

Unsure themselves of their jurisdiction in a case of this order, Wodnicki and Kelley notified the FBI, kept the house surrounded, and waited. When special federal agents arrived they, too, were unable to get in. Ralph was running, it seemed, from everyone. They could not convince anyone in the house that they weren't Crime Syndicate hit-men in disguise.

Near midnight Marrera's wife, Alberta, telephoned the Chicago FBI office, and was patched through to Stratton in his suburban home. She put Ralph on the line. "Look, Ralph. I haven't lied to you yet, have I?" Stratton said. "Those really are the good guys outside. The judge has signed a federal warrant for your arrest, and they're going to take you downtown, one way or another. Why don't you be smart, for a change, and let them in?" Marrera agreed to surrender, and the authorities were permitted to enter the house.

"Click," went the handcuffs on Ralph's wrists. "I really wasn't running," he protested. "I just got fed-up with all those questions and wanted to get away from it all. Give me my jacket and let me get out of here."

As Marrera was being led toward the door, clad in a matching denim trousers outfit, he turned to Wodnicki and asked, almost as an afterthought, "Where the hell are you taking me?" They took him to the Damen Area Headquarters, where he was booked, fingerprinted and photographed before being turned over to federal marshals. It was early Sunday as the two marshals placed an iron chain around Marrera's waist for added security and led him away. "Ralph, you look like a guy going to the gallows," Kelley commented.

Marrera was whisked out of the police building and secretly transported to the Winnebago County Jail in Rockford, 100 miles away. He was booked in at 5:15 a.m., and was assigned to one of the jail's two adjoining security cells.

He was returned to Chicago on Monday, October 28, under elaborate security measures, to be arraigned before Magistrate Sussman. Ralph's bond was set at $400,000 cash, and Marrera was remanded to the custody of the U.S. Marshal's Office, and then slipped back to the distant Rockford jail. Authorities planted a phony story that he was at Fort Sheridan in hopes of keeping their prized prisoner safe. As U.S. Attorney Jim Thompson explained to the press that morning, ". . . somebody might find him and squeeze him too hard."

"When somebody's accused of stealing four million bucks he's sure game for anyone who wants to take it away from him."

CHAPTER 15

Gushi's luck continues—all bad.

While Ralph Marrera was being returned to the Rockford jail, police received another windfall in the fast breaking case. James Lynch, of Columbus, Ohio, like most Americans, had been following the Purolator headlines with great fascination. It was a classic good guys versus bad guys case, and it looked like the good guys were closing in fast.

When he read of police speculation that the loot might have been flown out of the country, his memory was jogged by a curious incident that happened a week earlier. Lynch, the regional sales manager for Executive Jet Aviation, the airplane leasing firm at Port Columbus, checked his log and, sure enough, the incident occurred on the same day the mammoth theft was uncovered in Chicago.

He momentarily debated whether to tell anyone, and risk being laughed at. Then he decided he'd take a draw. The most it would cost would be a phone call. Lynch dialed the long-distance operator and asked for Illinois State Police Headquarters in Springfield. He told them this story:

"Last Monday morning, October 21, I got this phone call from a person who said his name was James Morini. He inquired about a charter flight for four persons to Grand Cayman Island, in the British West Indies.

"I told him it would cost him $4,600, and he made a reservation. That afternoon, about 3:15, Mr. Morini telephoned again and said he and his party would be at the airport within an hour. At around 4 p.m. he arrived with the three other guys. They came in two cars."

Lynch was asked if he remembered anything about the cars.

"Positively," he said. "One was a white Ford, and the other was a kind of black-over-blue Lincoln. A Continental Mark IV. In fact, they took off and left the cars behind. I distinctly remember the incident, because there was a conversation with the man who owned the white Ford. He didn't want to leave the keys behind, because he seemed afraid somebody might snoop in his car, but I told him that was necessary because we would have to be able to move the cars in case of emergency."

On the way south, Lynch said, the quartet got into a conversation about whether they had to pass through customs on the way out of the country, and decided to end their trip at Miami. They were given a $1,100 cash refund, since they had already paid the fare to Grand Cayman Island.

"And the automobiles are still there?" the state trooper questioned.

'One of them is," Lynch replied. "The guy with the white Ford showed up yesterday and got his keys from our dispatcher, Dorothy Gallen. But the Mark IV is still here on the lot."

"Can you give me its license number?"

"I jotted it down. It's got Illinois license plates, number KJ 5192."

The state police officer thanked Lynch and assured him his call was not considered foolish. He then relayed the information to the Chicago Police Department, which passed it on to the FBI in accordance with the share-and-share-alike agreement. Stratton seized the information with excitement as he recalled from IBI reports that an agent had spotted a Lincoln outside Peter Gushi's home on Saturday night, October 19, just 24 hours before the big score.

Referring to his files, Stratton was elated to find that the license number on the Mark IV seen at Gushi's was listed as KJ 5192! This was indeed another fluke in the bizarre case, since the IBI agent spotted the car a week after official surveillance had been withdrawn — while just out joy riding.

IBI Agent Patrick Durkin had taken his wife for a ride in the family car that Saturday night, because Mrs. Durkin wanted to get out of the house for awhile.

"Okay, I'll show you where I spent one week of my life," Durkin laughed, and headed out to suburban Oak Lawn to point out Gushi's house. "There is where I walked on surveillance," he said, pointing to an ordinary length of curb. "And over there are the bushes where I would sometimes watch from at night."

As they drove past the house, Durkin noted the Lincoln Continental parked outside, and dutifully jotted down the license number. Inadvertently, he had made the contact that would link DiFonzo to other accused gang members one day before the big theft.

If this wasn't enough to start Stratton's juices flowing, he recalled that Pollakov, the informant, had reported to Siragusa that the money from the "big cash score" Gushi had boasted about was going to be taken to Nassau or Grand Cayman Island, in the West Indies.

Grand Cayman, a tiny island with 188 banks, is to the Americas what Switzerland is to Europe — secret bank accounts, mostly in the names of phony companies. No questions asked. It is a tax haven for depositors the world over.

Finally, Stratton recalled Pollakov's report of overhearing Gushi discuss a man named Redmond, who was supposedly in the charter boat business in the Miami area. So, it all added up.

Stratton contacted the FBI office in Cincinnati, and the bureau in Columbus, and they went to work on Executive Aviation immediately.

Lynch directed them to the blue and black Lincoln left by "Mr. Morini." The auto checked out to the Kazmier Leasing Company of Lombard, Illinois, a western suburb of Chicago. Records at the agency showed the vehicle was leased to Louis M. DiFonzo, the man the FBI knew as "Luigi." A federal search warrant was obtained at Columbus, and the Lincoln was seized. Inside the car, agents found a walkie-talkie radio on which were several latent fingerprints. The prints were processed through the FBI Identification Division, and two of them checked out to the fugitive Pasquale Charles Marzano!

Meanwhile, back in Chicago, Gushi and Jimmy-the-Greek Maniatis were arrested on charges having nothing whatsoever to do with the Purolator case. Police nabbed the two of them in Gushi's Family Bargain Center as suspected members of a fencing operation which authorities said handled five million dollars worth of stolen goods annually.

"I've never done anything wrong in my life," Maniatis protested, as he was taken to Central District Headquarters at 11th and State Streets to be booked, mugged, and finger-printed.

Gushi was taken to Damen Avenue Headquarters for processing, and was read his constitutional rights. When asked to account for his actions the previous days, he had replied he had flown down South, "to get some sun and swimming under my belt. I was gonna stay longer, but I came back to be near my family."

Meanwhile State's Attorney Carey and "Charlie Cigars" Siragusa, whose agents had infiltrated the stolen property ring, called a joint press conference to announce that the Cook County Grand Jury had returned indictments charging Gushi, Maniatis, and three other men with selling 1,500 stolen wrist watches, valued at $37,500. These were the watches that, through Maniatis, Gushi had fenced to Pollakov at a profit of $3.50 per watch.

Carey identified the watches as part of a million dollars worth of jewelry and other merchandise taken July 24 in the robbery of a warehouse of the Douglas Dunhill Company, in southwest suburban Oak Forest.

Carey also announced somewhat sheepishly, that Charlie Marzano had been charged with possession of an invalid driver's license, one he obtained under an assumed name, Charles Rossa, in 1973. This charge, a misdemeanor, would allow federal authorities to hold Marzano as a fugitive if he crossed state lines to avoid prosecution.

Elated law enforcement officials display $1.4 million unearthed in the basement of the Chicago bungalow owned by the grandmother of accused Purolator vault guard Ralph Marrera. The man in the center is U.S. Attorney James "Big Jim" Thompson.

following page: Exterior of Purolator Security, Inc. on Chicago's Near North Side. Armored truck and unmarked police car are shown parked outside.

Floor plan of the Purolator money warehouse taken from Chicago Police Department drawing.

artwork: Sheryl O'Brien

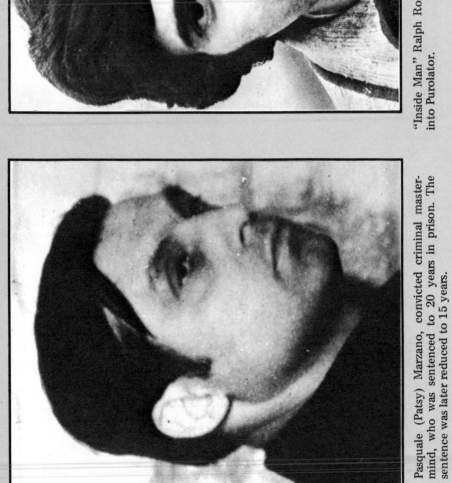

Pasquale (Patsy) Marzano, convicted criminal mastermind, who was sentenced to 20 years in prison. The sentence was later reduced to 15 years.

"Inside Man" Ralph Ronald Marrera; the key to getting into Purolator.

William (Tony) Marzano, Patsy's cousin who pleaded guilty and was sentenced to 7 years in prison. His sentence was later reduced to 5 years.

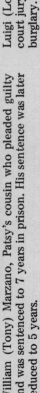

Luigi (Lou) DiFonzo smiles after his acquittal by a federal court jury that convicted Pasquale Marzano in the Purolator burglary.

above: Peter (Pete) Gushi, self-styled "master criminal" who turned government witness and was sentenced to 4 years in prison.

left: James (Jimmy the Greek) Maniatis who pleaded guilty and was sentenced to 18 months in prison.

opposite page: The one-ton door of the looted East Vault of Puro-lator Security, Inc. Thieves obtained the combination from an unwitting employee who had taped it on his personal locker.

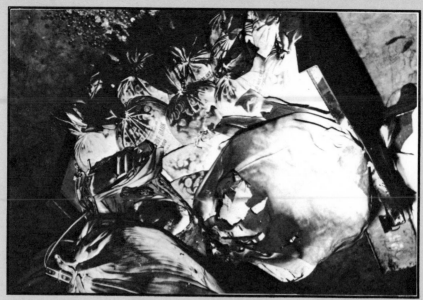

above: A handcart of charred money bags. Not one greenback was destroyed because lack of air in the vault doused the flames.

below: Three gasoline firebombs lie harmlessly on the floor of Purolator Security, Inc. after removal from the looted vault. Each plastic bag contained 1½ gallons of gasoline.

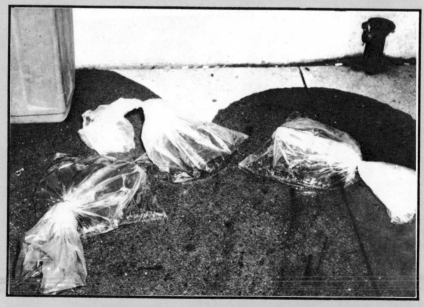

opposite page: Fire-damaged interior of Purolator vault from which $4.3 million — 1,000 pounds of money — was taken.

Purolator's Joe Woods, proudly displays the "Nixon fit" in wearing apparel.

---

opposite page: Charles Siragusa, the angry man of the Purolator probe.

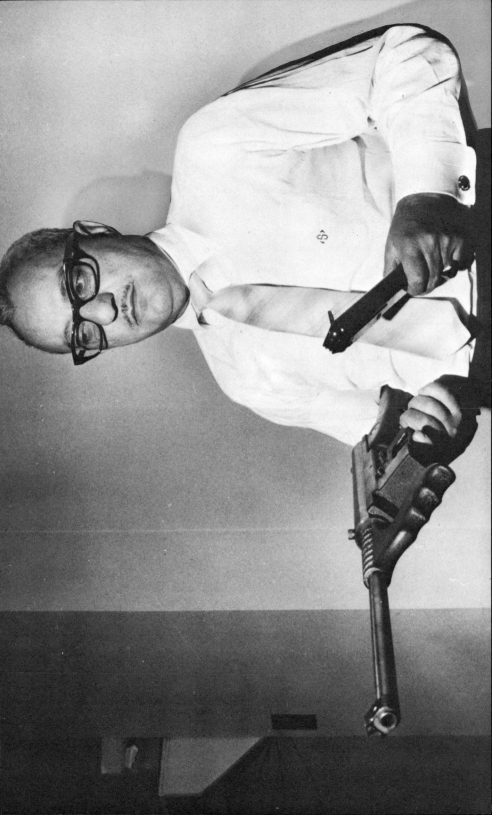

Chief FBI agent on Purolator case, Ramon Stratton (center, with cigar) confers with fellow lawmen in basement where more than $1 million of stolen money was found.

Chicago bungalow where $1.4 million of Purolator loot was found buried in the basement. The "Grandma Connection."

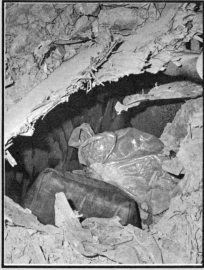

The Purolator fortune being unearthed from the concrete basement floor in the home of Marrera's grandmother.

next page: Detective Superintendent Derrick Tricker who led FBI agents to two of the Purolator theft suspects and part of the stolen millions in the British West Indies.

United States Attorney James "Big Jim" Thompson on his way to becoming Illinois governor.

Defense Attorney Julius Lucius Echeles. "Purolator . . . it was only a theft, your honor."

Trial Judge William J. Bauer, who passed a sentence of 20 years for the convicted mastermind Pasquale Charles Marzano.

Bernard Carey, Cook County state's attorney meeting with reporters.

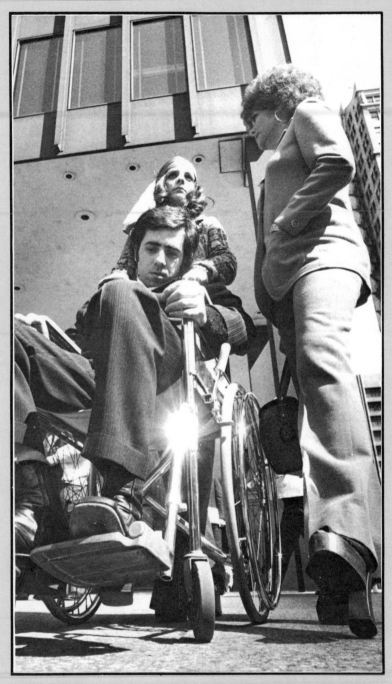

Ralph Marrera, the guard accused of taking $4.3 million from the East Vault of Purolator Security, Inc., is wheeled from Dirksen Federal Building, in Chicago, by his wife Alberta after a judge ruled him mentally unfit to stand trial. At right, Defense Attorney Jo-Anne Wolfson waits for a taxi.

Gushi was released on $100,000 bond on the stolen property charge, and told Maniatis he would get some more money and come back for him. Under Illinois law, ten per cent of one's bond money must be posted in cash to obtain release, meaning Gushi had to scare up another $10,000 for his Greek partner.

While he was going about this, the U.S. Attorney's office authorized the filing of a conspiracy complaint charging Gushi with bank larceny, bank burglary, and use of explosive during the commission of a federal felony, in the Purolator case. The complaint, like the one naming Marrera, was signed by Stratton.

On Monday evening Gushi returned to Police Headquarters with his lawyer, Werksman, and the $10,000 to spring Maniatis. But, as he got out of Werksman's car, he was arrested for the second time in one day. Chicago police ushered the unfortuante Gushi into the headquarters where he was detained overnight. The confused Maniatis, his bond having been posted, left the building alone, a free man.

CHAPTER 16
Gushi blows the whistle.

Chicago police turned Gushi over to federal agents first thing Tuesday morning, October 29, and Pete the prisoner was taken directly before U.S. Magistrate Sussman. He ordered a staggering one-million dollar full cash bond, and remanded Gushi to the custody of the U.S. Marshal's office.

Gushi met his limit, he had it. The perfect crime blew up when the gasoline bombs sputtered out; two carloads of mysterious hoods took his $300,000 in the dark of the night; his very own *compare* turned his back on him and told him he was on his own; the state's attorney jailed him on the stolen property rap — and now, this. How in the hell was he ever going to post a million dollar bond?

And these weren't all of his problems. Deep down inside he grieved for the return of his teen-age daughter, Pamela, who ran away from home May 18. He reported her disappearance to the Oak Lawn police, but they could do nothing. In August he got a letter from her, postmarked from South Carolina. He had heard nothing since.

Peter James Gushi was through running, through worrying, through hiding, and through fighting. He was whipped. He put in a call to Jerry Werksman. Late in the afternoon he and his lawyer met with Stratton's men and agreed to co-operate with the FBI and the U.S. Attorney's office. Gushi then sat down at a table opposite the smug Stratton and, while a court reporter took notes, he told the whole story.

The "big cash score" he had boasted to Pollakov was,

indeed, the Purolator burglary. It all began that summer when Charlie Marzano approached Gushi. "He asked me if I would be interested in holding some big money for him," the self pronounced master-criminal-turned-stoolie told Stratton.

Despite his grandiose boasts, Gushi insisted his only participation in the Purolator heist was to hold whatever money Marzano gave him, and to try to line up a boat in Florida to take the thieves and a large chunk of the loot to the British West Indies. He fulfilled neither task with success.

Chattering with almost reckless abandon, he told Stratton of the "Let's have breakfast" telephone call from Marzano, and of meeting Marzano in the parking lot alongside the Tri-State Tollway at 5:30 a.m. Also there, he said, were Marzano's cousin, Tony, and Lou DiFonzo.

Gushi told Stratton how they had made the jet connection in Columbus, and arrived in Miami that Monday evening. Gushi's job there was to line up a boat to ferry the men and their cargo to Grand Cayman, some 500 miles south of Florida. One operator he talked to was in drydock, and another skipper refused to put out in rough seas, eventually forcing the trio to revise their plan again.

While staying at the Crossways Airport Inn and plotting their next move, Gushi told Stratton how he ducked out to buy a *Miami Herald*, and noted the Purolator theft bannered in the headline. At that early stage, the loss was estimated at $3.8 million. Gushi handed the *Herald* to Charlie who scoffed, "Look how much they exaggerate! I wonder how much they pocketed themselves."

The next morning, Tuesday, DiFonzo — who stayed in Miami under the name of Keith Anderson — chartered a flight from Fort Lauderdale to Grand Cayman Island, paying $1,236 cash. He took with him two green suitcases containing approximately $1.5 million. The two Marzanos followed DiFonzo later the same day on a Bahamas Air commercial flight, while Gushi returned to Chicago, via New York City.

After Gushi completed his story, he was returned to the

federal lockup, by agreement with the FBI. His family was placed in protective custody. A complaint was filed against Maniatis, charging him with conspiracy, bank larceny, bank burglary, and use of explosives during commission of a federal felony. The white-haired Maniatis, the lone outsider among a mixed assortment of Italians, whose preoccupation in life until now had been prowling flea markets in search of bargains, offered no resistance when taken into custody in his home by Chicago Police and IBI agents. He was taken to the Central Police lockup, and detained overnight.

Meanwhile, Marrera's lawyer, Nussbaum, accompanied by a new legal entry into the case, Mrs. Jo-Anne Wolfson, a gifted criminal lawyer, went before Federal Judge Abraham Lincoln Marovitz to plead for a reduction in Ralph's $400,000 cash bond.

"Mr. Marrera is a working man, with no criminal convictions," the red-haired Mrs. Wolfson pleaded in asking that the bond be lowered to $25,000; "The defendant has no plans of becoming a fugitive, your honor. The only reason there was difficulty in locating him to serve the arrest warrant was that he had been constantly harrassed, surveilled and interrogated by the FBI for three days, until he had reached the point of exhaustion."

Assistant U.S. Attorney Michael King argued that Marrera must be kept in custody because Gushi had voiced "death threats to the witnesses and their families." He made no reference to the fact that Gushi was now himself in protective custody.

The 69-year-old Marovitz refused to interfere in the case, telling the lawyers to take their plea to Sussman, who set the bond in the first place. This was Nussbaum's last effort on Marrera's behalf. He turned the whole package over to Mrs. Wolfson, and withdrew from the case.

Minutes after Gushi had finished his narrative of events, Stratton called Mike Balgley, who was coordinating all information in the case. "Bags, what do we know about Tony Marzano and Louie DiFonzo?" Balgley came into Stratton's office, and handed him two manila folders. "I don't want to wade through all that crap right now,"

Stratton said, waving it aside. "Just give me the highlights on these two birds for the time being."

"William Anthony Marzano, 31, Charlie's cousin, used to be a fruit stand operator," said Balgley emphasizing the word "fruit" with a smile. "He's five-nine, wears a thick mustache, and is divorced. Tony considers himself to be quite a ladies man, and likes to hang around places like Faces, on Rush Street. Native of Chicago, unemployed, used to be a truck driver until somebody swiped his truck."

Now Stratton smiled.

"Ah, he's been indicted twice for theft from interstate shipments, and he's got a record of arrests for armed robbery and passing phony money orders," Balgley concluded.

"Luigi M. DiFonzo, 27, is a fast-talking, get-rich-quick opportunist. This kind of caper would appeal to him, I'd say. He's the son of a Fall River, Massachusetts, gas station operator. Came here last winter. Lou got himself a reputation as the boy wonder of the silver futures market. He opened an office out in Des Plaines, and began selling options to buy commodity futures contracts in silver bullion. He persuaded thousands to invest in North American Investment Company and North American Trading Company. These two outfits were flash fronts, nothing else."

"How'd he pull it off?" Stratton asked.

"Well, he told the suckers he had two masters degrees and that he'd made a million dollars before he was 21. Actually, he never even graduated college. He worked as a salesman and bill collector before coming to Chicago. But not long after opening his new office in Des Plaines he walked in and plunked down $190,000 — cash — for a home out in Oak Brook. He likes to live out in the western suburbs with the polo set."

"And then the shit hit the fan, I take it," Stratton interjected.

"It did," laughed Balgley. "The Securities and Exchange Commission started an investigation, and when his 'investors' heard about it they started yelling for their money back. So Louie closed up shop and filed bankruptcy. His assets were estimated at $18,000, and his liabilities at $2.5 million. So he goes back home to Massachusetts, tries to set up a commodities operation in Boston, and falls right on his ass. Next thing you know, he's back here."

"I guess that explains his part in the Purolator job," Stratton speculated. "He sounds like the kind of schemer these guys would bring in — somebody with enough know-how of international banking operations to help make large sums of cash difficult to trace. He's the guy our friend, Pete Gushi, says hopped a plane for the Bahamas carrying a couple of suitcases full of cash the day after the heist."

Stratton relayed the information to the FBI office in Miami, along with Gushi's story about trying to charter a boat.

It was quickly established that a man named George Redmond operated a charter boat business out of Islamorada Marina, in the Florida Keys. At the moment, however, he and his boat, "Willi-Wa," were somewhere in the Baltimore area. Special agent Edward Szweda of the Baltimore office of the FBI took it from there. He found Redmond and the "Willi-Wa" moored at Bal Harbor in Ocean City, on Maryland's Atlantic coast.

From Redmond's wife, Guinela, the agent learned that Gushi had telephoned on October 15, saying it was important that Redmond get in touch with him, immediately. Redmond said he made several unsuccessful attempts to reach Gushi at his home phone the following day, but gave up. At 7:30 on the night of the burglary, however, Redmond said he did get through.

"Mr. Gushi said he wanted to take a party of four on a seven-day trip to the Bahamas. He said a Mr. Charles Rossa and three other men would be going, for sure, but he was uncertain whether he'd be going himself. I told Mr. Gushi my boat was out of service for the season. He then said he'd wire me money to fly down to Florida to charter another boat for him. I told him this was impossible, because I was working up here, but I'd do what I could to try to arrange another boat for him."

Redmond said he contacted Billy Knowles, skipper of the "Queen Catcher," at the Holiday Isle marina on Islamorada.

Knowles agreed to take the assignment for one week, beginning October 22. He advised Redmond he would be berthed at the Bertram Yards in Miami on the twenty-first, waiting for the charter group. Redmond said he telephoned Chicago and relayed the information to Gushi. "That was the last I heard from him."

From Knowles the FBI learned that he had received a phone call on Tuesday morning, October 22, from a man who said he was the person in whose behalf Redmond had set up the trip. "I said the wind was blowing at 35 knots and the voyage wouldn't be safe," Knowles recalled. "The individual wanted to go anyway, but I refused to risk the boat. I wasn't about to go out on rough seas like that. I said, 'Why don't we wait a day and try it on Wednesday?' I offered to pick up the group at Fort Lauderdale. I told them they could spend the night on the "Queen Catcher" and we could take off the next morning for the Bahamas. This guy said he'd take it up with his associates and call me back. But he never did."

The trail now clearly led to the Caribbean.

CHAPTER 17
A call for help to Scotland Yard.

Run your finger down a map of the Caribbean. West-northwest of Jamaica are three small islands: Grand Cayman, Cayman Brac, and Little Cayman. They were discovered on Columbus' fourth voyage to the New World. Nearly 500 years later, two other Italians, Luigi DiFonzo and Pasquale Marzano, would make them famous, if not richer.

Not too many people had heard of these remote isles in the British West Indies until recent years, when articles about a new and better tax haven began appearing in newspapers and business journals. In 1964 there were only two banks on the islands. Ten years later there were more than 180 on Grand Cayman alone, the largest and most populated of the three islands. That's a lot of banks, considering the island's population of 12,600.

Most of the money came from points well beyond, and for good reason. In addition to being every bit as circumspect as Swiss banks, interest earned on deposit at the going rate was tax free under British law.

The climate is another draw to the islands, where the average winter temperature is 75 degrees, and the hottest days of summer are tempered by the ever-blowing Trade Winds.

The islands got their names in 1586 when Sir Francis Drake, fresh from sacking Santo Domingo, sailed by and reported seeing "great serpents called caymanas (crocodiles)." There are no crocodiles left on the Islands today, but the name Cayman remains. Sailors aboard Columbus' ships nearly a hundred years earlier called the islands Las Tortugas, meaning turtles, because tortoises abounded, and still do. A turtle is at the top of the Cayman Islands coat of arms.

Grand Cayman is the largest of the three islands, 22 miles long and 8 miles at its widest point. Its capital, George Town, overlooks a harbor on the west side, and was abustle in 1974 with construction. Mostly, multistory buildings for more banks and allied businesses. George Town is the hub of activity in the Cayman Islands, and its tiny Owen Roberts Airport handles small-size commercial jet traffic from Miami, a one hour flight over Cuba, as well as flights from Central and South America. A passport isn't necessary, provided that visitors from the States can prove their citizenship with a birth certificate or voter's registration card.

Visitors found to be carrying guns, drugs, or gambling paraphernalia (gambling is prohibited there, unlike other British possessions in the Carribbean) would find themselves guests of the island's top cop, Superintendent Derrick Tricker, a character out of the pages of Conan Doyle, with a bent-stemmed pipe, flowing bush mustache and round face.

It was to this island that DiFonzo came on Tuesday, October 22, with his two suitcases crammed full of cash, his chartered jet touching down at Owen Roberts little more than an hour after winging out from Fort Lauderdale. Although DiFonzo's stay overnight in the Miami hotel was under the name of Keith Anderson, he used his own name on the flight, and did the same when he passed through Grand Cayman customs, apparently because he had no identification to support an alias, and did not want to draw undue attention.

He cleared customs with barely a yawn. An immigration officer, Mrs. Kerry Nixon, noted his suitcases were "crammed with U.S. dollars." But, because of the island's tax-haven status, visitors bringing in large amounts of currency were not uncommon. Only a week before, another American came through toting an estimated eight million dollars, according to the island immigration officials.

Still, she could not help but notice the handsome American as he cleared customs with his cargo of green paper. She observed that Bruce Campbell, a local attorney, was anxiously waiting for him in the airport terminal, to give him a lift downtown with the heavy bags. The two men drove off in Campbell's car.

Ten minutes later DiFonzo arrived in George Town and checked into the posh oceanside Grand Caymanian Holiday Inn. The swank hotel, on the eastern side of the island across from North Sound, offered a sprawling complex of tennis courts, colorful stucco buildings, shrubbery and a bar-side swimming pool. The keepers of the inn liked to boast that, although the island's air, beaches, and water are unspoiled, "our guests are spoiled like crazy."

Records at the inn show that DiFonzo, calling himself James Morini, took room 57, on the ground floor, with a door onto the beach. He was soon joined by the two Marzanos, who checked into Room 216, on the second floor, overlooking the sea. They registered in their own names.

Next day the boys did some reorganizing. The Marzanos moved to Room 59, next to DiFonzo/Morini, with a connecting door to Room 57. During the following days, Tony Marzano was rarely seen outside the bar, while Charlie and DiFonzo divided their time between business in George Town, their rooms, and the thatched-roof outdoor bar and pool. There is no language barrier in the Caymans, and the men from Chicago had little difficulty doing business. The speech is a mixture of English and West Indian, with touches of Irish, Welsh, and American drawl thrown in. Island natives are mainly descendants of pirates, shipwrecked sailors, and slaves.

One evening shortly after their arrival, while at the Inn's main dining room, Charlie Marzano took the maitre d'hotel, Gian Franco Audieri, aside and asked him, "What are the best banks to do business with when you do business on the island?" Audieri recommended several, after which Marzano asked, "Is there anyway that your money can be taken out of the bank, you know, by the authorities?"

"No, sir. It's the same here as it is in Switzerland," the maitre d' replied. "Nobody can come in and take your money out."

"Good man," the smiling Marzano said, gently cuffing Audieri's chin. He tipped the hotel employee a $100 bill and returned to his table, where DiFonzo was chatting with a vacationing airline stewardess.

During the next few days, a total of $1,154,200, later claimed to be part of the Purolator loot, was deposited at 12 per cent interest in four banks in the names of so-called shell corporations, existing only on paper. The phony corporations, the banks, and the amounts deposited were as follows:

Ghengis Kahn, Ltd., in the Bank of Nova Scotia — $438,540.

Rural Investments, in the Cayman National Bank & Trust Co. — $35,000.

Development, Ltd., in the Swiss Bank & Trust Co., — $500,000.

Harlow Investments, Ltd., in the World Banking and Trust Corp., — $180,660.

Campbell, the attorney who helped the client who gave his name as Morini stash the money, also held the keys to four lockboxes in the Royal Bank of Canada, later found to contain $5,000. The boxes were numbered 112, 130, 131, and 132. They keys were kept in an envelope bearing the message: "This envelope is the sole property of Jim Morini and can only be dealt with by him."

There is little night life on the island. An official of the Department of Tourism summed it up this way:

"The Cayman Islands are not for everyone. We don't intend to-be. We don't have flashing neon, gambling casinos, or big night life. We prefer a different approach. We take life easy, soak up the sunshine, and relax in the sea breezes."

By Saturday, Tony Marzano had firmly established that the take-life-easy pace of the islands was not for him. Tired of sunshine and sea breezes, and longing for the sleazy din of Chicago's Rush Street, he decided to hop a jet back to the States, leaving Charlie with Room 59 all to himself. He booked a seat on the next flight to Miami, and took an island cab to the airport.

After paying the native cabbie, Tony realized he was still carrying between $500 and $600 in island "expense money"

— cash from the Purolator loot that he didn't want to be caught with on American soil. So he went directly to the men's room, whereupon he regretfully ripped the bills into tiny pieces and flushed them all down the toilet. Then he stopped in front of the mirror, brushed his hair, and disappeared.

Occasionally, during the next few days, Charlie Marzano and DiFonzo ventured out onto the beach, or took a dip in the outdoor pool. Hotel waiters recalled that they ate well, mostly steaks and fresh sea food. Marzano preferred an inexpensive Bordeaux wine called St. Emilion with his meals, and paid for everything with $100 bills. DiFonzo/Moroni drank only milk; an ulcer perhaps.

By Tuesday morning, October 29, the hotel management observed that the two men's bills were up to $1,200, and a clerk was asked to diplomatically call for "Mr. Morini" in Room 57, and request payment on the bill.

"Okay, sure, I'll be right down to settle up," he said. "We're gonna be staying here another five days." He did not come down as promised, however, and the clerk finally called the room again during the afternoon. He got no answer. At last, in late evening, the man called Morini answered the phone. "Well, sure, we're gonna pay. You don't have to worry. But we're having a problem with your laundry right now. We sent some stuff out, and we didn't get it all back.'"

"I'm terribly sorry about that, Mr. Morini," the clerk apologized. "That is not the Holiday Inn's laundry, however. It is an outside service. We've never had any trouble with them, and I'm sure they will discover your missing items and have everything straightened out in the morning. In the meantime, Mr. Morini, our policy is not to extend credit beyond a certain point, and the management would be gratified if you would come down and arrange a settlement. Your bill, at this point, is rather high. The amount is $1,188.40, to be exact."

"All right, all right, we'll be right down," Morini said. At about 10 p.m. DiFonzo and Marzano came down and settled their account, paying it with $100 bills.

Another incident shortly thereafter also caused hotel employees to remember the men. Charlie Marzano kept his money in a safe deposit box in the hotel office, and came down to ask a desk clerk to get it out for him. She did, and set the 22-inch by 4-inch long metal box down on the counter facing him, so he could turn the key in the lock. When the lock clicked, the girl lifted the lid, facing Marzano, in what she thought was a helpful gesture. Marzano far from thanked her, however. Instead, he raged, "I'm opening my own box!" He then clutched it toward himself and glared about the lobby. The clerk could see it was jammed with $100 bills.

As this mini-drama was taking place on Grand Cayman Island, FBI agents in Miami were checking out the final points of Gushi's story.

They determined that DiFonzo, Gushi, and the Marzanos arrived at Butler Aviation Terminal at Miami International Airport on the flight from Ohio at 7:30 p.m. October 21, and stayed overnight at the Crossways Airport Inn. DiFonzo, they established, left Fort Lauderdale's International Airport at 12:25 p.m. the following day, aboard a chartered jet, and arrived at George Town at 1:45 p.m. The Marzanos followed by commercial jet from Miami International Airport, arriving at George Town a short time later.

FBI agents Paul Rico and Anthony Amoroso of the Miami office located a City Cab Company driver, Marcel J. Robert, who recalled being dispatched by radio to the Butler terminal on the twenty-first to pick up four men. "They had three or four pieces of luggage. One of the suitcases was so heavy it took two of them to lift it into the trunk of the cab," the cabbie said. "They refused to let me lay a hand on it."

He drove the quartet to the DuPont Plaza Hotel on Biscayne Boulevard, where two of them went inside. A short time later they returned to the taxi and advised their companions that the hotel was full, and they could not get adjoining rooms. They ordered Robert to take them to the Holiday Inn, near the airport. On the way, however, they passed the Crossways Inn on 42nd Avenue and told the driver to stop. One of them went inside, and came back out to tell the others that rooms were available.

The agents showed Robert five photographs. From them he identified Peter Gushi as the passenger who sat in the front seat alongside him, and Louie DiFonzo and Charlie Marzano as two of the three men in the back seat.

Next, in going over the company logs, the agents located a Yellow Cab driver, Marcus Matijevic, who had been dispatched to the Crossway Motel the following morning, October 22.

Matijevic said he picked up three men at about 11:30 a.m., with several pieces of luggage. They directed him to take them to Pompano Beach, but changed their minds along the way and told him to head for West Palm Beach instead. While driving along Interstate Hwy. 95, Matijevic said, he received a radio message from his office instructing him to telephone his dispatcher immediately upon discharging his passengers. He said this appeared to un-nerve the trio, and they made him turn off his radio. They then directed him off I-95 at State Hwy. 84, and told him to proceed to Fort Lauderdale.

"Along the way, about three or four traffic lights past Sunrise Boulevard on highway A-1A they told me to stop at a grocery store," the cab driver said. "One of the guys in the back seat said they wanted to pick up some groceries to take to their motel. I asked them if they wanted me to wait, and they said no. The bill was $20.27, according to my log. They gave me $27 and said I should keep the change."

He was shown a group of photos, and picked those of Charlie Marzano and Peter Gushi as resembling two of the three men in the cab. He said Gushi sat in the front seat with him.

Checking records at the Crossways motel, the agents determined that five telephone calls had been made from the rooms the men occupied overnight. The first call was to a party in Miramar, Florida, and the second to Brookfield, Illinois. The third call was to Irving, Texas. The fourth call was to George Town, on Grand Cayman Island, and the fifth was to Joseph Oteri, a Boston lawyer who represented DiFonzo.

Meanwhile, FBI agent Alfred Lamanna of the Fort Lauderdale office had scored on DiFonzo. Mrs. Thelma Raniero, a secretary for Robert Graf, Inc., an aviation service, told him she had received a telephone call from a man identifying himself as DiFonzo on the morning of October 22, inquiring about a charter flight to Grand Cayman Island. She told him it could be arranged.

The man showed up at noon and made arrangements for the flight. The cost was $1,233, plus a $3 head tax. Mrs. Raniero said the customer paid the bulk of the fare with $100 bills, which he carried in the breast pocket of his sports coat. Prior to leaving, the man made a long distance call to Grand Cayman. He checked the cost of the call with the operator, and paid Mrs. Raniero $6.48. Records showed the plane, piloted by Michael Harris and Jeffrey Abrams, took off from Fort Lauderdale at 12:25 p.m., and set down at Grand Cayman at 1:45p.m.

Mrs. Raniero was shown several photographs of men. She picked a photo of DiFonzo as resembling the man who had chartered the flight.

Both Harris and his co-pilot, Abrams, identified photos of DiFonzo as the man who made the flight. Harris recalled that their passenger was carrying two large folding suitcases, that were "extremely heavy," and two smaller ones, a briefcase and an overnight bag.

"During the flight he asked me, "If someone came from Nassau to Grand Cayman, would he have to clear Miami customs?" I told him no, because that would constitute travel between two foreign countries flying the same flag. That was the only conversation we had," Harris said.

At the airport on Grand Cayman, Harris said, DiFonzo was met by a man, about 30, having light brown short, curly hair, and wearing slacks and a sports shirt. He said DiFonzo greeted the man by name, but did not recall what it was. The two then got into the man's car and left the airport.

Since the suspects had now been traced to British soil, it became necessary for the FBI to contact Britain's famed Scotland Yard. The Yard promised full cooperation. Officials of the U.S. State Department and Scotland Yard worked late into the night Tuesday, October 29, ironing out legal and diplomatic barriers that might hinder a search for the men and the money on Grand Cayman Island.

Early in the morning of Wednesday, October 30, special agents Patrick E. Farrell and Frank Pieroni of the Miami FBI office packed their suitcases and prepared to establish a beachhead at George Town.

CHAPTER 18

An arrest is made, Cayman style.

T he flurry of activity that went on Tuesday night in Miami picked up in Chicago on Wednesday, October 30, as FBI agents and federal prosecutors began to smell the end of the trail. Maniatis was turned over to federal agents by Chicago police, and taken to the Dirksen Federal Building where he was permitted to talk to Gushi.

After consultation with his friend from the bargain center, Maniatis decided that full cooperation for him, too, would be the best way out. The 58-year-old peddler, nervous about the caper from the very start, gave a written statement detailing his cameo role in Purolator. He described his purchase of the Ford van for Charlie Marzano, and told how, on the night of October 21, he helped Mary Jane Gushi hide the packages of money in the artificial flower planter while her husband was on the way to Florida with DiFonzo and the Marzano cousins. On Sunday night, while the actual burglary was taking place, he was at the race track. He cashed in several tickets, on the daily double, and the FBI was able to check them out.

Maniatis was arraigned before Magistrate Sussman, who set bond at $300,000 full cash, and remanded him to the custody of the U.S. Marshal's office. He, like Gushi, was placed in protective custody, and whisked to an undisclosed location.

Sussman then heard from Mrs. Wolfson who sought unsuccessfully to reduce Marrera's $400,000 bond.

While this was going on, a Federal Grand Jury sitting in Chicago indicted Marrera, Gushi, and Maniatis for bank burglary, bank larceny, and illegal use of explosives. The case was assigned for trial to United States District Judge William J. Bauer. Bauer, a former United States District Attorney for Northern Illinois, scheduled a preliminary hearing for November 14.

At the same time, based on information given by Maniatis, Special Agent Thomas Green went to the Gushi home to check the described hiding places. He retrieved what was left of the $400,000 turned over to Gushi by Marzano in the restaurant parking lot. It contained approximately $30,000 in $10, $20, $50, and $100 bills. This was the amount Gushi, decided at the last minute, to hold back from the pre-dawn extortionists who forced him to make the terrifying drop in the alley behind his home. Green found one bundle hidden in a nightstand in the master bedroom, and the other in the basement where Gushi had stashed it.

The agent thanked the bewildered Mrs. Gushi, and gave her a receipt for the cash. It was not until several days later, when she talked to her husband, that Mary Jane Gushi discovered the money stashed in the nightstand — $5,000 — was not part of the Purolator loot, but money from the discount store. The money Gushi actually held back the night he dropped the bundle in the alley totaled $24,610.

Authorities, meanwhile, launched what Stratton like to call a "full court press" for the elusive Tony Marzano. They knew that the white Ford left earlier at the airport in Columbus had been claimed, so it was logical to presume he was back on his native turf. Chicago police, checking Marzano's parents' neighborhood in Berwyn, spotted a white-over-white Ford LTD parked in the 1400 block of Home Avenue at 10:30 p.m. The license number, AF-9375, checked out to Anthony M. Marzano for a 1972 Volkswagen. A check with neighbors revealed the car had been parked there since 8 o'clock in the morning. The auto was placed under surveillance, in the event that its owner might return.

Considering that the auto was recovered not far from Ralph Marrera's home, in the 1400 block of Clinton Street, police speculated that Marzano might have been hiding out at Marrera's, thinking it safe since Marrera was in custody and nobody was apt to look there. Police questioned neighbors, and determined that an unidentified man had been seen to enter the Marrera home.

The investigating officers called their Damen Avenue headquarters for back-up assistance, and five more Chicago policemen arrived, along with a detail of officers from the Berwyn Department, in order to make the raid official. While police surrounded the home, Sgt. Ed Wodnicki and three other officers entered an inner front hallway leading to the Marrera apartment.

Wodnicki kicked open the door and shouted, "Police officers! We are looking for Tony Marzano, who has been named in a federal warrant!" A noise was heard at the rear of the apartment, and Wodnicki repeated his warning. Another sound was heard inside, and Wodnicki and his men burst in and conducted a rapid room-to-room search of the apartment, consisting of two bedrooms, a living room, and kitchen.

When they got to the kitchen they discovered that the noise was being made by police on an enclosed rear porch, trying to get in the back door. They also discovered something else.

On the south side of the kitchen was a large closet, that had no door. There, sitting on the floor in full view, pointing at the astonished policemen, was a Japanese made machine-gun with a fully-loaded clip.

Wodnicki stepped gingerly toward the gun and took a look into the room. On a shelf to his left was a 12-gauge Winchester shotgun; a U.S. Army .45 caliber automatic pistol; a .45 caliber Smith and Wesson revolver with a six-inch barrel; a .38 caliber Colt Cobra revolver; a .38 caliber Smith and Wesson snub-nosed revolver with a holster, and a .38 caliber Smith and Wesson revolver with a four-inch barrel.

Marrera had an arsenal large enough to start a brisk fire-fight. A check with Berwyn police revealed that none of the weapons was registered. Treasury agent Robert Zarek of the Bureau of Alcohol, Tobacco and Firearms was contacted, and the weapons were turned over to him.

U.S. Attorney James Thompson had now authorized the filing of complaints before Magistrate Sussman charging DiFonzo and the two Marzanos with bank larceny, bank burglary, use of explosives during commission of a federal felony, and a new charge — interstate transport of stolen property.

FBI agents Farrell and Pieroni, waiting for this development in Miami, took off for Grand Cayman Island on the next plane, armed with arrest warrants for the fugitives. They were welcomed at Owen Roberts Field by Derrick Tricker, the self-styled Sherlock Holmes of the West Indies, who offered them his full cooperation. Tricker promptly showed them several documents that assured them their trip had been anything but a waste of time. One was a photostat of a General Declaration Form bearing the official stamp: Immigration Officer No. 14, October 22, 1974. Entry Cayman Islands. The document read:

Owner and Operator:	Robert Graf
Registration:	N855W
Flight Number:	"Private"
Date:	October 22, 1974
Departure:	From Ft. Lauderdale, Fla.
Arrival:	At Grand Cayman
Total Number of Crew:	Three: Michael Harris, Jeffrey Abrams and Lou DiFonzo

"Well, it looks as though at least one of our guys is here for sure," Farrell said.

"Oh, that's not all," said Tricker smugly, obviously enjoying himself. "I do believe you are seeking the whereabouts of two other individuals as well." With that he handed the agents two immigration cards captioned "Cayman Islands — Immigration Entry." Farrell took the two cards and studied them:

```
Name:              Anthony Marzano
Date of Birth:     January 20, 1943
Place of Birth:    Chicago, Ill.
Address:           2430 N. 79th Ave., Elmwood
                   Park, Ill.
Passport No.:      M625-9214-3020
Employment:        Salesman
Date:              October 22, 1974
```

```
Name:              Charles Marzano
Date of Birth:     October 14, 1934
Place of Birth:    Chicago, Ill.
Address:           1803 S. 59th Ct., Cicero, Ill.
Passport No.:      M625-404(?) (?)253
Employment:        Business
Date:              October 22, 1974
```

Tricker also had a card for DiFonzo, listing his date of birth as December 19, 1947, and his business as "consultant."

"Well, you're certainly making it easy for us, superintendent," Pieroni commented. "Now all we have to do is find where these individuals are now."

Tricker smiled and handed them two more cards, which turned out to be photocopies of the Holiday Inn registration forms:

```
Number:            15622
Name:              Anthony Marzano
Address:           2430 N. 79th Ave., Elmwood
                   Park, Ill.
Miscellaneous:     In 10/22  Rm. 216  Out 10/23
                   Rates: $28.80  Paid Cash
```

```
Number:            15623
Name:              Charles Marzano
Address:           1803 S. 59th Ct., Cicero, Ill.
Miscellaneous:     In 10/22  Rm. 216  Out 10/23
                   Rates: $28.80  Paid Cash
```

"Where it says 'out,' they simply check out of that particular room, and into another one," Tricker quickly explained. "By the way, I also took the liberty to interview Mr. Bruce Campbell, who has offices in the Bank of Nova Scotia building. He is the gentleman who met your Mr. DiFonzo at the airport, you know. All he could tell me is that he met with all three of your chaps in the Holiday Inn, but the nature of any business they conducted, he felt, must be privileged communication between attorney and clients. Come along, gentlemen. Shall we drive into town?"

Back at the Holiday Inn, word that the fugitives in America's biggest cash theft might be on the island was picked up via Miami radio, and DiFonzo decided it was time to pack the suitcases for a hurry-up trip to Costa Rica. He was aware, perhaps because of the much-publicized disappearance there of fugitive financier Robert Vesco, that the Central American country had no extradition treaty with the United States.

His plan struck an immediate snag, however, when Marzano balked at leaving. "My laundry ain't all back," he complained. "Dammit, I haven't been throwing $100 tips around all week long just to get my monogrammed pajamas stolen."

"Jesuz Christ, Charlie. We'll get you some new goddamed pajamas in Costa Rica. They've got lots of pajamas in Costa Rica. It's famous for pajamas, monogrammed anyway you want them," DiFonzo argued.

"That ain't the point," Marzano protested. "The point is, I'm not leaving this hotel until they come up with my fuckin' pajamas. When we paid up last night they said they were gonna straighten it out in the morning, and now its morning, and dammit, they are gonna straighten it out!"

The angry Marzano, building up a full head of steam, got on the house phone and demanded to talk to the Holiday Inn's manager, George Salati. He filled Salati in on the missing pajamas caper, and a few minor items, and stormed, "Monday! Gone since Monday! And here it is, Wednesday. Your people said they were going to straighten this out. Now, Mr. Salati, I want you to go down and look for my pajamas yourself, understand? If I don't get them back, there's gonna be trouble."

"Jeez, Charlie, I'll buy you a new pair myself, just as soon as we get out of here," moaned DiFonzo, holding his head in his hands.

"No," argued Marzano. "No two-bit laundry is going to fuck me outa my silk pajamas. I'll be damned if some native spook is gonna be walking around this island wearing pajamas with MY monogram on them. No way! I'm gonna get those goddam pajamas back if I have to turn this place upside-down."

Marzano, once billed by the admiring Gushi as "the strongest man in the world," did not have to turn the hotel upside-down, however. At Salati's persistent prodding, the laundry located the misplaced sleeping attire, and several shirts, which were promptly returned to the delighted Marzano, who told DiFonzo: "What did I tell you? Huh? Those bastards had 'em all the time."

"Charlie, can we go now?" begged DiFonzo, at the point of exasperation. The two, after previously advising the hotel they intended to stay another five days, quickly checked out, and left no forwarding address. As they departed, Salati shook his head in Marzano's direction.

"He sure raised an awful fuss," he said to a night desk clerk. "And I thought he was such a nice man. He liked to talk about Blackbeard, and the other pirates who used to come here . . . "

A short time after DiFonzo and Marzano retreated from the Holiday Inn, the phone rang. It was Superintendent Tricker, himself, asking to speak to the manager. "I wonder if you could tell me, old boy, whether you still have a party by the name of DiFonzo, or Marzano, staying with you?" he asked. "You have? Marzano! Oh? Just checked out, eh? Hmmm. I see. Well, I am going to come right over with some photographs for you to look at. I'll see you directly."

Accompanied by the two FBI agents, Tricker drove over to the hotel, where Salati and his employees were shown pictures of the suspects. All identified the Marzanos and DiFonzo as their recent guests, although they knew DiFonzo by a different name, Morini.

"Very well," announced Tricker, turning to the G-men. "They're on the island, and they won't get away. I'm going home to pick up Karen. I'll drop you off at your residence so you can freshen up a bit, and I'll call for you later."

Tricker, 48, and his attractive blonde wife, Karen, spent all their evenings together, no matter what. They were frequently accompanied by Reg Holland, owner of the Royal Palms Hotel, and Holland's wife Meg, an old friend. That night, while Special Agent Farrell joined Caymanian police in combing the island for the fugitives, the Trickers took his partner, Pieroni, out riding with them.

At 9:30 p.m. a message was relayed to Tricker that Mike Adams, a ticket agent at Owen Roberts Field, reported two "suspicious acting men" loitering in the airport waiting room. A LACSA Airlines flight was due in from Miami shortly, and scheduled to take off for San Jose, Costa Rica, at 10 minutes after the hour. Adams said the two strangers had tickets on the outgoing flight.

"It's such a nice moonlit night. Shall we motor over to the airport?" suggested Tricker. "I think that would be lovely, Derrick," answered the statuesque Karen. Pieroni shook his head and smiled.

Everyone on the island knew Tricker, and when he entered the airport lounge his attention was quickly directed to two men who appeared to be ducking their heads so as not to be noticed. These were the two Adams called about, booked onto the Costa Rican flight under the names of J. Stewarte and M. Stewarte.

Tricker strode officiously across the lounge of the narrow frame structure, with its bare wooden floors, ceiling fans, and fish trophies on the walls. He immediately recognized the Stewartes as the fish he had been looking for — the men he had seen in photographs identifying them as Luigi Michael DiFonzo and Pasquale Charles Marzano. The two fugitives stared apprehensively at the quaint island cop as he marched up to them, puffing on his pipe, Mrs. Tricker at his side. Pieroni remained at a discreet distance, since the FBI had no jurisdiction on the British possession.

Approaching the suspects, Tricker politely removed his pipe before speaking.

"My card, gentlemen," he began, unfolding his wallet to display his credentials. "Won't you come to the office with me?" With that, Tricker turned his back and walked away. The stunned DiFonzo and Marzano follow meekly, while tall, blonde Karen Tricker brought up the rear.

Pieroni, watching incredulously, caught up with the parade and whispered to Tricker, "You didn't frisk them for weapons!"

"No need to," snapped Tricker. "We do not allow them on the island."

And the charge?

"Refusing to give me their true identities," replied the superintendent, matter of factly. "The suspects refused to answer my questions." In Tricker's domain, that was enough to hold anybody, and DiFonzo and Marzano were booked to spend the rest of the night in George Town's tiny, green stucco slammer.

But first they were relieved of their personal possessions. In addition to their clothing, Marzano was found to be carrying $9,960 in American money. DiFonzo had $13,067.80 more on his person, plus 65 cents Cayman.

Pieroni, still unable to accept the scenario he had just witnessed, commented to the Trickers after the Chicagoans were locked up, "Boy, I'd say that was really cutting it close. Ten minutes more and they'd have been on their way to Costa Rica."

"Oh, no," said Karen, smugly. "Derrick had called ahead, don't you see? The airplane was not going to leave until he had arrested them."

CHAPTER 19
But, where is the money?

The "action," as Americans say, had 'gone down' right in their own back yard, but residents of the tiny island learned of the arrests by remote control. On Thursday morning, October 31, radio Miami, the island's main source of news, beamed word that the suspects were behind bars. Some 300 curious islanders, expecting nothing less from Derrick Tricker than immediate ouster of the "American gangsters," lined the fences alongside the terminal at Owen Roberts Field hoping for a glimpse of his celebrated prisoners.

Law in the islands forbade extradition except in cases of murder and high treason, but Caymanian officials had been known, on occasion, to expel undesirables. They simply bundled them aboard outgoing planes without the pomp of extradition ceremonies. In this case, only Tricker himself determined that Charlie Marzano and Louie DiFonzo were not desirable. As they were taken from the dinky George Town jail, and turned over to Farrell and Pieroni, Tricker formally handed each prisoner a receipt for his belongings.

October 31, 1974

RELEASE OF PROPERTY

TO WHOM IT MAY CONCERN:

This is to certify that the following property, obtained by the arrest of LOU DEFONZO (sic) and CHARLES MARZANO, on 10/30/74, is hereby released to F.B.I. agents Patrick E. Farrell and Frank Pieroni.

1. 5 containers of sundry items of clothing.

2. 1 page of yellow note paper with sundry.

3. $9,960 from CHARLES MARZANO.
   $13,067.80 from LOU DEFONZO (65¢ CAYMAN).

4. One pair of cufflinks, one cigarette lighter, one gold wedding ring, one gold diamond setting ring and one Parker pen from LOU DEFONZO.
   One Bulova watch from MARZANO.
   One Wallet with I.D. card.
   One key ring.
   One gold type Longine watch from LOU DEFONZO.

With the receipt signed by Tricker, the two would-be millionaires were then placed unceremoniously in separate cars, and driven to the airport, where the island crowd had already assembled.

"Here they come!" shouted Jake Manderson, a cab driver who claimed to hold the island's first driver's license, issued in 1922. Manderson pointed to two green Austin-Healy unmarked police cars heading slowly for the terminal. The lead Austin was driven by Tricker, and contained Marzano and a Caymanian corporal. Di Fonzo sat glumly in the second car, along with the two FBI agents.

Tricker, obviously rather pleased with himself, waited calmly until all other passengers had boarded LACSA Flight 620 to Miami. Then he saw the two fugitives aboard, nattily attired, sun-tanned, sullen, and in handcuffs. They were accompanied by Pieroni and Farrell, who paid for all four tickets. Since the suspects could not legally be arrested by the FBI until they set foot on American soil, Corporal Eric Smith of Tricker's staff was sent along to make the trip official.

As the plane took off at 10:30 a.m., and Tricker waved good-bye, he displayed a broad smile beneath his bushy mustache. It had been a "good show," and he knew it. So did a Miami newsman, who had flown over for the event. Noting to fellow reporters that it was Halloween, he pointed at the police superintendent's smug grin and quipped, "Tricker treat!"

An hour and five minutes later the plane touched down at Miami International Airport, and Farrell and Pieroni officially took possession of the more than $23,000 the two men had been carrying. Then, as they escorted DiFonzo and Marzano down the passenger ramp they were greeted by FBI agents Eugene McKinney and Richard Gerrity, who placed the suspects legally under arrest.

The two men were processed in the Miami FBI office, and taken to the U.S. Marshal's lockup, where they refused to answer questions. Both were then brought before U.S. Magistrate Perter Palermo in Miami, who ordered DiFonzo held in one million dollar cash bond and Marzano in $500,000 cash bond. He scheduled a hearing for November 8 on their removal to Chicago, and remanded them to the custody of the marshal.

The ever-widening search for Tony Marzano ended abruptly, that same morning, when the last known fugitive in the Purolator caper walked into the Dirksen Federal Building, accompanied by his lawyer, Robert S. Bailey, and surrendered to the FBI. Marzano decided the night before to throw in the towel, after seeing his face on television during the 10 o'clock news.

"Well, Bill, you've really got your tit in a wringer this time,'" Ray Stratton remarked, when Marzano was brought into his office. "Anything you'd like to tell us?" Marzano shook his head. Negative. Nobody ever called him Bill except his lawyer. He figured the keen-eared Stratton must have heard them talking as they walked in. "O.K. Come on," Stratton beckoned.

Marzano was brought before Magistrate Sussman in a room jammed with newspapermen and television and radio reporters — every bit as curious as the crowd that had gathered on Grand Cayman Island earlier in the day — waiting to get a glimpse of the last of the Purolator fugitives.

"Do you have a job?" Sussman asked the 31-year-old prisoner.

"I worked in the cartage business, but my truck was stolen a couple of months ago," Marzano answered.

"Do you have a family?"

"My wife's in Florida, in Clearwater, I think. We're separated, and I'm paying $20 a week support for two kids."

"I don't think you're a very stable man, Mr. Marzano. I'm setting your bond at $375,000, cash," Sussman said. Marzano, who had been sitting on millions of dollars a week ago, couldn't come up with the scratch.

He was remanded to the custody of the U.S. Marshal, and a preliminary hearing was scheduled for November 8. Like DiFonzo and Charlie, he, too, refused to submit to an "interview" by the FBI.

It was not yet noon on October 31, only eleven days after the discovery of the biggest cash burglary in the history of America, and all six suspects were in federal custody. "Charlie Cigars" Siragusa, whose undercover agents first infiltrated the mob, offered an observation:

"The whole thing was a bit of a fiasco. If the IBI had followed through and kept up the surveillance, who knows? They might have caught the vault thieves right in the act. But, as it turned out, the case was salvaged. The bad guys were arrested, and charged, and some of the money was recovered. Thanks to us." Siragusa did not get where he was without blowing his own horn, even if only a little peep.

True, some of the money had been recovered, but it represented only a fraction of the missing loot. Finding the remainder could prove a tougher nut to crack than solving the case.

"I fear that virtually all of the loot taken from Chicago

to Grand Cayman by the defendants probably has been deposited in a number of the island's more than 180 banks," U.S. Attorney Thompson opined. "You know, one of these guys, Charlie Marzano, kept asking a lot of questions about pirates while he was down there. Some of that missing dough could even be buried somewhere under the beaches."

Publicity attendant on the DiFonzo-Marzano episode on the island was the first of any magnitude to raise questions about the banking procedures there. Government and bank officials on Grand Cayman reacted by imposing a news blackout on something that, by tradition, had always been secret information anyhow.

Referring to news stories about the hiding of the Purolator loot on the island, the Crown goverment's senior principal secretary, Dennis Foster, declared self-righteously: "We don't want their bloody money. We have a worldwide reputation at stake. Gangsters and their booty are not welcome here."

But would the talkative Foster back up his declaration with action, when the United States government asked for assistance in ferreting out the hidden funds?

"Our banking laws," answered Foster, "are completely secret." Nothing could be disclosed short of an order from the Queen, and the court process to obtain such an order was so detailed that it would drive even a Philadelphia lawyer up a wall.

"There is no shortcut to finding details of any transaction here," said one banking official. "You have to come into court with facts and figures."

One banker, Rodney Bond, general manager of the Swiss Bank & Trust Corp., admitted he had spoken with Charlie Marzano during his brief stay on the island, but was tight-lipped about any financial dealings they might have had. "I am not in a position — nor are any of the banks here — to make any comment on any financial matters," he insisted.

The official line put forth by spokesman for the island's huge banking industry was that none of the banks would think of touching stolen or embezzled money. But the Purolator treasure hunters refused to buy it. The banks on

Grand Cayman were there for one reason: To lure money.
And the more the better.

On Thursday night, while islanders young and old celebrated a West Indies Halloween by donning lavish Devil
costumes, Tricker took his wife, Karen, to the Royal Palms
for dinner. Two newsmen from the States, sent down to
cover the arrests, were also in the room.

Tricker was pleasantly sociable, and obviously pleased
with himself over apprehending and deporting the two
Chicago burglary suspects, as he raised his glass to his lips.
On all of Grand Cayman Island, Derrick Tricker knew no
peer when it came to the consumption of good Scotch.
But anyone who foolishly thought it might loosen his tongue
was soon disappointed.

"This is a social evening, really," he told reporter John
O'Brien of the *Chicago Tribune,* who attempted to casually
ask him about the Purolator case. Scotch and water in
hand, Tricker quickly turned the tables on the newsman by
asking questions himself.

"Tell me about Chicago," he begged. "I was stationed
there for awhile by the Royal Navy. There were some,
ahem, ladies I knew in the suburb of Blue Island." He
allowed only small talk, and asked reporter Arnold Markowitz of the *Miami Herald,* "Tell me, do you play naughts
and crosses?"

"Naughts and crosses?" Markowitz struggled, giving
Tricker a blank look.

"Here, let me have your pen," Tricker said impishly.
"There! After you."

He had drawn a tic-tac-toe diagram.

CHAPTER 20
Now it's a treasure hunt.

Tracking human prey is almost elementary compared to trying to find the wherabouts of more than four million dollars in unrecorded bills, part of it being, authorities were convinced, in secret numbered accounts in any one or all of the Grand Cayman banks.

Federal agents returned to the island that Friday, the day after Halloween, to begin the search. They were there unofficially of course, having no jurisdiction in British territory. But Derrick Tricker basked in the company of fellow policemen. And they seemed to enjoy his Sherlock Holmes demeanor.

The British Criminal Investigation Department, under Tricker, was seeking the missing money on three fronts:

1. The conglomeration of banks, several of which DiFonzo and Charlie Marzano were known to have visited while on the island.

2. The island's postal facilities, which could have been used by the suspects to mail some of the money back to the States, where the untraceable cash could already be back in circulation.

3. Remote jungle cottages, which could have been rented during the suspects' stay, as hiding places for the loot until after the investigation cooled down.

In addition to trying through his own sources, to determine whether DiFonzo and Marzano opened secret bank accounts, Tricker attempted to determine whether they might have also rented safe deposit boxes in one or more of the banks, to simply put the booty in storage.

At the Swiss Bank & Trust Corp., he scored. A portion of the loot was deposited there. Recovering it might take years of legal maneuvering by lawyers for the American interests involved, but the British sleuth now knew he was on the right trail. He immediately ordered an investigation of credit information and references the burglary suspects might have supplied when they opened the account, to determine whether British banking laws were violated.

That evening, the delighted Tricker celebrated by treating the FBI agents to a merry party, complete with calypso band, at the Royal Palms.

On Saturday, November 2, State's Attorney Carey, in Chicago, announced an investigation of Jimmy the Bomber Catuara, Gushi's neighbor and *compare* to determine whether the hoodlum had knowledge of the Purolator theft. Catuara, 67, an upper level Crime Syndicate chieftain in Chicago, according to police, attended a September 23 meeting between Gushi and another mob figure in suburban Oak Lawn, where they were observed by IBI agents. Carey said surveillance at that time showed the two-hour meeting was followed by a series of sessions between Gushi and DiFonzo.

Some investigators felt that Catuara might have brought the two men together. Gushi's connection with top echelon mob figures would explain how professional criminals, each an expert in his own field, were recruited to pull off the master heist and move the money out of the country. The surveillance of Catuara was stepped up when federal agents learned he had put his home on South Kilbourn Avenue, Oak Lawn, and the next door home of his son, Carl, up for sale. It was a package deal, both houses and lots for $200,000. because the aging mobster reportedly wanted to fly out to Phoenix and retire in the sun.

With much of the Purolator loot still missing, one theory was that Catuara knew where it was, and law enforcement agents did not want him to drop from sight.

Authorities were also taking a fresh look at Allen Wainer, the 69-year-old Prohibition era bootlegger. Wainer's name

appeared in intelligence files gathered by Siragusa's infor-
mers, as having met with Gushi, and possibly being the
person who put up the front money for the Ford van and
traveling expenses.

This was the kind of detail work that follows the solution
of any major crime. It frequently goes nowhere.

On Monday, November 4, two of the defendants, Gushi
and Maniatis, were brought before Judge Bauer, who would
hear the case. They pleaded innocent to all charges, and
Bauer scheduled a hearing for November 27, to determine a
trial date.

Later that same day, at another hearing, Bauer reduced
Marrera's cash bond from $400,000 to $250,000. But he
rejected a plea by Marrera's new lawyer, Jo-Anne Wolfson,
to cut it any more.

"The court agrees that the government has superb reasons
for asking such a high bond," he commented. Mrs. Wolfson,
bangles dangling from her ears, placed one hand on her hip
and announced, "I'll take the decision before the U.S. Court
of Appeals."

Reporters who covered the federal courts in Chicago were
elated at the entry of Mrs. Wolfson into the case, and looked
forward to a colorful trial. She was a flamboyant red-head,
addicted to jangling bracelets and Indian jewelry, and once
worked as the "Little Indian Girl" on whom the trained
elephant would sit in the Gene Holter Wild Animal Show.

She took up law after marrying Warren Wolfson, a top
criminal lawyer, and many now considered her his equal in
courtroom performance. Once, on noticing that a drug addict
she was defending was nodding to sleep in front of the jury,
she called for a recess and dragged him out of the courtroom. Astonished witnesses saw the fiesty red-head drag the
startled defendant over to a drinking fountain, knee him,
and crack his head against the spigot, as she threatened,
"Don't you dare screw up my case!" Marrera chose his
counsel well.

On Tuesday, November 5, Tony Marzano went before
Magistrate Sussman with his lawyer, to plea for a similar
reduction in bond. Sussman agreed to cut it from $375,000

to $225,000, since Tony had "voluntarily surrendered" to federal authorities.

The next official action in the case came Thursday, November 7, when the Federal Grand Jury in Chicago returned a twelve-count indictment naming the six men in custody. All six were charged with conspiracy to commit bank larceny. All except DiFonzo were also charged with bank larceny, bank burglary, and the use of explosives in committing a theft. DiFonzo, the two Marzanos, and Gushi were also charged with interstate transportation of stolen property.

There was also official action in the Caribbean on that day. R.N. Donaldson, acting attorney general of Grand Cayman Island, filed a petition in Grand Court for an unprecedented court order. Officials of five banks were told where the Purolator loot was believed to be hidden and they were asked to provide details of any mysterious deposits in their banks.

"We want to see how much money was put where," he said. "It is not our policy to cover up crime in Cayman Island."

Donaldson requested the order, he said, because of "certain allegations" that part of the Purolator loot was stashed in the banks by DiFonzo and the Marzano cousins during their stay on the island. He explained the court order would enable authorities to learn how much money was deposited in each bank, and under what circumstances.

Information from Tricker's investigation indicated that $1.1 million was deposited in four of the five banks in the names of phony or "structured" companies, existing in name only, and formed on the island just before the loot was banked.

He identified the four as the Bank of Nova Scotia, the Swiss Bank & Trust Corp., the Cayman National Banking Trust Co., and the World Banking & Trust Corp., Cayman Ltd.

He added that the rest of the money brought to the island by the fugitives, some $300,000, was believed stashed in four separate safe deposit boxes in the Royal Bank of Canada.

An American insurance company initiated legal steps to recover the stolen money on Grand Cayman Island on Friday, November 8, even before Donaldson's petition was acted upon. Robert F. Doran, attorney for Commercial Union Insurance Co., of New York City, arrived on the island to confer with officials of the Grand Court to determine what steps had to be taken to assure return of the cash to its rightful owner. Commercial Union, along with Lloyds of London, insured the Purolator loss.

Magistrate F.E. Field, who would have to rule on Donaldson's petition, announced he would delay his decision until Tuesday. He did so after attorneys for the banks argued in chambers that issuing the order Donaldson requested would "jeopardize the island's structure as a tax haven." Such an order, they insisted would violate guarantees assuring depositors their identities and the sums on deposit will be kept secret.

An interested party to the arguments in Magistrate Field's chamber was Louie DiFonzo, who, from his jail cell in Miami, had hired a Grand Cayman barrister to represent him at the hearings. He hired the lawyer under the name of Jim Morini, the same alias under which he stayed at the Holiday Inn on the island. Under Caymanian law, not even the name of the lawyer could be divulged because the proceedings before the magistrate were not public.

While the point of order was being argued on Grand Cayman, the first trace of the Purolator loot was discovered in Miami. The more than $400,000 that had been deposited with the Bank of Nova Scotia in George Town was returned by that bank to the Federal Reserve Bank in Miami during a routine business transaction. Although the money, in $10, $20, $50 and $100 denominations, was not recorded by serial numbers when it was stored with Purolator, the cash was recorded when deposited on the island.

"Unfortunately there is not going to be any quick recovery of the money, even though we know where it was placed," stated an FBI spokesman. "The barrier to the recovery is establishing that the hidden money is, in fact, the money that was stolen."

This was also the day scheduled for DiFonzo's and Marzano's hearing in Miami to determine whether they should be returned to Chicago for trial. This time they made it easy for Uncle Sam, and waived the court hearing, agreeing to go north in the custody of federal marshals. Allen Lindley, chief deputy marshal in Chicago, said the prisoners would be returned over the weekend, but cautioned: "I can't say exactly when and how they will be brought back. Our biggest worry is watching out for somebody wanting to wipe them out and silence them."

On Tuesday, November 12, Magistrate Field announced his decision in George Town. It went against the government. Efforts to recover the more than a million dollars secreted in the island bank depositories were dashed when he ruled, without explanation, that he was refusing to order the banks to open their records for investigation.

He based his decision on arguments by the five banks' lawyers that such disclosure would violate the Swiss-style secrecy under which the banks operated, and on the assertion by DiFonzo's lawyer that the court lacked authority to issue such an order. Field took comfort in the fact that the theft occurred outside his jurisdiction, and no one had yet been convicted in the case.

"Well, there are other methods open to disclosure." Donaldson said, after his petition was rebuffed. "I will file my finding with the Grand Cayman Executive Council, which itself can order a disclosure of the banks' records. Another route, he said, would be to file criminal charges against one or more of the banking officials, charging they knew the deposited money to be stolen.

A breakthrough in the frustrating search for the money came three days later, on Friday, November 15. Donaldson requested, and was granted, a search warrant naming the George Town branch of the Royal Bank of Canada. Based on information provided by the FBI, the warrant authorized British police to seize and inspect any money concealed in several safe deposit boxes in the bank.

In anticipation of what might be uncovered, the FBI jetted a team of specialists from Miami to the island, armed with copies of palm and finger print charts of each of the Purolator suspects.

Attorney General Gerald Waddington of Grand Cayman, back from a holiday in London, relieved Donaldson, and stiffly announced, "We are collaborating as far as we can with the FBI in order to bring the perpetrators of the crime to justice and recover as much of the money as we can. We are working very assiduously and not leaving any stone unturned."

Donaldson added, "The attitude (of the court) has changed in the past three days, since it has been advised that insurance companies have repaid the victim of the theft for the loss, and are now trying to recoup their payment from banks in which some of the money is believed held. The stolen money now belongs to the insurance companies." One of the major carriers, of course, was Lloyd's of London.

After obtaining the search warrant, Donaldson turned it over to Tricker for execution. The FBI advised Tricker that they had turned up information that as much as $300,000 of the loot would be found in the safe deposit boxes rented in the name of Jim Morini.

But the opening of the boxes, in the presence of Tricker and FBI agents, only proved the wily cunning of the thieves. There was no $300,000. There was only $5,000. From island sources Tricker learned that the man called Morini did secrete $300,000 in the four boxes shortly after arriving in George Town, but removed the bulk of it on the following day because, he said, he wanted to deposit it in a cash-disbursing commercial account.

Checking out the boxes was not a wasted effort, however. The containers were processed for latent fingerprints, and several were identified as being identical to the prints of Luigi Michael DiFonzo.

Later that same day the Commercial Union Insurance Co. of New York City filed suit for injunction to restrain the four banks in which DiFonzo and Marzano were believed to have deposited the loot from disbursing any of the funds. All four banks voluntarily froze the funds, totaling $1,154,200, pending disposition of the suit.

On Saturday, November 16, DiFonzo and Charlie Marzano were removed from the Dade County Jail in Miami under heavy guard and flown to Chicago. The move, for security reasons, did not begin until a full week after the two had waived extradition proceedings and were reported on their way home.

The following Monday the two Marzanos and DiFonzo were arraigned in Chicago before Judge Bauer in Federal District Court. Each pled innocent to all charges.

Bauer set December 6 as the date to rule on motions, including one by Charlie Marzano and DiFonzo that their appearance before him was improper, on grounds they were "kidnapped" from the British West Indies by the FBI.

CHAPTER 21
The treasure hunt leads underground.

The "Caribbean Connection" and the romantic lore of real pirates who once hid booty there, could not help but inspire talk that the Purolator loot might, indeed, be buried beneath the sun drenched sands of Grand Cayman Island. U.S. Attorney Jim Thompson had suggested as much, and he wasn't far from wrong — only about 1,600 miles.

A sizeable portion of the loot was unearthed on Thursday night, November 21, buried deep in the sand. But not in the British West Indies, as some believed, but under the basement floor of an ordinary bungalow on Chicago's far Northwest Side.

From almost the minute the staggering Purolator loss was established, Ray Stratton and his fellow FBI agents, along with Chicago police and the IBI, had been pumping their confidential informants ("CIs") to get a handle on anyone who might know the whereabouts of the missing millions.

The Purolator building itself was gone over from top to bottom, old rusty water tanks were looked into, and the homes of innocent people were searched when anyone, who carried a grudge against them, phoned-in their names. Finally, in mid-November, agents picked up a tip from "a reliable source" that as much as two million dollars could be found cemented under the basement floor in a house formerly occupied by Ralph Marrera's grandmother on the Southwest Side, in the vicinity of Western, Ogden and Taylor. "I can't tell you the old lady's name, because I never heard it. But the info is legit," the informant whispered into the phone.

In an effort to determine the identity of the "old lady," an exhaustive documentary search was begun of birth and marriage records in Chicago. Old telephone books were pored over meticulously, and street directories going back years were scrutinized.

Using bits and pieces of information from this source and that, Stratton, Special Agents Thomas J. Green and Robert E. Hall, and Special Clerk Jack Ridenhour, painstakingly reconstructed the family trees of both Marrera and his wife, the former Alberta Lee Gardi.

They determined that both Alberta's maternal and paternal grandmothers were deceased, as was Ralph's maternal grandmother. That left only his paternal grandmother, Mrs. Dorothy Marrera. Records indicated that, for the last twenty years, she had lived at 2045 N. Natchez Avenue. This was in an industrial neighborhood, a far piece from the old-world Italian community clustered around the location earlier hinted at.

FBI agents discreetly interviewed neighbors around the neat, one-story brick bungalow, and learned that the well-kept home had been vacant for about two years; since Mrs. Marrera, an elderly widow, became ill and moved in with a daughter.

"Oh, but *they* watch it though," Cecil Pigg, the 58-year-old night watchman for the gear works on the corner, told the agents. "Every night about 2 a.m., until this last month, this fellow in a station wagon would come by to check if the door was locked. But he never went in."

Other neighbors told of men coming by regularly throughout the summer to mow the lawn, both in front and in the fenced-in back yard, and to do whatever else needed fixing up around the place. "Last month they said they had a repair job down in the basement," one neighbor recalled. "I don't know what they were doing, but they said something about fixing a drain."

"I'll tell you what they were doing," Stratton told his partner, Balgley. "Those were the highest paid chore-boys in history. They were working around the house over a long period of time to avoid arousing suspicion over any sudden activity. And I'll bet my ass they weren't fixing any drain in that basement, either. Those buzzards were digging a hole. That's what they were doing!"

Grandma Marrera's home, three doors away from the gear factory, sat back only 12 feet from the sidewalk, and four feet from the homes on either side. Any activity, then, would hardly have gone unnoticed. Stratton took his store of information to Assistant U.S. Attorneys James Breen and Michael King, who went to work on a thirteen page affidavit for a search warrant.

"Oh, boy," Stratton said, looking at his watch: "It had to be tonight of all nights, didn't it."

"It was just one month ago today that the burglary was discovered," Balgley noted.

"Yeah, and it's also my Boy Scout night. That's what I'm talking about," Stratton said.

"The scoutmaster's got to be there," Balgley joked. "You go ahead home and get into your uniform. We can take care of this, and I'll give you a call and let you know how it turns out."

"Over my dead body," Stratton retorted. "I've gone all the way with this one, and I'm not pulling out now. If and when that money is found, I want to be there."

"Do you want us to put it off for a night?" Balgley asked.

"Hell, no! Just give me time to make a phone call. My assistant scoutmaster can take care of the meeting as well as I can. If that money's really there, somebody else could go into that house and dig it up while I'm teaching square knots."

At 7:30 p.m. Stratton, Balgley, and the two federal prosecutors drove to the North Side apartment of U.S. Magistrate James T. Balog, and presented their petition. He read it thoroughly, and was obviously impressed.

"This is a classic job of sleuthing if I ever saw one," Balog commented. "You fellows have taken one little bit of information and parlayed it into a string of evidence that ultimately leads you right to the house. You definitely establish probable cause, and I am issuing a search warrant for 'Family residence at 2045 North Natchez, Chicago, Cook County, Illinois, including basement thereof and area beneath cement floor of basement, a one-story red brick bungalow.'"

Balog was reading the wording of the petition as he talked. The warrant, as requested in the affidavit, explicitly directed that it could be served at any time, day or night, since the house was vacant and a search would not disturb anyone's right to privacy. It also provided authority to "break cement on the basement floor reasonably necessary to effect search."

Ninety minutes later, armed with sledge hammers, shovels, and picks, Stratton, Balgley, the two prosecutors, along with fourteen other FBI agents, Chicago police officers, and IBI investigators, pulled up in a caravan in front of the darkened bungalow at 2045 North Natchez, ready for a pounding workout.

Stratton officiously walked up and rang the front doorbell, like a vacuum cleaner salesman, and waited impatiently, knowing full well that nobody was home. "We gotta go through the motions," he said over his shoulder to the curious array of lawmen now bunched behind him on the porch steps. "The law requires we knock first." Again Stratton rang the bell, dramatically thrusting his index finger forward for the benefit of onlooking neighbors. Then he knocked loudly, several times. Having satisfied the law, he declared in mock surprise, "I guess there's nobody home. Open her up fellas."

Attempts to pick the lock failed in the next several frustrating minutes, so police Commander Vrdolyak, who had been alerted by Lt. Nickels to be on the scene, trotted around to the back where he forced open an unlocked window on the enclosed rear porch.

Moving quickly through the home, noting it was immaculately kept and free of dust, he found the front door with his flashlight, swung it open, and beckoned the somewhat startled Stratton inside.

"Some things you never forget," explained Vrdolyak, a former burglary detective.

The hunting party went directly to the basement. Someone found the light switch and Balgley pointed to a sandy residue in a nearby laundry tub. Several plastic buckets, also containing sandy residue were observed.

"Looks like somebody might have been mixing cement, doesn't it," Stratton commented.

In the southwest corner of the basement, upended over a patch of recently poured cement, was a large cardboard box that once held an artificial Christmas tree, with removable aluminum branches.

"Merry Christmas, gang," quipped Stratton. "Let's see what Santa left under the box."

He then turned to Maureen Higgins, the only female FBI agent among the treasure seekers. "Ladies first."

Higgins, her hooped ear rings bouncing with each swing, wasted no time in striking the first honorary slams with a ten-pound sledge.

Now others moved over the discolored floor patch, wielding sledges of their own at the spot marked by Mo Higgins. Breaking through the surface they encountered a layer of chicken wire embedded in the cement. The wire was cut away, as the process was photographed, and the lawmen resumed the downward struggle until they came to a layer of plywood.

Stratton and Balgley hunched over the opening, their hearts pounding, as the plywood was carefully lifted out of the way and pushed aside to reveal a wooden compartment built into the ground, 16 inches wide, 26 inches long and 61 inches below the floor level, Crammed into the dank vault were several canvas bags.

"Boy, we've got it," Stratton beamed, savoring the moment. "If I could only see *their* faces now."

Five olive drab Army duffel bags, each encased in plastic wrap, were hoisted from the compartment. The plastic was removed, and the bags were opened, but not dumped out. As hoped for, each was stuffed with bundles of United States currency, tied with string or rubber bands. Four of the bags contained bundles of $10 bills, and the fifth appeared full of $20 bills. On the outside of each duffel bag was a strip of masking tape, with numbers written on the tape in crayon. Stratton totaled the figures, and came up with 2.2 million dollars!

"Leave a receipt and let's get going," he told the incredulous Balgley. "The law requires that when something is taken pursuant to a warrant, a receipt is supposed to be left."

As Balgley was working in his notebook, another agent poked the beam of his flashlight into the pit and yelled, "Hey, there's something else down in this hole." The agent dropped to his knees and fished out two bags of moisture-absorbing compound.

"Will you look at that," whistled Stratton. "How could they be so smart to think of something like that to protect the money from mildew — and still be so dumb they didn't realize there wouldn't be enough air in the vault to keep the fire going?"

The five duffel bags were loaded into Stratton's car and taken directly to FBI headquarters. There the contents were spread out on a large conference table in the office of Richard G. Held, special agent in charge. Wearing plastic gloves, agents removed the bundles of money from each bag, arranging the piles of bills in neat stacks of green. The top and bottom bill from each bundle was then carefully removed and processed by examiners brought in from the Latent Fingerprint Section of the FBI's Identification Division in Washington. One one bill, and one piece of cardboard included in one of the bundles, was found the fingerprints of Tony Marzano. He couldn't resist touching the money!

It was now 1 a.m. Friday, November 22. Special Agents Thomas J. Green and Thomas H. Greene, the same two who responded to the bomb scare in the First National Bank the morning after the burglary, were assigned to guard the money until 8 a.m., when it would be inventoried. Shotguns cradled in their laps, they positioned themselves in the hallway, at the only door to the conference room, and nobody went in or out all night. As they whiled away the hours with small talk, Green commented, "That son-of-a-bitch Stratton has a weird sense of humor, hasn't he?"

"What do you mean?" asked Greene.

"Picking you and me to baby sit with all this 'green' stuff."

That morning a guard in the Winnebago County Jail in Rockford, who had caught the early morning newscast, greeted Marrera with his breakfast and the tidings, "Hey,

Ralph. I hear they dug up a whole pile of money in your grandma's basement."

Ralph lurched from his bunk and strode across his cell to the portable TV set and snapped it on. As the picture tube lit up he frantically flipped the tuner from one station to another, looking for a news broadcast. Breakfast was ignored.

CHAPTER 22

The long count comes up short.

Surprisingly, the fortune found in grandma's basement was a hot potato — nobody wanted to be stuck with. The FBI turned the whole kit and kaboodle over to U.S. Attorney Jim Thompson just as soon as he arrived for work Friday morning. Thompson was immediately besieged with telephone calls from the news media for details of the discovery. He called a news conference so he could get it all over with in one telling.

"This recovery is far bigger than I thought we could get," he openly admitted. "It's an extraordinary recovery, particularly in light of the total amount stolen. As far as I've been able to tell, two-point-two million dollars is the biggest recovery of stolen money in United States history."

Thompson explained that Marrera's whereabouts were unknown for several hours on the Monday the theft was discovered, between the time he left the Purolator warehouse, and the time the FBI picked him up for questioning. His story was that he'd been puttering around the family-owned hotel. More than likely, though, he was stashing the loot, the prosecutor hinted.

"We believe that is when he made contact with his accomplices, and took the two-point-two million to his grandmother's vacant home. The hole in the basement floor was probably dug before the theft took place. All they had to do after the money was dumped into it was pour fresh cement over the top, and position the cardboard box to hide the patchwork."

Agent Held revealed that straps on the bundles of $10 and $20 bills had been traced to the Central National Bank of Chicago and to the Jewel Food Company, both of which used the Purolator service for transporting money.

As news of the find was flashed across the nation, FBI Director Kelley telephoned from Washington to personally congratulate Held and Stratton.

Magistrate Balog, meanwhile, ordered the 13-page affidavit on which he based issuance of the search warrant suppressed in order to protect the identity of the informant who tipped investigators to the Marrera mother-lode.

"This information will never be made public," said Stratton. "Certainly not in the lifetime of anyone around now."

Throughout the day, the heavily-guarded money, spread out on a large table in the FBI office, was displayed — at a respectful distance — to photographers from the various newspapers, television stations and news agencies, clamoring to take photos of more money than most of them would ever see again, no matter how long they lived.

Shortly after 4 o'clock Friday afternoon it occured to the busy Thompson that the weekend was coming up, and he still had more than two million dollars spread out on the desk in $10 and $20 bills — far more than could possibly be crammed into the small FBI vault, where stolen money is normally kept. At 4:30 p.m. the telephone rang in the office of Rob Wrobel, credit officer and assistant to the president of Amalgamated Trust & Savings Bank, 100 South State Street, a short distance from the federal building.

"Hey, Rob. This is Jim Thompson," said the ever ebullient United State's attorney. "I've... ah... got sort of a problem."

"What's the matter, Big Jim? Somebody you sent to the can getting out?"

"No, it isn't that. It's just that I hadn't realized until right now that it was so late in the afternoon, and it seems I have a considerable sum of money over here. I was . . . ah . . . wondering if maybe we could sort of store it in your nice big vault over the weekend."

"Gee, Jim," answered Wrobel. "Couldn't you just put it

in a shopping bag and take it home with you?"

"Quit kidding, Rob," Thompson laughed nervously. "The fact of the matter is, you might say I'm frantic."

"Okay, okay, Jim. You send the dough over and I'll try to work something out."

"I'm not sending anything over. The FBI will bring it in person."

"Hey, are we talking about all that Purolator money?"

"Now, I didn't say that, Rob. I just said the FBI will be over with lots of money in a few minutes."

Wrobel hung up and got moving. It was almost time for the bank to close. Eugene Heytow, Amalgamated's president, was in Cambridge for the Yale-Harvard football game Saturday, so Wrobel tracked down Larry Bloom, senior vice president. He briefed him on what had transpired, set the wheels in motion to received the money, and went down to the State Street lobby to await its arrival.

Shortly after 5 p.m. a well-dressed man approached the banker and showed him his FBI credentials. "We'll be bringing the material in through the Monroe Street entrance," he said matter-of-factly.

Wrobel hurried over to the side door, from where he could see three cars now parked near the entrance. On a signal from the agent in the lobby, several men wearing dark raincoats jumped out of the first car and began directing traffic away from the area. There'd be hell to pay if this money was stolen a second time.

Other agents quickly got out of the second and third automobiles, opened the trunk of the middle vehicle, and removed five bulky mail sacks. They half carried and half dragged the heavy sacks into the bank. One was so bulky it got stuck in the revolving door.

"That damned money is cursed. It's given us nothing but trouble since this whole burglary business began," grumbled the agent, struggling to free himself and the bag from the door trap. "I'll be glad when we get rid of it."

Wrobel conducted the agents to the bank vault, and the five sacks were placed in a safe within the valut. A key to the safe was handed to Stratton, who remarked, "Thank you, sir. We'll be coming back for it Monday."

"I'll be glad to get rid of it," quipped Wrobel. "What a way to start a weekend."

"Ha! I know somebody who is going to feel a lot worse than you do about this," laughed Stratton. "Maybe a couple of guys, as a matter of fact."

The FBI retrieved the money on Monday morning, as promised, and returned it, under heavy guard, to the federal building. Later that day Harold T. Berggren, assistant vice president of Commercial Union Insurance Company of New York City, presented Thompson with a "hold harmless" agreement, asking that the money be held for the insurance firm, which had quickly reimbursed Purolator for the loss. On instructions from Thompson's office, Stratton deposited the money in a special account at the Northern Trust Company of Chicago, pending disposition of the case. During the next three days, tellers meticulously inventoried and counted the piles of cash, a monumental task that did not end until the afternoon of Wednesday, November 27 — Thanksgiving Eve.

To Stratton's surprise — to everyone's surprise — the bank reported a grand total of only $1,454,140 — more than $700,000 shy of the 2.2 million dollars the government believed it had recovered. Events happened so quickly the night of the discovery, there was no time to count the incredible volume of currency, so Stratton and his aides simply totaled the amounts in crayon noted on the outside of each of the five duffel bags.

"Well," snorted Stratton. "If Johnnie can't read these days, neither can the bad guys add, huh?"

After the correct total was verified, the FBI removed $21,890 to be held and processed as evidence. The initial recovery and the event following were reviewed, and authorities were convinced that no one could possibly have lifted the $700,000 which they thought they had.

"Wait a minute. Try this for size," suggested Stratton. "We aren't dealing with dummies. We know that. It's highly unlikely these birds could have made a $700,000 mistake. My guess is that maybe Marrera's share of the loot was seven hundred grand for setting the thing up. Maybe Ralphie skimmed his hard-earned wages off the top and stashed it elsewhere before dumping the sacks into the hole for safe keeping. What we have left is $1,454,140."

The agents nodded in agreement. They would have to talk to Marrera again. Now that he knew a big chunk of the loot had been recovered from his own grandmother's basement he might open up and get the rest of the story off his chest in hopes of cutting a deal for a lighter jail term.

Of the $4,374,398.96 known to have been taken just over a month before, the FBI had now recovered or accounted for $3,161,355.76. This included the cache dug up in Grandma Marrera's basement; the bundles found in Gushi's home; money turned over to Gushi's lawyer for bond purposes; and the cash Charlie Marzano and Lou DiFonzo were carrying the night of their arrest.

Stratton tallied the money recovered as follows:

From 2045 N. Natchez, Chicago	11-21-74	$1,454,140.00
From Atty. Gerald Werksman	10-29-74	28,680.00
From Atty. Gerald Werksman	10-30-74	7,000.00
From Mary Jane Gushi	10-30-74	6,250.00
From Mary Jane Gushi	10-30-74	18,360.00
From Atty. Gerald Werksman	10-31-74	1,800.00
From Luigi Michael DiFonzo	10-31-74	13,062.80
From Pasquale Charles Marzano	10-31-74	9,960.00
Total Recovered:		$1,539,252.80

Also Located:

Bond money on deposit by Peter James Gushi	10,000.00
Bond money on deposit by James A. Maniatis	10,000.00
Seized by Grand Cayman Police from DiFonzo's safebox	5,000.00
Pending civil suit, four bank Grand Caymans	1,154,200.00
Additional Total Located:	$1,179,200.00

Identified as securities in loot	442,902.96
Grand total accounted for:	$3,161,355.76
Total Loss:	4,374,398.96
Total Unaccounted For:	$1,213,043.20

The total unaccounted for included the approximately $300,000 Gushi said he left in the alley behind his home to be picked up by the midnight terrorists, plus about $25,000 which could be documented as having been spent for plane fare and gracious living in the West Indies.

Meanwhile, the last Purolator burglary suspect to be taken into custody, Tony Marzano, became the first released. At a hearing before Judge Bauer, Marzano's bond was reduced from $225,000 to $100,000, and he was advised he could be freed, pending trial, by posting the required 10 per cent in cash. A short time later Marzano, the unemployed truck driver, posted $10,000 cash, all in $50 and $100 bills, with the federal court clerk's office, and walked from the building accompanied by his attorney, Robert Bailey.

CHAPTER 23
Mystery illness fells star witness.

Thanksgiving Day, 1974, was not a particularly happy day for Ralph Marrera, as he sat within his 10-foot-square cell. It was a dingy place, without windows, but plenty of graffiti scrawled on the fading yellow walls to ponder. Ralph played a game of checkers through the bars with Mark Gardner, his 18-year-old cellmate in the adjoining cubicle. Tiring of that, they watched the pre-Christmas parade on the portable TV set brought to Marrera by his wife, Alberta.

Marrera had been in this cell since 5:15 a.m. October 27, one month and one day following his arrest by the "pizza man" at his in-laws' home. The only visitors permitted had been loyal Alberta, and Ralph's two lawyers, first Nussbaum, and later Mrs. Wolfson.

He had been taken into custody by the FBI within days of the theft, as a manhunt for other suspected members of the gang spread across the nation, throughout the Western world, and finally came to focus on tiny Grand Cayman Island in the picturesque British West Indies.

Marrera miserably failed the lie-detector tests, and that told the FBI their prized prisoner was harboring all the vital information they wanted to know: Who hatched the scheme? Who carried it out? When? How? And, where did the money go? He was ordered held under $400,000 bail and, in a highly unusual action, a federal magistrate declared that he could not return to the streets pending trial until the entire sum was posted in cash, rather than the customary ten per cent established by federal court rules.

Uncle Sam was taking no chances on anyone trying to silence this guy.

"Marrera obviously knows so much there's a real concern that either his confederates may want to bump him off, or some other hoods trying to learn where the loot is may find him and squeeze him too hard," explained Thompson, the state's future governor.

Marrera was known as a guy who liked to impress people, and the feds wanted to keep him under wraps as long as possible, so he wouldn't try to impress the wrong crowd. They planted a story in the press that he was being held at Fort Sheridan, the sprawling military reservation north of Chicago. This was done, authorities explained, to put the Army between Ralph and anybody who might have ideas about putting him in the past tense.

The mob could have blasted their way into Fort Sheridan with tanks and not found Ralphie, however. He was actually being held incommunicado in a maximum security cell of the Winnebago County Jail in Rockford, 100 miles west of Chicago.

In the past month he had been taken out of the jail by federal marshals for FBI questioning and court appearances five times, October 29 and October 30, and again on November 1, 4, and 13. There was little to do, and Marrera slept much of the time. He arrived with $12.21 in his pockets, and he still had $10.01 in the brown envelope at the front desk where the personal belongings of prisoners were kept.

Young Gardner, who would later be convicted and imprisoned for breaking into the home of an elderly Rockford woman, binding her, and robbing her of six dollars, had been Marrera's cell neighbor throughout his incarceration in Rockford.

Fate brought the two together — one accused of a violent crime in which his reward was a paltry six one-dollar bills, and the other charged with involvement in the most sophisticated and lucrative operation of its kind in America.

A troublesome prisoner until Marrera's arrival, Gardner had taken a strong liking to Ralph, and no longer caused problems for his jailers with outbursts of temper. Like Marrera, he had become a "model prisoner." He looked up to Marrera like a big brother, and told his jailers, "Ralph, he's real cool."

Marrera, himself, had shown signs of being disturbed only once, and that was the previous Friday when Jail Officer Paul Shimaitis brought him the news about the money discovery in his grandmother's basement. He had flicked on the television set, but could not find a news show at that early hour, so he borrowed Mark's radio to monitor the hourly newcasts out of Chicago. The news made him extremely nervous and irritable, and more talkative than he'd been since his arrival.

"The FBI is framing me because of my gangster friends," he told Shimiatis and Gardner. "They planted that dough in my grandmother's house, that's what they did. Crap! You know, that whole burglary was some sort of ruse, concocted by the Watergate gang. I had nothing to do with it all. I was only their goddam patsy.

"Hell! You know why they got Joe Woods there at Purolator? His sister works for Nixon! That fuckin' outfit has come up short fourteen times before, and this burglary was just another cover-up. Nixon's Committee (to Reelect the President (CREEP)) got Woods that job there so they could launder their lousy illegal campaign funds."

"That's a good story, Ralph," Shimaitis laughed. "The only trouble is, you're selling it too hard. Nobody's gonna buy it."

Marrera had had a week to cool down now, and to brood about the money being found. A million and a half dollars could have taken him a long way, once he got out of the slammer.

"How about another game of checkers, Ralph?" suggested the admiring Gardner.

"Nah, not right now," answered Marrera. "I just want to lay on the sack and do some thinking."

At noon the traditional Thanksgiving Day meal of turkey

and cranberry sauce was brought in, a special treat for prisoners. But, somehow, it wasn't like home. After dinner, Marrera requested permission to use the telephone.

Jail officer Floyd Bauer conducted him from his cell to the telephone station, and reminded the prisoner, "Don't say anything you don't want us to hear." All calls were routinely monitored, with voices broadcast over a speaker at the guard station. A sign at the telephone advised inmates of this.

Marrera placed a collect call to Alberta, in Berwyn, and told her it had been one hell of a Thanksgiving, but he'd been thinking of her.

"Ralph, Honey. I just don't know what to do, I'm so worried," the woman's voice responded over the phone.

"Just take it easy, Hon. That's all you have to do," consoled Marrera. "And don't worry about what anyone thinks. Remember, I didn't have a damn thing to do with what happened. They're trying to set me up. All you have to do is keep your mouth shut, and don't talk to nobody. Nobody!"

"Well, since this happened, I've been running around a lot, and . . . "

" What the hell do you mean, 'running around?' " Ralph interrupted, harshly. "What kind of running around, huh? Christ, here I am in the shithouse and you're out running around."

"No, Honey. No, Ralph. You got it all wrong. Please listen to me, will you?"

"Okay, I'm listening."

"Ralph, like I say, I've been running around like crazy, trying to get bond money for you, and seeing the lawyers to find out what I'm supposed to do. This whole thing, Ralph, it's got me so confused. And the children miss you . . . "

"Okay, okay, I'm sorry I blew up," answered Ralph. "It's just that I don't like being in this lousy jail. I haven't done anything, and you have to believe that. I miss you and the kids, and I worry about you.

"The main thing, Honey, is to take care of yourself, and the kids. You hear me? Take care of yourself and the kids.

Funny things happen in places like this."

Jail Officer Michael Pollare, who had monitored the call, asked Marrera, after he had been returned to his cell, "What did you mean when you told your old lady that funny things happen in places like this?"

"Oh, nothing," shrugged Marrera. "I'm gonna take a nap."

The next morning, shortly before 11 o'clock, Marrera carefully arranged photographs of Alberta and their two children on his bunk, along with the many encouraging letters he had received from her during the past month.

At 11:05, Shimaitis, the only jailer on duty at the moment, heard Gardner shouting, "Hey! Shim! Ralph's trying to hang himself." The shouting was also heard down in the jail's medical room, where Bauer was assisting Dr. Mayor Larson, the jail physician, and the two rushed to the fourth floor. Along the way they picked up Jail Officer Walter Smith. Shimaitis already had the cell door open when the others arrived, Marrera, his back to the bars, was hanging limply by a sling, fashioned from a strip of blanket, two inches wide and 30 inches long. One end was looped about his neck, and the other tied to a horizontal bar, just above his head. A low, gurgling sound came from his throat.

Bauer grabbed the prisoner's legs, and lifted upward, to release the pressure on the noose, while Smith whipped out a pocket knife and cut the blanket strip. Marrera flopped forward, over Bauer's shoulders, and the prisoner was laid out on his back on the floor.

Dr. Larson quickly revived the stricken man with a resuscitator, and gave him an arm injection of five miligrams of valium, a tranquilizer. Marrera was placed on his bunk, where he appeared in a relaxed state, breathing heavily. He was relieved of his belt and shoe-laces, to forestall another attempt at taking his life.

The jail officers left to make their reports, and advise Head Jailor Joseph Thomas of the incident. Since Marrera was a federal prisoner, Thomas notified FBI Agent Jerry Nolan of the Rockford Field Office. Nolan hustled over to the jailhouse to personally look in on the government's valued property, and that probably is why Marrera is alive

today. As Shimaitis ushered the federal agent into the cell at
11:40 a.m. the two gawked in amazement at what greeted
them. Marrera, wearing only his underwear, was kneeling on
the concrete floor with his head rammed as deep as he could
get into the toilet bowl.

"My God! Is he drowning himself now? Get this door
open," Nolan barked incredulously.

"Get Mayo again," Shimaitis called down the corridor.
"He's done it again." After a few moments the prisoner
gagged, coughed, and belched a mouthful of water, and went
into convulsions. Dr. Larson returned, shook his head in disbelief, and administered a sedative.

"That ought to put him to sleep for awhile while you
gents figure out what to do," Larson said. "I have other
business to attend to. This isn't my only patient, you know."
With that he picked up his bag and left.

Marrera was then carried into Gardner's cell and placed
on the bunk. This cell was visible from the central guard
station, and jailers could easily keep an eye on the prisoner.
The bewildered Gardner was moved to other quarters.

After being placed on Gardner's bunk, Marrera soon went
into convulsions, his whole body trembling and lurching to
the point where Bauer commented, "He's bouncing clean off
the cot." Larson was again called, and he administered 250
miligrams of phenobarbital, another tranquilizer.

In discussing the two incidents with Nolan, the jailers
themselves, were in disagreement over their own observa-
tions.

"I tell you, his feet were completely off the floor when he
was hanging there, " said Shimaitis. "Personally, I think he
was trying to go down the tubes. He was unconscious to
me — wasn't talking, except making those gurgling sounds."

"Well, it seem to me it was poorly executed," argued
Bauer. "Any time he wanted to he could have stepped on
his bunk, which wasn't an inch from his feet, and taken the
pressure off his neck. And his hands were free. He could have
reached behind him and grabbed the bars. It was a lot of put-
on to me. But then, again, you don't know what goes
through a person's mind. He appeared unconscious, and the

doc had to give him that injection after he was down on the floor."

Smith, a former Rockford policeman with 25 years experience in "white cars," as police call ambulance duty, said, "I've seen a lot of suicides, but this one, I don't know. Like when he had his head in the crapper. He appeared unconscious, but if you start losing consciousness, you fall over.

"And another thing. When you start to go, your body muscles relax. You urinate and defecate, and I didn't see anything like that there. There was no soiling, and this kind of struck me as odd."

"Well," added Shimaitis. "When Jerry Nolen and I went into the cell and found him in the toilet bowl, he was completely limp. His body was not tense. It was loose. For a guy who is supposed to be faking it, if that's what you think, I've never seen anything like it. When I pulled him out of the toilet, he started these severe convulsions."

While the guards were debating whether Marrera really meant it, Judge Bauer in Chicago was conducting a hearing on bond reduction for two of the other defendants, DiFonzo and Charlie Marzano. He agreed to reduce DiFonzo's million-dollar bond to $500,000, and to cut Marzano's $500,000 bond in half, to $250,000. He also ordered that they could be released upon posting 10 percent of the bond in cash, and surrendering their passports to the clerk of the Federal District Court.

FBI agents met with U.S. Marshal John Twomey of Chicago, and agreed it would no longer be advisable to keep Marrera in Rockford. Marrera was taken from the Winnebago County Jail on a stretcher, and was returned to Chicago, making the 100-mile trip by private ambulance.

Marrera celebrated his arrival at Cermak by taking a punch at a resident physician the moment the restraints were removed after he was carried from the ambulance. He was quickly subdued by attendants, held flat on a bed, and strapped down. After two suicide attempts in Rockford, authorities were taking no chances. For the remainder of his time in the jail's psychiatric ward, Marrera was kept under heavy guard, sedated, and bound with restraints. Then it happened.

The Windy City was being swept into the Christmas spirit on the evening of Wednesday, December 4, when Marrera, presumably under heavy police guard, quite suddenly, unaccountably and mysteriously lapsed into a deep coma from which he never fully recovered. It lasted four days. His body temperature soared to 106 degrees, and in the language of the west side streets where Ralphie grew up, "his fuckin' brains was fried."

Nathaniel Brown, House of Corrections superintendent, said one other prisoner, James Roundsville, 19, was taken from Cermak to the County Hospital at 6:20 a.m. Thursday, suffering from similar symptoms as Marrera. His condition was not considered serious, however. Brown explained 21 other prisoners in the psychiatric ward, all receiving the same medication as the two stricken men, showed no unusual symptoms. The medication Marrera was taking included a tranquilizer, Thorazine, and another drug, Cogentin, which cushioned the effect of the first.

Ralph was the one man whom the federal government wanted very much to keep alive. And, even as the doctors desperately worked over him, some of the top dons of the city's underworld were cursing and praying that the little West Side dago dandy would soon wake up in Hell. He knew far too much to stay healthy.

Doctors at Cook County Hospital where Marrera was taken, conducted extensive tests of his blood and urine, and found nothing abnormal. Everyone who had anything to do with handling of food for Cermak Hospital patients was questioned, including inmates who took food carts from the nearby County Jail to the hospital, and those who dished food out on trays.

While not discounting the possibility that someone deliberately tried to get Ralph out of the way, Brown suggested that the illness could have been caused by a reaction to the tranquilizers. The unconscious Marrera, meanwhile, was transferred downtown to Northwestern Memorial Hospital, where private physicians fought to save his life.

The next morning Cook County Prosecutor Bernard Carey called a press conference, ostensibly to annouce new indictments against Marrera and the five other suspects in the super theft. But news of the unfortunate Marrera's condition had also leaked out and the Chicago reporters, never noted for their elegance of manner, clamored for details, even though it wasn't part of Carey's program.

"Come on, Bernie. What the hell happened?" they demanded. "Wasn't this guy supposed to be under a 24-hour guard? What went on there? Did he take some pills, or did somebody slip him something — or what?"

As the television cameras whirred and the badgering continued, Carey obliged. In a dramatic voice he observed:

"A serious question exists as to whether he was capable of arranging to obtain drugs to make a third attempt at suicide. It would appear . . . that someone has deliberately tried to take his life."

During Marrera's five-day stay in the hospital he, like other inmates having violent tendencies, was repeatedly injected with a repressant. One theory advanced was that he might have been allergic to the drug. The other theory, based on knowledge of how easy it has always been to smuggle almost anything in or out of the Chicago correctional facility, was that someone — not a doctor — had doctored Ralph's medicine.

In any event, whether it was by accident or design, the $4.3 million secret was now locked in the muddled brain of the $4.30 an hour guard forever.

Jesse James, Cole Younger, and the Dalton Gang never stole as much as the Purolator bandits. Nor did the infamous John Dillinger, or Bonnie and Clyde. Freebooters of the Spanish Main sacked whole cities without matching the value of the Purolator plunder. Sir Francis Drake, Blackbeard, Morgan the Terrible and Captain Kidd captured galleons laden with Aztec gold, but never in one fell swoop equalled the score of one night's work for Ralph Marrera.

Ironically, he never got to spend a penny of it.

CHAPTER 24

Derrick Tricker gets a treat.

W hile some of the country's best doctors were applying their medical talents to save Ralph Marrera's life, someone unknown to authorities stepped forward to give Charlie Marzano and Luigi DiFonzo a new lease on theirs. Somebody quite miraculously came up with $75,000 cash, sufficient to win their release on bond from federal custody.

Where it came from was anybody's guess. They would not be foolish enough to lay out Purolator money, Marzano had no visible means of support, and DiFonzo had recently declared bankruptcy. The best guess was that it was coughed up by the crime syndicate in exchange for a piece of the action.

Only Peter Gushi and James Maniatis remained behind bars, where both were being held for their own protection.

The December Grand Jury of the Circuit Court of Cook County, meanwhile, indicted all six suspects on local charges in the Purolator case. This action was in addition to the federal charges already pending. Maniatis, the least involved, was charged with obstruction of justice, for helping to conceal the stolen money in the Gushi's living room planter.

DiFonzo, Marrera, Gushi, and the two Marzano cousins were charged with burglary — specifically the theft of $1,720,353, which was the Hawthorne Race Course money. The two Marzanos and Marrera were also charged with arson and armed violence — the use of explosive materials — while committing burglary and theft. And all except the reluctant Maniatis were charged with conspiracy to commit theft.

Both U.S. Attorney Jim Thompson and State's Attorney Bernard Carey conveniently agreed that, in their opinions, the Purolator offenses could be separated and prosecuted in both state and federal courts. They also agreed that it would be useless to attempt to prosecute the mysterious Allen Wainer since, if there was a conspiracy, Wainer withdrew from it early in the game to be replaced by DiFonzo.

The first defendant to go before the court was Maniatis. On Thursday, December 19, he stood nervously before Judge Bauer in the United States District Court and pled guilty to charges of bank larceny and conspiracy. In exchange for his saving the government the expense of a trial, the prosecution agreed to dismiss the remaining counts of the indictment against him.

Maniatis' lawyer, Werksman, in arguing for a light sentence, characterized Jimmy the Greek as "a flea market peddler, and a hard working family man," whose only involvement in the theft was in obtaining the van used to haul the money away.

Judge Bauer concurred that Maniatis was only "peripherally involved" in the nation's biggest cash theft. He sentenced the defendant to 18 months in federal prison.

The following day, Friday, Maniatis appeared before Judge John F. Hechinger in Criminal Court, where he pled guilty to the state charge of helping to conceal the stolen money. He was sentenced to one to three years, to run concurrently with the federal term.

Before Maniatis could be sent up, however, there was one more matter pending. It was the sale of those stolen watches to Marty Pollakov, the undercover man, for which he'd been indicted, along with Gushi, in October. On Friday, December 27, two days after Christmas, he went before Judge Philip Romiti in Criminal Court and pled guilty to a charge of possession of stolen property. Romiti sentenced him to another one to three years, to run concurrently with his other jail time.

Jimmy the Greek was sent off to the federal maximum

security prison at downstate Marion, Illinois, to sit out his concurrent federal-state time. From the day he became involved in the multi-million dollar plot the grumbling Maniatis had been nervous. He knew it would never work, and he was right.

The trials of the other five defendants coming up, the state moved to forestall a plea by Marrera's lawyer that he was mentally incompetent, by obtaining a court-ordered psychiatric examination through Chief Judge Joseph A. Power of Criminal Court. Dr. Edward J. Kelleher, chief of the Circuit Court Psychiatric Institute, reported that he did not know what was wrong with Marrera, because doctors at Northwestern Memorial Hospital had advised him the patient was still far too ill to be psychiatrically examined.

His attorney, Mrs. Wolfson suggested that he had suffered brain damage during the four-day coma, from which he had never fully recovered. Dr. Richard Abrams, Marrera's psychiatrist, announced he was working with Mrs. Wolfson to prepare a statement on the patient's condition. Kelleher went before Judge Power on January 9, to ask that the matter be continued "until the time when the patient is fit to be examined." The case was put over to January 30.

For his trial lawyers, DiFonzo, the suave New Englander, selected three of his own region, Boston lawyers Joseph Oteri, Thomas Troy, and Martin Weinberg. Each would have a specific job, once in court. Oteri, with his clipped Bostonian accent and salt-and-pepper beard, would handle the cross-examining of government witnesses. Professorial in appearance, he was known as a smooth operator — always smiling, always friendly — quick, courteous, and to the point. Troy, a former policeman, would question witnesses called in DiFonzo's behalf, if any. Weinberg, junior member of the team, would be called upon to cite cases on legal points raised by the defense, and to monitor the proceedings for technical flaws, should an appeal become necessary.

To the delight of newsmen waiting to cover the trial, Charlie Marzano selected as his champion Julius Lucius Echeles, 60, a flamboyant peacock of a lawyer who had never turned his back on a tough case. An ex-convict himself,

Echeles fought for his clients with bulldog determination because, as his liked to tell a jury, "I know what it's like behind those gray stone walls."

Echeles served ten months in federal prison in 1952 for using influence to obtain jobs for persons in the Chicago Post Office. In 1964 he was convicted by a jury of procuring perjured testimony in a federal narcotics trial, of a man named Broadway Arrington. He was sentenced to five years in prison, but the United States Court of Appeals reversed the conviction. He was retried, and the judge acquitted him after the jury reported it could not reach a verdict.

Echeles' clients in the past included a group of Chicago policemen-turned-burglars, in one of the city's biggest scandals; and Richard Cain, former chief investigator for the Cook County Sheriff, who went rotten and subsequently got his head blown off by a shotgun blast in a pizzaria.

In August, 1968, Echeles was sentenced to death by mob loan shark Sam DeStefano, a psychopathic weirdo whom Echeles had unsuccessfully defended in a perjury case. From his hospital bed DeStefano, who was feigning illness, also ordered the executions of the judge who heard the case, and the assistant state's attorney who prosecuted him. The hired killer later described how he walked into Echeles' office on a Saturday morning to assassinate him, but could not get rid of Julius' secretary long enough to do the job. He then broke with DeStefano, and went into hiding himself, to escape his former employer's wrath. DeStefano, still fighting jail, was cut down by a withering shotgun blast in his garage in April of 1973, and no one was known to have shed a tear.

With Julius Lucius Echeles in Marzano's corner, the trial promised to be no dull affair.

Derrick Tricker, the Holmesian cop from the West Indies, who had expressed an interest in seeing Chicago again, got his wish on Friday, January 24, when the goverment flew him in to testify at a crucial pre-trial hearing for DiFonzo and Charlie Marzano.

Lawyers for the two hoped to avoid going to trial by arguing that DiFonzo and Marzano should not be there in the first place. They contended that the defendants were "improperly detained" on Grand Cayman Island by British authorities on "trumped-up" immigration charges, and were "illegally expelled" from the island. In effect, they claimed they were kidnapped. For that reason, Troy and Echeles argued their clients' arrest by the FBI, when their plane touched down at the Miami airport, was "illegal and unconstitutional."

The lawyers were basing their hopes on a decision handed down in May of 1974 by the U.S. Court of Appeals in New York, in the case of James Toscanino, an Italian-born resident of Uruguay. After being convicted in Brooklyn on federal charges of smuggling narcotics into this country, Toscanino contended he was arrested abroad and forcibly returned to this country, where he was tried illegally. He said U.S.—directed agents in Uruguay kidnapped him and smuggled him into Brazil, where he was tortured, and then shipped to the United States without a hearing.

A three-judge panel in the Second Circuit U.S. Court of Appeals ruled that Toscanino was entitled to a hearing on the charges, and if he could prove them, he had to be freed and returned to Uruguay. The crux of their decision was the allegation that Toscanino had been physically abused by authorities, and the country from which he was "illegally" taken had formally protested against the action to the United States.

At the DiFonzo-Marzano hearing Inspector Tricker, the star witness, related how DiFonzo arrived on Grand Cayman Island two days after the Purolator burglary carrying suitcases "crammed with U.S. dollar bills." He told how DiFonzo, assisted by Bruce Campbell, the island lawyer, deposited $1.5 million in various Grand Cayman banks in the names of fictitious corporations. Making no mention of the FBI being present, he told of arresting the two only ten minutes before they were to board a flight for Costa Rica.

"The following day I told Mr. DiFonzo and Mr. Marzano that I had two plane tickets for Miami, and wanted them to leave the island," he related, amid snickers from Marzano, who appeared to be on the verge of open laughter. "I said I

though it would be a good idea if they went voluntarily."
More guffaws from Marzano. "I couldn't force them. If they
didn't want to go, I didn't know what would happen."
Marzano was almost rolling in the aisle, but Judge Bauer
pointedly ignored the performance.

Then, as Troy began cross-examining Tricker, Echeles
leaped to his feet with a flourish and loudly objected.

"Your honor! It is becoming very difficult for me to
defend my client. I can't understand those other lawyers,
because they have Boston accents, and I can't understand
this, er, policeman, because he has a British accent, and
furthermore...."

That was as far as Echeles got. Judge Bauer, who had seen
him in action before, banged his gavel and admonished,
"Julius, I can't understand you, because you have a West
Side accent."

After completing his testimony the impish Tricker paused
briefly at the defense table, on his way to the rear of the
courtroom, and whispered to the amused Marzano, "Good-
bye, Charlie. I'm going back to the land of the sun, now."
Before returning to his island paradise, however, the British
Sherlock enjoyed a night on the town with his new found
chum, Ray Stratton.

Judge Bauer took the case under advisement, and issued
his ruling on Tuesday, January 28. The defense motion to
dismiss the charges was denied. In no way, Bauer ruled, "did
the United States government illegally or forcibly abduct the
defendants from the British West Indies." The way was now
paved for the federal trial to begin.

On January 28 Dr. Kelleher finally won permission to
examine Marrera in the hospital, and determined that Ralph
was, indeed, mentally incompetent to stand trial. In a written
report to Judge Romiti in Criminal Court, Kelleher stated:

"The above named defendant's examination was completed on Tuesday, January 28, 1975, by the undersigned
psychiatrist. Based on the above examination, it is my
opinion that this defendant is suffering from organic brain
damage. He is, however, not suffering from psychosis. He is
suffering from a neurological state whose symptoms are

severe enough to interfere with his ability to assist defense counsel. He, therefore, classifies as an individual UNFIT TO STAND TRIAL because of his physical (neurological) condition. It is my opinion that he is being properly treated for such condition, and should remain under his present treatment for at least several weeks."

Judge Romiti scheduled a hearing for February, for another status report on Marrera's condition.

Up to this time, no one had really made any money on the Purolator heist, except for a handful of defense lawyers, but at last somebody saw a pot of gold. Herb Rodgers, producer-director and owner of Rodgers Production, Inc., announced on March 18 that the caper would be made into a movie entitled: "THE GREAT CHICAGO ROBBERY."

"I mean, this is a funny, funny story . . . this robbery," he explained at a press briefing in the John Hancock Center. "This story is going to make people forget their problems. It'll, well, make everyone laugh. It's certainly not a tragedy, right? No. It's gay, light, frivolous, musical . . . people love fantasies about money."

He emphasized, of course, that all of the characters would be fictionalized, to which his associate producer, Silver Smith, added, "Yeah. We've made them more fun."

The film would be shot both in Chicago and on Grand Cayman, with George Nowak, a West Indian calypso singer, chanting the title song, "Where Has Me Money Gone?" according to Rodgers.

Joe Woods coolly refused permission to shoot the burglary scene in the actual Purolator vault. "We don't need any more publicity like that," he growled. He failed to share Rodgers' opinion that the affair was nothing more than a "light, frivolous" fantasy. The hilarious movie, to star George Hamilton and former Playboy centerfold model Barbie Benton, was never made.

Any humor in the situation was also lost on the real life characters in the case.

With Maniatis already serving time for his part, Gushi reluctantly made his move. On Friday, April 11, the weekend before the trial was scheduled to begin, the self-styled "master criminal" appeared unannounced before Judge Bauer in the afternoon in a nearly empty courtroom.

Flanked by federal marshals for his own protection, the perspiring Gushi withdrew his earlier plea of innocent and offered a guilty plea to charges of conspiracy to loot and then destroy the Purolator vault with firebombs. He answered with a nervous "Yes, sir," to each of Bauer's questions as to whether he did, in fact, commit the crimes, and was confessing voluntarily.

Gushi's sentencing was deferred to May 9 — a move designed to insure his cooperation with federal prosecutors — and Bauer cleared his desk for the trial to begin on Monday, April 14.

CHAPTER 25
Stratton counts his fingers.

The United States vs. Marrera, et al. Case Number 74 CR 806, opened in the court of Judge Bauer in the Federal Building on Monday morning. Fifty prospective jurors were on hand to have their number whittled down to twelve.

In the corridor outside Bauer's courtroom a last-minute dispute erupted between DiFonzo and Charlie Marzano. The usually placid DiFonzo was having second thoughts about spending the best years of his life behind bars. In view of all that had happened, he suggested it might be wiser to plead guilty and hope for a light sentence.

"Nobody cops a plea," Marzano ordered angrily. "You never know what a jury's gonna do. If we get just the right people on there, we'll be free. We take our chance. Period."

Marzano, vigorously chewing gum, was dressed in a gawdy tan, green, and red suit, white shirt, and tie. He looked more like the friendly maitre d' in a neighborhood Italian restaurant than the man the government hoped to prove masterminded the theft of more than four million dollars.

A newspaper reporter, who overheard the exchange with DiFonzo, sidled up to Marzano in an attempt to engage him in light conversation. "I'm told Gushi regards you as the strongest man in the world," the newsman commented.

"Not the strongest," smiled Marzano, popping his gum. "But the strongest minded."

DiFonzo, wearing his usual tinted glasses, smiled broadly

at the rejoinder, but remained silent. He'd had his share of bad publicity in the past year, between his ill-fated commodities caper and the Purolator heist, and he was doing nothing more to get his name in print any more than necessary. His full head of hair was so perfectly coiffed it appeared to have had the attention of a hairdresser. And his flashy plaid suit caused one spectator to quip, "He looks like the successful owner of a hairdressing salon."

Tony Marzano stayed apart from the other two defendants. He walked into court wearing a full beard, and dressed casually, in a brown v-neck sleeveless sweater, white open-necked shirt, and tan trousers. A woman TV sketch artist purred, "Oh, he's sexy."

Before the selection of the jury began there was the expected eleventh-hour legal maneuvering, and one more surprise in this case that already had come up with more twists than a carnival pretzel.

Tony Marzano, accompanied by his lawyer, Bailey, stepped solemnly before the bench, and withdrew his innocent plea. He said he was indeed guilty of all ten counts of the indictment against him.

Under questioning by Judge Bauer, Marzano told the court he was fully aware that, in pleading guilty, he could be sentenced to 115 years in prison and fined $110,000. He averred, through Bailey, that he had not been threatened, nor had the government promised him anything in return for his plea.

What had happened was quite simple. He, like DiFonzo, had done a lot of soul searching and had seen the handwriting on the wall. Unlike DiFonzo, however, he did not fear his cousin, Charlie, who had ordered, "Nobody cops a plea." Tony was not a stupid person. How was he going to convince the judge and jury he had nothing to do with the biggest heist in history when his fingerprint was found on the money recovered from old lady Marrera's basement?

He had worn surgical gloves during the actual theft, and had taken great pains to make sure no evidence as to his identity was left at the scene. But the goddam rubber gloves felt like a condom on his hands and he had peeled them off while helping to count the loot in the basement of a friend's home, before it was divvied up.

"The G's got me by the fuckin' balls," he told his lawyer. "I don't care what Charlie says. I'm throwin' in the towel. I wanna cop a plea and get out when I'm still young enough to enjoy life."

As the astonished co-defendants looked on, Judge Bauer recited each of the charges in all ten counts of the indictments against Marzano, and asked the swarthily handsome man standing before the bench if he did, in fact, commit them.

"Yes, I did," replied Tony, speaking to the courtroom floor, in an effort to avoid his cousin's eyes.

The judge set sentencing for May 9, and ordered a presentence investigation, asking for a detailed report on William Anthony Marzano's background.

Bailey, a former prosecutor in the Organized Crime Division of the U.S. Attorney's Office, told the court that the government had recommended, in talks with him, that Marzano be sentenced to seven years in prison. "They think seven is right, and we think five is right," he protested.

He also told the court that Tony Marzano, though admitting his own guilt, "will in no way agree to testify if called by either side. We are laying all our cards on the table, and if Mr. Marzano is called by either side he intends to rely on his privileges under the Fifth Amendment." He explained that, although Marzano had pleaded guilty to the federal charges, there were still companion charges pending in the state court. Tony's business in this court was now completed, for the time being.

While the court proceedings were officially entitled "Marrera, et al . . . " the star of the show obviously was not in attendance. Mrs. Wolfson rose to tell Judge Bauer that her client was now at home in Berwyn, where he was being treated as an out-patient from Northwestern Memorial Hospital. She asked that he declare Marrera incompetent to stand trial.

Judge Bauer agreed to sever Marrera from the trial, because of his condition, and set a hearing for April 28 on the competency issue. Of the six original defendants, now only Charlie Marzano and Luigi DiFonzo were left. Before the trial could commence there was a flurry of defense motions, all of which were denied.

Echeles asked for a postponement of the trial on grounds he had contracted asthma over the weekend and was on medication. Echeles objected to what he described as "newspaper people and sketch artists in the well of the courtroom, whose presence magnifies the importance of the case." Judge Bauer agreed to remove the media from the special area that had been set aside for their convenience, and positioned them in the front row of spectator seats.

Next Echeles moved for a separate trial for Charlie Marzano, saying his defense strategy was incompatible with DiFonzo's. In trying the case, he argued, the defense lawyers would be legally fighting one-another as well as the federal prosecutors.

"I did not learn until yesterday what their strategy will be," he protested. "The defense of DiFonzo will be antagonistic and detrimental to my client, Marzano."

The best Echeles could do on this one was to win separate tables, one for him and Marzano in the area the press had been cleared from, and another for DiFonzo and his trio of Boston barristers.

Judge Bauer then permitted a short hearing on a defense motion — which he denied — to suppress photographic evidence in the case. The first witness called for the hearing was FBI Agent Pieroni, who journeyed from Miami to Grand Cayman Island to observe the arrest of the two defendants by Derrick Tricker. Echeles, in questioning Pieroni, concluded by observing:

"Special Agent Pieroni, you bear a remarkable resemblance to Efrem Zimbalist Junior!" There was laughter in the courtroom over the comparison of the handsome real-life FBI agent to the star of a television show, then in reruns, that portrayed G-Men and their triumphs as something more than reality.

"Remarkable restraint," interrupted Judge Bauer, rapping his gavel impatiently.

Echeles also played games with another FBI agent called as a witness, Alfred LaManna, of the Fort Lauderdale office. While questioning LaManna, Echeles said, in mock awe, "So, you are a special agent! What is a special agent of the FBI?"

"We are all special agents, answered LaManna, sheepishly.

"Ah," observed Echeles, triumphantly. "So, then, there is nothing special about special agents."

"Objection sustained," announced Judge Bauer, as the young prosecutors, Michael King,Gordon Nash, and James Breen all rose irritably in defense of Bureau titles for its agents.

Echeles reveled in his fun, but as the session ended for the day, FBI Agent Pieroni cornered him in the corridor for the final word. "Say, it's not Efrem Zimbalist that I remind you of. It's Petrocelli." The reference was to another TV character, this one a very Italian defense lawyer who wins them all.

Tuesday, April 15, was spent laboriously empaneling the jury. To speed things up, Judge Bauer personally took over the questioning of potential jurors. Jury selection was completed at 3:45 p.m., as both sides agreed on nine men and three women, and two alternate jurors.

Judge Bauer admonished the jurors not to read of or listen to broadcast accounts of the case, nor to mingle with anyone connected with the case during the trial. He directed them to use the north bank of elevators when coming to court, while everyone else was ordered to use the south bank.

The jury selected, and court adjourned for the day, Echeles mischieviously pulled a small gold box from his jacket pocket, held it in the palm of his hand, and instructed a group of newsmen huddled around him, "Watch me."

He gave a tiny handle two quick turns, and music began to tinkle from the miniature device. Echeles ebulliently sang along, "If I Were A Rich Man . . . dum, da, da, da . . .

"Now, gentlemen," snapped Echeles, secure in the knowledge that he had captured his audience completely. "I have figured out the logistics of this thing quite precisely."

He explained that there comes a moment in every trial when a good lawyer can both surprise and please a jury, and this was what he would like to do. "I have it worked out so that I can wind this music box, put it back into my pocket and walk all the way to the jury box while it plays this beautiful tune from 'Fiddler on the Roof.' I have it figured out, in fact, so that the music will stop playing at the exact moment I reach the lectern to begin my cross-examination."

He beamed triumphantly. Every good magician knows that, in order for a trick to be successful, he first must prepare his audience.

The next morning, as DiFonzo and Charlie Marzano arrived for the first day of their trial, they were met in the corridor by a jovial Ray Stratton, the agent who broke the case, and to whom they now owed their very presence in the building.

Stratton marched up grinning, and shook hands with each defendant. They returned the gesture, not knowing what else to do, as Stratton remarked, "Yesterday Charlie looked upset. Today you do, Lou." Stratton then mockingly counted each finger of his right had, as if one or two might have disappeared during the handshakes.

The defendants uneasily headed for their respective tables in the courtroom, as the twelve jurors and two alternates filed into the jury box and took their designated seats. The drama was about to begin.

As court was called to order, the opening statement for the government was offered by Breen, a slightly-built man with a carefully trimmed mustache in a conservative gray suit. Talking in a boring monotone, he told the jury the government's case was "akin to building a house — one board, one brick, at a time. Here it will be one witness and one document at a time."

He talked for 35 minutes, without theatrics, outlining the prosecution's case, and advising the jurors they would hear testimony from Martin Pollakov, a government informer, and Peter Gushi, "a man who has been involved in crime for a good portion of his lifetime." He continued:

"The evidence will show that during July, 1974, Charlie Marzano was planning a score, a burglary that would net a tremendous sum of money. He enlisted the aid of Peter

Gushi and asked Gushi to arrange with Al Wainer to launder a large sum of money." However, the plans with Wainer did not work out, Breen explained, and Marzano, through Gushi, "went to DiFonzo, who agreed to wash the cash for Marzano in the Cayman Islands," in return for 15 per cent of it — "knowing it was stolen."

In concluding, he told the jury, "You will see the entire chain of events, from the beginning to the end. We are confident of proving this case beyond a reasonable doubt."

In contrast to the bland-talking-appearing Breen, Julius Lucius Echeles strode to center stage, resplendent in a midnight-blue velvet smoking jacket, green slacks, green shirt, and a green and yellow striped tie.

"In order to depend on Peter Gushi, you should have a full picture of the man," he lectured the jury in his deep, very theatrical, voice. "Our evidence will show that, in addition to crimes of violence, such as murder, he has the type of mind that engages itself in large swindles."

He told the jury he would show how, after Gushi arrived home from Florida, his home and store "were surrounded by concentric circles of law officers from the FBI, the IBI, and the Chicago Police — and yet, a little 10-year-old boy slipped through and handed Gushi a note."

His voice rising dramatically, he mockingly described the threat on Gushi's life if he didn't hand over the $300,000 he had hidden in his home.

"Notwithstanding his reputation as a killer, Gushi trembled in fear, and then did what he was told. The government would have you believe he tossed the suitcase loaded with money over his fence, and watched as a car drove up, and a man got out and picked it up, and then drove away."

Echeles had the jurors on the edges of their swivel seats. He turned smartly toward them, raised his right hand high for effect, and thundered, "Peter Gushi's credibility will be the issue in this case!"

Finished, he turned abruptly and walked quickly to his chair. There were few lawyers in Chicago who knew Gushi as well as the man who had just issued the array of damning statements against him. Thirteen years ago, when Gushi was sentenced to ten years in prison for hi-jacking, and ad-monished by a federal judge for threatening to kill a govern-ment witness, Echeles was his defense attorney.

The next, and last to address the jury was Oteri. He took barely four minutes in his crisp, Boston accent, to explain that he would present a "somewhat complicated defense" that would show why DiFonzo traveled to Grand Cayman Island with Marzano. He suggested DiFonzo was unaware the money was stolen, and his only role in accompanying the Marzanos to the Caribbean was to help them establish an international commodities firm.

The opening statements completed, Judge Bauer glanced toward the prosecution table, "Gentlemen, you may call you first witness."

CHAPTER 26

"Hurry up, I'm watching McMillan & Wife"

As promised, the 32-year-old James Breen set out to build his case brick by brick, and board by board. He had a grand total of 85 government witnesses on tap, each with one scrap of information or piece of evidence to pile on top of the other, until the entire fat package was assembled.

The first brick was laid by Fireman Edwin Nelson, who told of arriving at the Purolator plant in answer to an alarm shortly after 1 a.m. on October 21, only to be barred from entry by Ralph Marrera. The Second Battalion chief told how the guard finally relented and permitted him to take six men inside, with axes, portable extinguishers, and one hose. He described the futile search for the fire until the indicator light was noticed on the alarm board, and told of the seemingly endless wait while Russell Hardt, the Purolator official, was routed from his bed to come down to open the vault.

Hardt, questioned by Prosecutor Gordon Nash, testified that, on the night he was called down to open the vault, it took him three tries, he was so nervous. On the third attempt, he swung the door open and "a billow of black smoke came out. The first thing I saw was currency laying on the floor. Some tankers were open. Firemen entered and brought out six shopping bags filled with gasoline."

On cross examination by Echeles, Hardt acknowledged the combination to the vault was usually changed every six months. The last time it was changed before the burglary, however, was fourteen to sixteen months earlier.

"And why was that?" questioned Echeles, smiling.

"Because I hadn't done my job," replied the embarrassed official.

He was then questioned by Echeles about loose security procedures at Purolator, and the fact emerged that at least nine persons were known to have the combination of the safe! He evoked some snickers from the audience when he testified that it was "a good practice to have Wells Fargo monitor the alarms" at Purolator, because "we felt much more comfortable in having them."

He evoked more chuckles from the courtroom when he finally testified, "Marrera was supposed to be guarding the building, and observing all the police and firemen there."

George Mikell, evidence technician for the Chicago Police Department, told of arriving at the money warehouse at 3:20 a.m., and finding Marrera and one other guard on duty with shotguns. "The smell of gasoline was very strong within the safe. It was my opinion that if I were to take a picture inside that safe, an explosion might occur," he said.

Asked whether he saw anything unusual in the tankers, Mikell replied, "Yes. On top of a Federal Reserve tanker I noticed a white powdery gray substance, approximately six inches long and three inches wide."

FBI Agent Timothy Mahoney, of the Crime Laboratory in Washington, said the substance could have been the device used to trigger the gasoline explosions, possibly dynamite. He told the jury it appeared to have been an "improperly constructed incendiary device."

The fourth day of the trial, Thursday, April 17, found Marzano in a jovial mood, bantering with news reporters before beginning his day in court. "You know, I was really big on sports when I was a kid," he boasted. "Particularly baseball. We had a sandlot team, and I was the catcher. Nobody ever stole on me. Haw-haw!"

The prosecution opened with the testimony of Dennis McConnell, manager of the Purolator Currency Department, who explained how the millions of dollars were handled at the firm daily.

Another witness, Mrs. Betty Burke, an attractive redhead who worked in Purolator's currency department, related a conversation she had with Marrera just a month before the burglary. "I was inside the East Vault, putting some money away, and Ralph asked about the money. I was putting some $10 bills in a bank footlocker when he asked me what I was doing. I told him, and he said, 'Why only $10 bills? Where are the big bills? Where do you keep them?'"

She said Marrera showed a particular interest in the foot locker she was working on, four feet long, three feet wide, and two feet deep. "Is it heavy?" he asked her. Then he proceeded to lift it, and appeared delighted when he got it off the floor.

Further insight into the man, Marrera, was provided by Purolator vault worker Robert Quill, who was present when the East Vault was locked for the weekend on the evening of the October 19 party. He told how Marrera sold Illinois lottery tickets to fellow employees, although he was not licensed by the state to do so.

Quill's testimony, drawn out by Breen, was designed to show how Marrera worked to earn the good will of his fellow employees, possibly as an excuse for contact and conversation, so he could pump them for information.

On Friday the government led off with Kenneth Johnson, another Purolator vault man, who described the movement of money between the main warehouse and a small Purolator facility on Chicago's South Side, at 39th Street and Wabash Avenue. Echeles, through his line of cross-examination, suggested the money may have been stolen before it ever arrived at the warehouse. He then asked Johnson:

"How many Purolator employees were in the vault area on the night of October 19, when the East Vault was sealed?"

"Seventeen or eighteen."

"Any suspicious activity?"

"No."

'Did you see Ralph Marrera."

"Yes."

"Was he suspicious?"

"No."

Johnson was followed on the witness stand by Patrick Sugrue, a Purolator truck driver. Under cross-examination by Echeles he admitted he had told the FBI that Purolator did not always enforce its own rules against unauthorized employees in the vault area.

He recalled that when he drove his truck into the money building on Saturday night, Marrera asked what was in certain bags he had brought in from the Metropolitan Bank & Trust Company. He testified that the conversation took place inside the East Vault, which was supposed to be off limits to guards.

The next witness was the vault coordinator, Philip Layne, who had the combination to the East Vault taped inside his locker door. Questioned by Nash, he told of closing the vault door at 9:26 p.m. October 19, and placing it on alarm. He said Marrera was present when the steel door was shut, having punched in for the day at 12:49 p.m., and out at 9:37 — just eleven minutes after he observed the vault being locked. Layne also testified that Marrera made unauthorized entries into the East Vault on at least two occasions in September and October, and that he had reported this to Hardt.

He recalled that when he arrived at Purolator at 3:45 a.m. on October 21, to help clean up the mess caused by the explosions, he again found Marrera inside the vault, and told him, "You have no business in here."

The final witness of the morning was Mildred Bivens, who came to work at midnight, October 21 only to discover that Angela Hughes had already gone home. She described for the jury the hissing sound she heard just before firemen arrived.

"It was really dull and slow that night, wasn't it?" suggested Echeles.

"So-so," she answered.

After lunch the prosecution called the attractive Angela Hughes. She appeared wearing a smart, well-fitting pants suit, and her Afro hairdo was now closely cropped. She identified herself as a "former" Purolator alarm board operator, who indeed knew Ralph Marrera. "We worked together."

In the months preceeding the burglary, she said she and Marrera worked the evening shift together every third Sunday. Prior to the night of October 20, when she ducked early, she recalled she left her job before quitting time on at least five other occasions, all with Marrera's permission. Cross-examined by Echeles, she said an alarm board operator's responsibility was to monitor alarms from scores of "currency exchanges, stores, and professional offices." She said Marrera agreed to watch the board for her when she ducked out before completing her tour of duty.

Oteri then approached the witness, smiling, and asked politely, "Have you ever been threatened with prosecution unless you cooperated?"

"No, not really," smiled the striking Angela. "They said that if I didn't tell the truth I'd probably lose my job." The understatement of the trial. Angela was fired two days after the theft was discovered.

The second week of the trial started on Monday, April 21, with a motion by one of DiFonzo's three attorneys, Martin Weinberg, that his client be given a separate trial from Marzano. It was, in essence, the same motion Echeles unsuccessfully offered a week earlier.

"A strategic difference has developed between counsel," Weinberg explained. "The great bulk of the government evidence is being directed at Marzano." He said he feared DiFonzo would be "buried" by the evidence against his co-defendant. Judge Bauer, as before, denied the motion.

The government then called Joseph Vick, who testified he quit his part-time Purolator job as a vault guard one week after the theft because "I didn't want any more involvement in incidents like that." Under cross-examination by Echeles, he conceded there were "some irregularities" in security procedure at Purolator. Judge Bauer quickly sustained a government objection to a question by Echeles as to whether he was aware that a sum of money between $300,000 and $400,000 turned up missing at Purolator in 1973. No basis for that particular question was given.

Next into the witness chair was vault guard Robert Woolsey, who was relieved by Marrera on the evening of

October 20. He related how Marrera showed up 40 minutes early, punched him out, and urged him to leave. Asked whether he had the combination to the Purolator vault, Woolsey replied, "No, I did not have it, but — I guess I could have gotten it if I wanted to."

Some rather interesting testimony came from a man named Nick Wassell, who on the night of October 20 was installing a burglar alarm for Purolator in a South Side tavern, the Cozy Corner. The alarm was being rigged directly to the money warehouse, and to make sure it was working properly, Wassell made two telephone calls to the Purolator Building to check the system. Each time he called, Marrera answered the phone, and appeared impatient and on edge.

"He kept interrupting me, saying, 'Are you finished? Are you finished?' He asked me that, maybe four or five times," Wassell recalled. "I asked him why he kept interrupting me, and he said he was in a hurry because he was watching McMillan and Wife on his TV set. I told him the same show was on at the Cozy Corner, too. It was a good one."

In an attempt to show that the bandits apparently conducted several dry runs weeks before the actual theft, the prosecution called David Binning, operations manager for Wells Fargo, who explained the operation of the alarms system between his firm and Purolator.

He said Wells Fargo employees watch lights on their monitor boards from what is referred to as "The Hole," a U-shaped hallway in the Wells Fargo office. From there, they noted that the burglar alarm sounded in the East Vault at Purolator on at least three occasions, September 8, September 29, and October 21 — all nights Marrera was on duty. The Wells Fargo employee, on each occasion, was Ashok Patel, the Indian, in the U.S. on a visa. He registered the September alarms as false.

Binning was asked by Echeles what Patel actually did when the lights flashed in September.

A. "He just shut the light off, and did not call the police."

Q. "Was that unusual?"

A. "Every light received in our office is not reported to the police."

Q. "How does the monitor know?"

A. "By the deflection in the meter's electronic current."

Q. "Did Wells Fargo, in its inspection of the Purolator Vault, find anything to have been tampered with?"

A. "Didn't look like anything had been tampered with."

Patel was then called to the stand to give his version of what happened on the night of October 20. Testifying in a part Indian-part British accent, he nervously admitted that the Purolator burglar alarm had, indeed, activated a light on his monitor board on the night of America's biggest cash theft.

"And, what did you do, Mr. Patel, when you saw the light?"

"I shut the light off. I didn't look at the meter. I did not call Purolator or tell the dispatcher, or make a report."

"Why did you fail to do this?"

"I saw no action in it. These things happen."

Patel also admitted he lied to the FBI on October 22, when he told agents that, at no time, had the Purolator light gone on, on the night of the theft. He corrected his statement on the witness stand, and said the light did go on.

"Why did you tell the FBI agent, when he questioned you, that the light did not go on?" asked Echeles.

"It was a mistake. When the FBI came to me, I had a fear I might lose my job."

Echeles, during his cross examination, likened Patel to the Dutch boy, trying to stop a flood by sticking his finger into many holes in the dike. Patel testified that he had no less than 1,100 lights to watch, all registering individual clients. In a harried tone, he described how his work at times becomes frustrating, saying, "Sometimes more than one light flickers on at the same time."

Breen, continued to set each brick and board in place as he built his case, then called the truck salesman who sold the Ford van to Maniatis for $3,887, cash, on September 27.

He was followed by Edward Doyle, the ex-Marine who worked as an undercover agent for the Illinois Legislative Investigating Commission, who told how he penetrated Gushi's fencing racket, and how he overheard Gushi boast of "a big cash score."

Two IBI agents next took the stand, to tell of their surveillance of Charlie Marzano during the period Doyle was working in the store. The first, James Harte, told of watching Marzano at a suburban motel on September 12. Marzano, he said, was sitting in his auto, monitoring the IBI radio band on a walkie-talkie.

IBI agent Patrick Durkin testified that on September 27 and 28 he followed Marzano, who was driving the green Ford Econoline van. He recalled that Marzano was wearing gloves, apparently so as not to leave fingerprints. Durkin evoked laughter from the courtroom when he described the later surveillance of Gushi's home, on his own time, while taking his wife out for a joyride.

The prosecution was methodically leading up to its big guns, the keystones in the brick-by-brick construction. On Tuesday, April 22, the slight, dour-faced Pollakov shuffled self-consciously up to take the oath to tell the truth, the whole truth, and nothing but the truth, "so help me, God."

He testified for more than two hours, always staring hypnotically at the back of the crowded courtroom, never making eye contact with either prosecution or defense attorneys. Interest in the trial had been building, and there was not an empty seat in Judge Bauer's court as the one-time juice victim who later made his living as a $200-a-week informant for Charlie Cigars told how he infiltrated Gushi's operation.

Though obviously uneasy, his role as an informer now out in the open, and his life on the line, Pollakov testified in a calm manner, his voice never breaking. the two defendants, Marzano and DiFonzo, never took their eyes off the witness during his entire time on the stand.

The witness told of meeting daily with Gushi in a number of places, throughout the month of September. Charlie Marzano was present at some 20 of the sessions. During one of these meetings, according to Pollakov, Al Wainer was also present, and Gushi asked him, "Do you know who we're dealing with?"

"Yes," Wainer replied. "Lou DiFonzo."

Under cross-examination by Echeles, Pollakov admitted receiving a sum of money from Siragusa, between October of 1974 and April of 1975 — the interval between the burglary and beginning of the trial. Echeles persisted in determining exactly how much, and Pollakov finally set the figure at "probably under $10,000."

His ordeal now seemingly over, the undercover man was about to step down after Echeles announced, "I have no more questions." However, DiFonzo's lawyer, Oteri, came forward with one more of his own.

"Mr. Pollakov," he asked politely, an almost friendly smile on his bearded face. "Isn't it true that you have applied in writing for the $40,000 reward offered by the Purolator people for information that would solve this case?"

For the first time, Pollakov took his eyes from the back of the room, and looked around for some sort of unseen help. Then he stared directly at Oteri and answered, "Yes. It's true. I've applied for the reward."

Oteri turned and smiled triumphantly in the direction of the jury box.

The witness seat was then taken by IBI Agent William Biros, who testified that, as a result of information Pollakov turned over to Siragusa, the IBI put Gushi, Charlie Marzano, and several other suspects under a lengthy surveillance. The operation was discontinued, however, about a week before the theft. "We were ordered to terminate the surveillance at that time. The directive came from the superintendent of the IBI (Kerstetter)."

Echeles: "Did you know Ralph Marrera, at that time, was a guard at Purolator?"

Biros: "I didn't know that."

During the IBI surveillance, all six suspects later indicted for the Purolator burglary were observed at one time or another, IBI Agents Roger Shields, Edward Cisowski, and Richard Tetyk testified in turn. The agents were called by the prosecution to provide details of the surveillance, specifically following one or more of the accused men at various times from one location to another.

Tetyk told of observing DiFonzo driving a white-over-blue

Mercedes Benz sedan with Massachusetts license plates. On other occasions, DiFonzo, always dressed elegantly, in the latest style and usually with a vest, was seen cruising from place to place in a leased Lincoln Continental.

Echeles ended his cross-examination of each agent with the same question, but none was able to explain why the surveillance was abruptly cancelled a week before the theft.

CHAPTER 27
The braggart babbles on his buddies.

T he courtroom silence was broken by "The United States calls Peter James Gushi." The government's star witness, whose uncontrolled boasting — more than any other factor — eventually led to the solution of the nation's biggest cash theft, lumbered into the courtroom through a rear door. He was accompanied by three beefy U.S. deputy marshals.

It was 10:25 a.m. Wednesday, April 23, as Gushi, wearing a conservative blue suit and tie, and a white shirt, walked deliberately to the witness stand to be sworn. He jabbed his horn-rimmed eye glasses back on his nose with his left index finger, and spoke in a low tone as he raised his right hand and whispered, "I do."

Nearly 185 spectators were squeezed into every available space in the gallery pews, watching his every move, straining for his every word. Pete Gushi, the well-known loud mouth, was now barely audible.

Lest there be any chance that the witness might possibly be mistaken for a choir boy or a Boy Scout leader, prosecutor Breen beat the wily Echeles to the punch by leading the tall, chunky Gushi, through a series of questions to establish that he had been convicted of felonies on four occasions.

The first time came in 1964, when he pleaded guilty in Chicago to a federal narcotics violation involving the sale of heroin. He was sentenced to two years in prison. In October, 1962, he was convicted of interstate transportation of stolen property, and sentenced to ten years. He was again convicted in April of 1963 of theft from interstate shipment, and given another 10-year sentence, to run concurrent with the earlier one. Remarkably, he was paroled in July of 1965, after serving only two years, following the abortive attempt to take his life while in Leavenworth Penitentiary, in Kansas. The fourth conviction, he revealed, was in the Purolator case, for which he was yet to be sentenced on his guilty plea.

Now Gushi got down to the business of describing events leading up to the Purolator caper. Perspiring heavily as he talked, and frequently wiping his bald head with a neatly folded hankerchief, he told how in mid-July, 1974, he and Charlie Marzano, whom he had known for 25 years, were comparing their debts.

"I told him I was in debt at the time for between $100,000 and $125,000," Gushi related. "Charlie said, 'Guess how much I owe?' I said, I dunno. How much do you owe, Charlie? He said, 'Two-thirty.' I said, 'Two-hundred and thirty thousand?' Charlie said, 'No. Two hundred and thirty dollars!'"

He testified that Marzano then told him he needed someone to launder a large amount of money he was about to come into, and if Gushi could line up someone to do the job, he would be given a $40,000 "commission."

The jury sat spellbound as the 47-year-old Gushi weaved a tale of how he offered to talk to his friend, Al Wainer, in Marzano's behalf. "Al later talked to Charlie, and told him that Grand Cayman Island was now the so-called Swiss bank program of the Western Hemisphere," he said. "How do you get the money onto the island?" he quoted Marzano as asking Wainer. "You just carry it in on your person," Wainer replied.

Wainer's cut was to be ten per cent, Gushi added. But, for some unexplained reason there was a disagreement, and Wainer bowed out. His place was taken by DiFonzo, who offered to take the money to the islands to be "laundered" for a return of fifteen per cent.

Gushi then testified that he and Charlie Marzano had a

conversation with DiFonzo at the Hickory Hills Country Club, in suburban Hickory Hills. "I asked Louie, 'Can you wash money?' He (DiFonzo) asked how much money are we talking about, and Charlie told him maybe $300,000. He said, 'I think I can handle it. I've got a law library which I will research, and get back to you.'"

Gushi said DiFonzo, whom he referred to as Louie, did get back to him and Marzano, and said, "Grand Cayman is okay." Gushi's surly, deep voice trailed off repeatedly as he testified, and he had to be reprimanded by Judge Bauer to speak louder so the jury could hear him. "Sure, Judge," and "Yes, Your Honor," he obeyed.

Gushi continued:

"Louie asked, 'Is this a score?' and Charlie told him, 'Yes, it is.' Louie asked, 'How much money, Charlie?' and Charlie said, 'Maybe $500,000.' Then I asked Charlie, 'Is it a bank?' He said, 'No, I don't fool around with no banks.' I said, 'Charlie, you're good, but are you that good?' He told me, 'I'm getting a little help.'"

On October 19, the Saturday night before the theft, Gushi related he met with DiFonzo and the two Marzano cousins in the kitchen of his home in Oak Lawn, to make final arrangements for disposing of the money. He said Charlie advised him the score might possibly come off the following day.

"If so, I would get a call on Sunday morning, October 20, or Monday morning, October 21, from Marzano, and I was to notify DiFonzo. The code words in the telephone call were gonna be, 'Let's have breakfast.'"

They were still discussing the arrangements, Gushi said, when he noticed it was 7 o'clock, and he excused himself to go into the living room to switch on the television set. His favorite program, "All in the Family," was on. "Charlie and Tony came in to watch it with me, but I don't remember if Louie watched it, or if he stayed in the kitchen." The courtroom erupted with laughter, and Judge Bauer attempted to conceal his amusement. Gushi dabbed his damp pate with a handkerchief.

Last minute conniving for the biggest cash theft in the history of America was delayed for 30 minutes while they watched Archie Bunker trade insults with his son-in-law. This done for another week, the four returned to their chairs around the kitchen table and reviewed their plans one more time.

At about 5:30 a.m. Monday, October 21, Gushi testified the anticipated "Let's have breakfast" phone call came from Charlie, after which he met DiFonzo and the Marzanos at the restaurant parking lot along the Tri-State Tollway. The prosecution attempted to identify the actual burglars by asking Gushi how his three companions on the trip to Ohio were dressed.

"Well, Louie was dressed up, but Charlie and Tony had on leisure clothes. They both look tired, and when we stopped at this diner, in Indiana, Tony laid his head on the table and closed his eyes."

After arriving by chartered jet in Florida, Gushi said he changed his mind about going on to the West Indies, and returned to Chicago "to hide the money" that was stashed in his home.

He then recalled the terrifying phone call, and the sinister voice that told him, "There's going to be blood, Charlie's ass and yours." He was sweating profusely as he told of his unsuccessful attempts to get help from Jimmy the Bomber Catuara, and how he finally packed the several hundred thousand dollars into a suitcase, and dropped it in the alley behind his home.

Asked by prosecutor Breen why he did not follow instructions and personally hand the money over to the men in the car, instead of dropping it and running into the house, Gushi deadpanned, "I did not feel it was in my best interests."

This concluded the government's presentation of Peter James Gushi. Judge Bauer looked toward the two defense tables and asked, "Is there any cross-examination?"

Julius Lucius Echeles was on his feet like a lion tamer. He strode toward the witness stand, darkness in his eyes, as he shouted his first question, "What did you do with the body of the man you killed with an icepick?"

Breen leaped from his chair, objecting heatedly, as Judge Bauer sustained the government's objection, and cautioned

that there was nothing about an icepick murder in this case.
"Did you ever brag that you killed Tony Dichiarinte?"
Gushi: "I never killed any man."
Echeles: "You did not tell Pollakov that you killed
Tony?"
Gushi: "No, sir."
Echeles: "And you, of course, never killed anybody."
Gushi: "That is correct."
Gushi explained that he met Tony Dichiarinte only once,
in 1952, and only for five minutes, adding, "I never seen
him thereafter."
The decomposed body of reputed crime syndicate figure
Anthony (Tony D) Dichiarinte, 54, under federal indictment
for income tax evasion, was found in the trunk of a car in a
west suburban Chicago motel parking lot on June 15, 1974.
He had been dead for about a month. The slaying was
never solved.
Echeles' line of questioning was designed to hint that the
prosecution might have struck a bargain with Gushi — not
to bring him to court for any possible murders in return
for his testimony in the Purolator case. Echeles pressed
on:
"Did you ever threaten to kill a cash register salesman?"
Gushi: "No."
Echeles: "Did you ever show a knife to anyone, saying
that you were going to kill the salesman?"
Gushi: "No, sir."
The witness explained that there had been a cash register
salesman in his Family Bargain Center, and "I told him to
leave. I didn't like his attitude."
Echeles: "Did you ever tell Pollakov you were going to
cut up two guys?"
Gushi: "No, sir."
The witness was obviously irritated. He was saving his
skin by blowing the whistle on his pals, but somebody
else had been talking about him. That goddam Echeles had
good sources, the son-of-a-bitch!
Echeles then led Gushi through questioning about claims
that he was going to beat up Pollakov's children. Smiling

for the first time, Gushi replied, "Aw, I was only joking."

Then, half to the judge, half to Echeles, Gushi explained, "What I meant was I only wanted to wrestle with Pollakov's kids. I even play in a fighting sort of way with my own kids."

Echeles: "You have a fear of going to prison, do you not?"

Gushi: "A dislike."

Echeles: "Did you attempt to commit suicide while in prison once?"

Gushi: "Yes. I couldn't take the prospect of 25 years in prison."

Echeles then asked Gushi if it was true that he once told Pollakov that he was going to "take out (kill) any cop that got in the way" of the big cash score.

"I don't recall. I might have said that. I was joking. I wasn't going along, so if I said that, it didn't matter anyway."

Echeles, in a frustrated tone of voice, finally asked Gushi just exactly what he did in preparation for the score, "since you seem to be blaming everyone else."

Gushi related, that he put up 20 percent of the money to purchase the van, and that he tried, unsuccessfully, to make arrangements for the boat trip to Grand Cayman Island. Also, he had introduced DiFonzo to Marzano.

Echeles, seemingly dissatisfied with the answer, asked incredulously, "Is that all?"

The entire courtroom, Judge Bauer included, rocked with laughter at Gushi's straight-forward reply:

"Well, I musta done somethin', or why else am I sittin' up here?"

Bauer decided to adjourn on that humorous note, and the cross-examination of Gushi was put over until the following morning. Echeles began his questioning Thursday with, "Do you know how many years you face by pleading guilty to all ten charges in the indictment?"

"Yes, I do," replied Gushi. "One hundred and fifteen years."

Echeles continued to press Gushi over various aspects of his earlier testimony, heaping scorn on the witness, dripping sarcasm whenever possible, and displaying incredulity. But Gushi's story remained unchanged.

After four and a half hours of cross-examination, Echeles sat down in a mock display of utter disgust with the witness and turned the floor over to the suave Oteri.

The Boston lawyer asked Gushi whether he and DiFonzo, a year ago, planned to put together a world-wide commodities trading corporation, and Gushi replied, "Yes, that was true." He also admitted DiFonzo briefed him on the "basics" of such a business, along with the "principles of leverage," and the "large tax benefits from a commodities trading business."

Oteri: "Did you consider him a financial genius? A financial wizard?"

Gushi: Yes. I thought he had a lot going for him."

The witness also testified to talks with DiFonzo in which they discussed purchasing seats on the various boards of trade, and conceded that the two had talked of chartering a corporation, for commodities trading, in either Lichtenstein or Costa Rica. DiFonzo's cut for taking the money to Grand Cayman Island, about $50,000 was to have been "seed money for the new trading venture.

Oteri sat down. His strategy, with each witness, had been to work quickly and courteously — to give the jury just a few important points to remember. Nothing more.

Breen asked several quick questions in redirect examination. He got Gushi to insist that he had, indeed, told DiFonzo, "This is going to be a score." This was done to emphasize that DiFonzo did know the money he was going to dispose of was stolen.

Gushi also insisted that he had never been promised anything by the government in return for his testimony. "I was given no idea," he said. "Nothing was said to me about what my sentence might be. After I agreed to testify, an FBI agent just shook my hand and said, "I wish you luck."

Gushi wiped his forehead one more time, then stepped down from the witness stand after nearly six hours of testimony over two days. It had been his worst ordeal since that night in the alley, when those mysterious bastards muscled him out of 300 grand.

CHAPTER 28
Tricker returns, with friends.

Gushi's testimony ended, the government set to the task of topping off its case. Only a few bricks and boards remained to be put into place.

Mrs. Kerry Nixon, the West Indian immigration officer who checked DiFonzo through customs when he landed on Grand Cayman Island, was brought to Chicago to tell her story.

"When I looked into his suitcases, I saw lots of money," she said. Asked if she could identify the individual who brought in the suitcases of currency, she stood in the witness box and pointed to DiFonzo. "That man, there." DiFonzo's lawyers waived cross-examination. Luigi had never denied taking the money to the island.

Another brief witness was Mrs. Nixon's boss, John Bostock, a tall, good-looking, tanned Anglo with a head of thick, black hair. He produced records to show that, in addition to DiFonzo arriving on October 22, the two Marzanos flew in. Bostock came all the way from Grand Cayman to spend less than two minutes on the witness stand. As he walked stiffly from the courtroom, Echeles stage-whispered to news reporters, "They're starting to pad their case!"

Gian Franco Audieri, the maitre d' of Grand Cayman's posh Holiday Inn, appeared next. He told of the conversation in which Charlie Marzano asked his advice about the best banks to do business with on the island. His testimony,

too, was brief — nothing to punch holes into, but the ir-
repressible Echeles saw one of those rare moments to amuse
the jury.

"Do YOU have a numbered bank account on the island?"
he asked.

"No," Audieri replied wistfully.

"If you are a maitre d' long enough, don't worry, you
will."

Echeles, pleased with his own advice, was about to return
to the defense table when he thought of one more point.
"Mr. Audieri. Did you receive a satisfactory tip from Mr.
Marzano in return for your advice?"

Audieri smiled as he recalled the $100 bill. "It was more
than adequate."

It was now 2:28 p.m. Thursday, April 24, and the television sketch-artists' pencils flew across the paper as the next
witness was called: Detective Superintendent Derrick Tricker.

The mustached Britisher stood rigidly before the witness
chair after taking the oath to tell the truth, and had to be
reminded that, in American courts, witnesses were permitted
to testify while seated. Twice during his testimony, Tricker
caught himself referring to Judge Bauer as "M'Lord," as
British judges are addressed.

He described the arrest of DiFonzo and Marzano on Grand
Cayman by himself and his wife, Karen, and of bundling
them off on a non-stop plane to Miami.

"I asked their names, and they refused to say anything
to me," he testified. "Refusing to identify oneself to a
police officer is a crime on our island."

Tricker's testimony was precisely 25 minutes in length.
He had made his second trip to Chicago in four months for
this. As he left the courtroom, wearing his conservative
striped gray business suit, he turned toward the defense
table where DiFonzo sat and, without breaking stride,
winked confidently at the accused, and Defense Attorney
Thomas Troy. Troy acknowledged Tricker's wink with one
of his own. The uneasy DiFonzo flopped both his lids.

Next came the quickest witness of them all, one who
came all the way from Grand Cayman to spend less than a

minute on the stand. It was an assistant inn-keeper from the island Holiday Inn, who produced registration cards to show that Charlie Marzano registered at the hotel under his own name, and DiFonzo signed in as James Morini.

He was followed by George Redmond of Baltimore, operator of the charter boat, Willie Wa II. He told the jury that, on the night of October 20, Gushi telephoned him and asked to arrange a trip from Florida. But he could not accommodate him because his boat was in drydock. Another brief witness was Mike Harris, the handsome pilot who flew DiFonzo from Fort Lauderdale to the island, who testified that during the $1,100 flight he asked DiFonzo what he did for a living, and DiFonzo told him, "I travel around for clients."

Amid yawns from spectators, the government then called the cab driver who picked up the two Marzanos, Gushi, and DiFonzo when they arrived in Miami from Ohio. "They carried with them two heavy suitcases," he testified. "They weighed so much I asked them what they contained, maybe mechanics tools? One guy said, 'Sort of.'"

The government next turned its attention to the discovery of the $1.4 million in grandma Marrera's basement. FBI agent Mike Balgley gave the jury details of how police broke up the newly-poured concrete, and brought the sacks out of the hole in the floor. In giving a description of the surroundings, Balgley noted there was, among other things, a television set in the basement, next to the hole.

Echeles, pouncing on another opportunity to brighten the jury's day, asked, "Was 'All in the Family' playing at the time?"

On Monday, April 28, the start of third and final week of the trial, the government put on its 80th witness, Julius Jones, a FBI fingerprint specialist from Washington. He told of examing DiFonzo's rented Lincoln at the Port Columbus airport, and of finding a walkie-talkie radio in the vehicle. He also testified that he accompanied Tricker on November 15, when lock boxes at the Royal Bank of Canada were opened and found to contain $5,000 in cash. In dusting the boxes, he said he found latent fingerprints of Luigi DiFonzo.

The government called upon Robert J. Hart, director of mutual clerks at Hawthorne Race Course, for the purpose of establishing that the money dug up in Grandma Marrera's basement was indeed part of the Purolator loot.

Hart explained how, after money was tabulated and listed on computer printout sheets following each of the nine daily races, the cash was separated into various denominations, and fastened with different colored paper straps for identification purposes. For example, $10 bills were wrapped in blue straps, $20 bills in yellow. A purple rainbow strap was used to bundle the $50 and $100 bills. Parimutuel clerks then initialed the top bill in each stack with a heavy black lead pencil, indicating the amount of currency in each bundle.

This procedure was followed on the night of October 19, Hart testified, and the money was placed in the metal foot-locker for shipment to Purolator. The footlocker was pad-locked by Charles McCann, Hawthorne's money manager, using his personal lock.

Echeles had a field day with Hart on cross-examination, drawing out the fact that the lock used by McCann cost no more than six dollars, and was the type that bore numbers on the bottom. Anyone looking at the numbers on the lock could buy a key for it at any hardware store.

"Is there some reason why Hawthorne race track buys locks with numbers on the bottom of them?" Echeles asked sarcastically. Without waiting for a reply, he continued, "If the number is on the bottom, a person can go to a store and buy a key for it, is that right?"

Again, not waiting for an answer, Echeles gave the jury a knowing glance, walked over to the defense table, and sat down.

Three Hawthorne mutuel clerks identified their personal markings on several bills shown to them. Some of the bills they were shown came from the cache in Mrs. Marrera's basement, and others were seized with the arrest of Marzano and DiFonzo on Grand Cayman. With that the government rested its case.

The usual defense motions, including one for a directed verdict of innocence, were made. Arguing their case before Judge Bauer was the expert on legal precedent, Martin Weinberg. Weinberg summed up DiFonzo's defense by telling the court that the "score" was never explained to his client by the other defendants. "He did not know that Purolator was to be the score."

Bauer denied all motions forthwith, and directed the defense lawyers to present their case. It was to have been the task of the third Boston lawyer, Troy, to put on witnesses in DiFonzo's behalf. Instead, Troy announced the defense was not calling witnesses for DiFonzo. He returned to his table, turned sideways to face the prosecution table, lifted a paper cup of water in toast to the government lawyers, and smiled, "Here's mud in your eye."

Judge Bauer nodded to Echeles, who took less than an hour to present the defense for Charlie Marzano. His tack was to attempt to remove suspicion from Marzano and cast it in the direction of Purolator employees. The first witness he called was Ronald Tomko, a vault coordinator for the money firm. Tomko conceded that, at the time of the theft, Purolator did not have in operation in the vault room area any closed circuit TV monitors. These widely-heralded protective devices were not activated until after the massive theft.

He also pointed out that, since the theft, a time lock had been installed on the East Vault, and a time lock on the West Vault, that had not been in use, had been reactivated. It was late afternoon, and Echeles said he had several more witnesses to present. Judge Bauer adjourned court until morning.

On Tuesday, April 29, Echeles surprised the prosecution by calling one of the government's main witnesses, Pollakov, to also testify for the defense. Echeles questioned the police informer about statements Gushi had once made to him, about killing Tony Dichiarinte, in an effort to discredit Gushi.

Pollakov testified that it was during a breakfast meeting with Gushi on September 13, that Gushi boasted of having murdered "a man named Tony" by stabbing him with an icepick in the head and chest. He told me that he grabbed Tony in an alley while Tony was emptying the garbage. He said that he killed this Tony because Tony had raped his sister-in-law."

After Pollakov retired, Echeles pulled another surprise from his bag. He called the wife of the government's star witness — Mary Jane Gushi — to the witness stand. She entered the courtroom wearing a forest green pants suit, and her red hair newly coiffed. Throughout her testimony, she referred to her husband as "Pete."

She related how, on the morning of October 21, she accompanied Pete to a parking lot on West 95th Street near the tollway, where Charlie Marzano handed Pete a suitcase containing a large sum of money. Her husband instructed her to take it home and hide it, telling her he would telephone with further instructions. "I took the money home and hid it in the base of a large flower planter," she testified. "I just got scared."

After Gushi's arrest, she said she turned some of the money over to her husband's lawyer, Werksman. "On one occasion when I went to Mr. Werksman's office he was not there, so I put about $10,000 in a brown bag behind a sofa in his waiting room."

The Gushis appeared to be big on leaving large sums of money lying around, Pete in darkened alleys, and Mary Jane in empty offices in brown paper bags. She told of turning other cash in the hoard over to the FBI, along with $5,000 of the Gushis' family funds, which she surrendered in her "confusion."

"The FBI returned the $5,000 after Pete and I both protested that it wasn't part of the other money, but was the proceeds from the Family Bargain Center."

Echeles contended, however, that the return of the $5,000 amounted to a government payoff in exchange for Gushi's unflagging cooperation. The defense attorney also attacked Gushi's amazing story of taking the $300,000 out to the alley behind his home, and then leaping the backyard fence and sprinting to safety when the ominous pickup autos appeared.

Echeles introduced blow-up photographs of Gushi's back fence, showing it to be three feet, six and a half inches, in height, to challenge the claim that Gushi, a very large man, was able to leap the barrier. He showed another photograph of the yard, to attack the claim that Gushi was able to observe the money pick-up from behind a window in his kitchen, because the large weeping willow would have obstructed his view.

In one final surprise before calling it a day, Echeles called on the man credited with solving the Purolator burglary, FBI Agent Ramon Stratton. Stratton had been sitting at the prosecution table during most of the twelve-day trial as its case expert. But he as not called by the government. Now he was hailed by the defense.

What Echeles hoped to accomplish through Stratton was not clear. He spent less than a minute on the witness stand, with the government objecting to all questions asked about the use of the Purolator loot by Gushi and Maniatis, and whether any of the money they put up for bond had been returned to Purolator.

Stratton stepped down, and Echeles announced he had concluded his case. It was 11:40 a.m. The other attorneys for the defense and prosecution told Judge Bauer they had no further witnesses. Court was adjourned until Wednesday morning to give both sides time to prepare closing arguments.

CHAPTER 29
And the verdict is...

Prosecutor Breen dryly summed up the case for the United States as court convened on Wednesday, April 30. He talked in a hypnotic monotone, and some of the spectators dozed in their seats as he droned on about the "overwhelming evidence of conspiracy" to steal $4.3 million from the Purolator vault on the night of October 20. "Charles Marzano was the mastermind, and Lou DiFonzo the financial wizard, was the 'launderer,' assigned to 'wash' the money by exchanging it for cash that could not be traced," he told the jury.

Breen took nearly two excruciating hours to painstakingly review almost all of the government's 85 witnesses and 115 exhibits, including the "crushing piece of evidence" — the $1,454,140 found in Ralph Marrera's grandmother's basement. "The prosecution's case is airtight — as airtight as the Purolator vault that snuffed out the fire intended to conceal the crime," he said.

Citing Echeles bitter attacks on Gushi, he concluded by reminding the jurors that Gushi was not on trial, and it was their job to decide on the guilt or innocence of Marzano and DiFonzo, nothing else. "Gushi was telling the truth. There is no doubt of that." Then, pointing to the two defendants, he proclaimed, "They are guilty!"

Julius Lucius Echeles sprang to his feet barely before Breen had time to retire to the prosecution table, and wasted no time resurrecting his attack on the woe-begone

Gushi. Awakening the dozers with a jolt, he thundered, "The government's case depends 90 or 95 per cent on Gushi's testimony. His middle name should be Judas, instead of James. It's not Peter James Gushi. It's Peter Judas Gushi! The government's so-called key witness is a man with a Machiavellian mind . . . a sharp, shrewd, cunning man who has spent a lifetime in crime."

Echeles, his voice ringing in anger, recalled Gushi's boast of having killed a man with an ice pick, and asked the jury, "Which Gushi are you going to believe? Gushi, the killer? Or Gushi who got on the stand and denied those statements?"

He attacked the government's case as "padded," referring to the almost endless parade of two-minute witnesses, from cab drivers to immigration officers. And he sarcastically described Purolator Security, Inc., as "Purolator Insecurity," and lambasted company officials for firing monitor Angela Hughes "instead of the head of security and the chief of alarms."

"Marzano was guessed into the Purolator case," he roared. "Gushi wanted to get himself off the hook! He constructed his testimony from beginning to end. He was the mastermind, and he structured the case for the FBI. He made a patsy out of Marzano when he lured him to Florida."

Then, again exhibiting his flair for dramatics, Echeles turned to the jury and, mimicking Gushi's voice and mannerism, shouted, "I'll fuck Marzano!"

Echeles did everything but dance a jig before the jurors in his final statement. He recited a poem, and regaled them with a song — one he said he sang as a boy at summer camp. It was the story of a bunch of little sausages. "And, if you believe Gushi's story about the $300,000 payoff to the men in the alley, you will be dancing like little sausages," he said. "Gushi is an infamous scoundrel, a liar, weird, Machiavellian, shrewd and jungle-like. Rat-like. And a courtroom swindler!"

Then, hanging his head in the manner that Gushi did during much of his testimony against his former pals, Echeles spat, "Poor, blushing, gushing Gushi!"

Oteri taking the floor in DiFonzo's behalf, came on like

a refreshing breeze after Echeles' bitter wordstorm. His remarks were brief, almost friendly.

"Mr. DiFonzo had nothing to hide," he began. "He had conducted himself as a legitimate businessman in his dealings with Marzano and the others. He had, indeed, taken a large sum of money to Grand Cayman Island. The place is a tax shelter, and Lou DiFonzo, a smart businessman, was taking it there to invest. He had no idea it was stolen. Lou was cast in the role of a fool, and was taken for a ride by a slicker (Gushi)."

As in all trials, the government had the final word. Gordon Nash wound up the presentation with a brief defense of the prosecution's key witness, telling the jury, "Nobody said the people involved in this case would be choir boys." He came down hard on the use of aliases and code words by the accused, such as the "Let's have breakfast" signal that the job had been pulled off. Nash also ridiculed the notion that anyone carrying more than a million dollars in his suitcases to Grand Cayman Island was going there on a legitimate business venture.

The final arguments ended, Judge Bauer instructed the jury on law, and advised that the testimony of convicted felons and informants must be weighed "with greater care" than that of other witnesses. He also explained that there was nothing legally wrong with the use of aliases, unless the jury concluded that they were used for purposes of committing a fraud. The instructions were completed at 5:45 p.m., and the two alternate jurors were excused. The twelve remaining panel members went to dinner, and returned to begin their deliberations.

After the jury of nine men and three women left the courtroom, Judge Bauer, the three prosecutors, the four defense lawyers, and several newspaper reporters retired to Binyon's Restaurant for dinner and cocktails around one long table.

The pressure was over, and the men who were at each other's throats only hours before tried to relax, and enjoy one another's professional fellowship, laughing and joking self-consciously as they nervously awaited the jury's decision.

Back in the Dirksen Building the jurors, after three hours of deliberation, decided to retire for the night to a nearby hotel, to resume their discussions in the morning.

The verdict came in at fifteen minutes after eleven on the morning of Thursday, May 1. After nearly seven hours of debate the jurors filed in, and their 46-year-old foreman, James DeJonge, a field service engineer for a foundry equipment firm, handed the verdicts to Judge Bauer. He opened the first envelope and read aloud.

To the charges of conspiracy, bank burglary and larceny, and transporting stolen money across state lines, Pasquale Charles Marzano was found guilty. To charges of planting firebombs in the Purolator vault to cover the theft, the jury found him innocent.

It was an incredible decision. The jurors, in their wisdom, declared that Charlie Marzano had nothing to do with setting off the firebombs in the vault, but went in and took the money.

Marzano, who elected to take a draw with the jury, but didn't testify in his own behalf, blinked his eyes, then shook his head disconsolately as the verdict of guilty on eight of the ten counts was read. He stared straight ahead as Judge Bauer opened the envelope containing the fate of his co-defendant.

Luigi Michael DiFonzo, his face white with fear, gripped the arms of his chair and prepared for the worst as Judge Bauer read the verdict. It was more incredible than the Marzano decision. The wheeler-dealer commodities speculator was found one hundred per cent innocent of conspiring to commit the greatest cash theft in the history of America, and to transport the stolen money across state lines.

When DiFonzo heard the magic words he sighed audibly and slumped back in the plush leather chair at the defense table. His brown haired wife, Diane, burst into tears.

Members of the news media looked at one-another in amazement and there were amused giggles in the courtroom. The jury heard all of the same evidence against the two defendants. Marzano and DiFonzo were arrested together in the West Indies, they were caught disposing of the loot, yet after hearing the whole case laid out for them the jurors found one of them guilty and set the other free.

The late Clem Lane, famed city editor of the old *Chicago Daily News*, a quarter century ago, liked to say, "Chicago is a 'not guilty' town." He would have enjoyed the verdict, as would the late George Wright, old time Criminal Courts reporter for the *Tribune*, who always warned rookie journalists, "Never trust a jury or a precinct captain,"

The Purolator case, right down to its final moment, had been a series of bizarre surprises.

As reporters ran for their phones, Judge Bauer ordered DiFonzo discharged. The ex-defendant lost no time departing from the courtroom, followed by his three lawyers and his sobbing wife. Then, over the government's objections, the judge ruled that Marzano could remain free on $250,000 bond, pending the usual post trial motions. Sentencing was set for May 26. Marzano quickly left the building, without comment. The loquacious Echeles, always a hard loser, grimly told newmen, "Obviously, the jury compromised."

Outside the court a beaming Oteri and DiFonzo stopped to hold an impormptu press conference. "I am very grateful," DiFonzo announced. "I want to thank the government, and the prosecutors, and the FBI, for their fairness. I believe in my heart in the concept of due process of law. I feel in my heart that Mr. Marzano will also be found not guilty, on appeal." Then it was Oteri's turn. "You know, this is always the hardest moment in a lawyer's life — waiting for the verdict to be read. You start to wonder if you've made any mistakes. You wonder if you're going to send a guy to jail . . .

"The jury's verdict showed that Lou had no knowledge that he was involved in a criminal venture, but I can tell you this: He'll be much more careful in his business dealings in the future."

The jury foreman was talking to the press, too. "The government just did not prove a case against DiFonzo," explained DeJonge. "The evidence was nothing definite, just inferences. And you can't go on that. I, for one, feel that justice was done. I don't think anybody sitting on any jury wishes to hang a man."

And in the press room, Samuel K. Skinner, first assistant United States Attorney, read a statement on behalf of Thompson: "This office, and particularly Jim Breen, Gordon Nash, and Mike King, can be pleased with the over-all results of the Purolator case. Four of five individuals available for trial were convicted, and a substantial portion of the monies was recovered. If we had these same results in all our cases, we'd soon be out of a job."

Outside the Federal Building, DiFonzo was still chalk white. The blood that drained from his face as he heard Marzano pronounced guilty, and was awaiting his own fate, was slow in returning. He drew deep breaths as his lawyers pushed him ahead, through the crowds, across Jackson Boulevard and down Plymouth Court. He walked with his head down, hands jammed deep into his pockets, as though he still couldn't get used to winning one at last.

Suddenly it hit him. Luigi DiFonzo jumped into the air like a high school basketball player who had just broke a tie game. "Yaaa-Hooooooo!" He slapped his lawyers on their backs, hugged the three of them, and shouted his hallelujas all the way to Van Buren Street.

"We're going to get drunk as skunks tonight," laughed Oteri as the victorious group headed east toward State Street, and hailed a Yellow Cab.

As the four men were about to pile into the taxi, a red, white and blue truck lumbered slowly around the corner. They stood transfixed — Oteri, Weinberg, Troy and Luigi DiFonzo — as they made out the lettering on the side of the ponderous vehicle: PUROLATOR SECURITY, INC. Suddenly, DiFonzo doubled over, convulsed with laughter. He looked up, roared with glee, held out his right hand, and gave the Purolator truck the royal finger!

Stella Novy did not sleep well that night. While the bankrupt DiFonzo and his expensive Boston lawyers were out getting "drunk as skunks," she tossed fitfully in bed in her suburban home, as she would for countless nights to come. Mrs. Novy, 58, a housewife and the mother of four, was not sure she had done the right thing. She was on the jury that acquitted the silk-suited financial wheeler-dealer, and now the entire trial kept running through her mind like a Grade B movie. The jury took four ballots before reaching its verdict on DiFonzo. On the first three, the vote was eleven to one, for acquittal, with Mrs. Novy being the lone holdout for guilty. On the fourth ballot she gave in. She went along with the rest, and now she was having conscience pangs. On Friday morning, the day after the trial ended, she telephoned *The Chicago Tribune* and told a reporter:

"He's guilty as sin, but the pressure on me was terrible. I was the only one who said 'guilty,' and then right away I started to get pressure from the other jurors.

"They all started saying that the government's chief witness was a liar, and that the government never proved that DiFonzo knew the money was stolen. I agreed that it was never proven that DiFonzo conspired to commit the robbery, but I believed that he was smart enough to know that the money was stolen money . . .

"I should have insisted that what I felt was right, and stood my ground. I guess I was tired. I didn't want to be stubborn. And I had a bad toothache. Anyway, I buckled, and I'm sorry.

"I'm calling to help get the whole thing off my mind. I'm confused, and angry, and I can't sleep. It's ridiculous, this thing. The trial keeps going on in my mind. There was another lady on the jury, and when I asked her why she didn't see it my way, all the evidence, she said she was 'against the whole entire establishment.' The government, too. If I ever was charged with something, I wouldn't want a jury like the one I was on to decide my fate. Anyone in their right mind could see he was guilty."

But the bushy-haired DiFonzo was home free of the federal Purolator rap. The government does not have the right of appeal.

Federal investigators announced, however, they would resume their securities fraud investigation of DiFonzo's ill-fated silver futures trading operation in Chicago. He was suspected of having ducked out of town with as much as two million dollars from his bankrupt investment firms, but the government held off on its probe so as not to interfere with the Purolator prosecution.

While the conscience stricken juror was pouring out her heart to *The Tribune*, DiFonzo, walking with the aid of a silver-grip cane, hobbled into Federal Court to arrange for the return of the $25,000 he miraculously posted to meet the required ten per cent of his $250,000 bond, now that he was a free man.

"Hey, what happened, Lou? Fall off a bar stool?" asked a news reporter.

DiFonzo chortled and started to open his mouth but Oteri moved in protectively. "He sprained his ankle yesterday afternoon," the Boston lawyer explained. "Playing touch football with Marzano's kids."

CHAPTER 30
The handing out of just desserts.

There was nobody left but Ralph Marrera. It was Friday, May 9, and he was scheduled to appear before Judge Bauer for a competency hearing. "I want to determine if Mr. Marrera is capable of standing trial, or not," said the judge. Newsmen arriving on the Federal beat early that morning were startled to find the lone defendant already there, in the still darkened courtroom.

It was a pathetic figure they saw, slumped awkwardly in a wheelchair, his stubbly chin resting on his chest as he gazed unflinchingly at the floor. His wife, Alberta, was the only other person in the room. She clenched Ralph's hand in her lap with one hand, and brushed his face and hair with a handkerchief held in the other.

Neither said a word as reporters entered the room, and one of them flicked on the light switch. As the fluorescent glow sputtered on, newsmen were caught by the contrasting appearance of the two silent figures. The once dapper Marrera, slumped motionless in the chair, had a day's growth of whiskers on his puffy face, and his hair was tousled as though it had become a stranger to the comb. He wore a rumpled dark gray suit over a thick woolen sweater. His eyelids drooped, as if to shut him out from the scene.

Alberta wore a large, red bandana, tied around her forehead, with a wide bow hanging down to her right shoulder. She had on a bright red and blue ski jacket, and silver-studded blue jeans. Her toe nails and finger nails were painted a glistening, gaudy blue.

Red-haired Jo-Anne Wolfson joined them, and as Judge Bauer entered the room, she helped Alberta push the wheelchair to the bench. Marrera's head flopped lazily to rest on his left shoulder as he appeared oblivious of his surroundings. Judge Bauer advised Prosecutors Breen and Nash that he had received a letter from Marrera's psychiatrist, Dr. Richard Abrams, who told the court Ralph was suffering from organic brain damage, had difficulty communicating and concentrating, was incapable of cooperating with his counsel, and, in his opinion, "is not fit to stand trial."

The government lawyers asked for time to review the psychiatrist's findings, and Judge Bauer gave them until May 30, to decide whether they wanted to hold a competency hearing. Before adjourning the session, Judge Bauer leaned forward and asked the catatonic Marrera — the nice guy who used to be "fun to be with" — two questions:

"Who's your doctor?"

"Dr. Abrams," the wheelchair figure mumbled in a barely audible tone.

"How often do you see him?"

"Whenever he comes."

Forty-nine of the fifty states celebrated Memorial Day on Monday, May 26, in 1975, but the legislators of Illinois stubbornly held out for the traditional May 30, so they could take two holidays in one week. Confusion reigned, with all federal courts and offices scheduled to be closed on the 26th, and state and county offices announcing they would be closed on the 30th.

Possibly with this in mind, Judge Bauer moved the Marrera hearing up one day, to Thursday, May 29. The defendant was not present, but Breen reported that it was Dr. Abram's opinion that more testing of Ralph "would be beneficial," although he was unable to determine, at that point, whether the organic brain damage will subside."

Judge Bauer granted a delay of four months, scheduling the next hearing for the end of September.

The Marrera matter temporarily disposed of, Judge Bauer

turned to the convicted mastermind of the Purolator job, Pasquale Charles Marzano, who now stood before him for sentencing.

Prosecutor Breen dryly urged "a substantial sentence" for Marzano, whom he described as a man of "extreme cunning and resourcefulness." Echeles dramatically pleaded for lenience, and asked Judge Bauer to consider the case merely as one of theft! "It's only a theft of money," he reasoned. "True, a lot of it, but still only a theft."

Marzano stood before the bench, his broad shoulders thrust back and his hands clasped before him, waiting for his medicine. "This is the time to say something, if you want to," Judge Bauer told the defendant. But Marzano stood mute, as he had from the start.

In passing sentence, the jurist described the massive theft as "mind boggling," and pointedly observed that more than one million dolllars taken in the burglary was still missing. "This is not a type of case for leniency."

The sentence: Five years in prison on the conspiracy conviction, ten years on the series of theft counts, and ten years for transporting stolen money out of the country. The first two sentences to be served concurrently, and the latter consecutively. Total: Twenty years in the federal penitentiary.

Marzano was also ordered to pay the cost of his own prosecution. Over the objections of the government, Judge Bauer permitted him to remain free on his $250,000 bond, pending an appeal, but ordered him to report in person to the federal marshal once every week.

Monday, June 2, dawned cool and damp, and it would stay that way through the day. This was the day of reckoning for Marzano's chief accuser, Peter Gushi, the self-styled "master criminal" with the admitted, fatalistic fear of the big house. It was also the day that Tony Marzano, who pleaded guilty to the biggest cash burglary in America's history, but refused to cooperate with the government, would learn his fate.

Gushi greeted the day nervously from his protective custody somewhere in the city. There was an outside chance, he figured, that the judge might give him probation, in appreciation for the help he gave the prosecution, and he could go somewhere far away and start life anew. He and Marzano arrived in court separately, but at the same time. Gushi was wearing the same dark blue suit he wore on the witness stand. Tony was dressed casually in blue jeans, a white shirt, and a red sleeveless sweater. At 10 a.m. Judge Bauer entered his Federal courtroom for the last time. He had been elevated to the United States Court of Appeals, and his personal effects had already been moved to his new office.

Tony Marzano was called to the bench first. He stood erect, his hands clasped behind his back, as Robert Bailey, his lawyer, told Judge Bauer Marzano had had no previous convictions except for being placed under one month court supervision in 1966 after a disorderly conduct arrest. He added that Tony and his former wife "are now back together, attempting a reconciliation," and asked the court to show mercy in handing down the sentence. "Make it as short as possible, Your Honor."

Prosecutor Nash reminded the court of the "tremendous amount of money involved," and urged that this be weighed in passing sentence. As his cousin, Charlie did the previous Friday when he got his twenty years, Tony shook off a chance to speak in his own behalf. He had no interest in prolonging the ordeal, nor of even talking about it. Judge Bauer flipped through the federal pre-sentence report. He noted that Marzano at one time "tried to avoid contact with members of the criminal element," and commented: "It's a pity he failed, and became involved in one of the most daring, outstanding and carefully-planned crimes that has ever come to my attention."

The sentence: Seven years. Judge Bauer gave him seven years for the six counts of theft, five years for conspiracy, and five years for taking some of the money out of the country, all to be served concurrently. He granted a stay of execution of the sentence to July 2, so to permit Marzano time to wind up his personal affairs.

Now it was Gushi's turn. He approached the bench nervously, bald head bowed, and rubbing his chin apprehensively. Security was tight. Three deputy marshals slipped forward almost from nowhere, and surrounded the turn-coat hoodlum as he stood stoop shouldered before the judge.

Gushi's lawyer, Werksman, called the defendant's participation in the heist "limited," and followed with such phrases as "good family man . . . no trouble with the law since 1961." He urged leniency, pointing out that, in testifying for the prosecution, "Gushi has crossed a bridge and started down a road from where there is no return. He has become a pariah in certain parts of the community." Prosecutor Breen joined in recommending leniency, saying Gushi "testified with complete candor and honesty." But he stopped short of suggesting a specific sentence. Gushi, like the Marzano cousins, had nothing to say in his own behalf. He said it all on the witness stand, and hoped to God the judge remembered the agony he sweated through.

Judge Bauer was not inclined to be lenient with this man, however. "It is surprising and an accident that someone did not burn, or get killed in the fire," he said. The sentence: "Four years. And, as with Marzano, Gushi was given until July 2, to wind up his affairs. Judge Bauer left his familiar courtroom for the last time, without looking back.

The book on the biggest cash heist in America's history was almost closed. Of the six men originally arrested for the massive theft:

James "Jimmy the Greek," was already doing his 18 months deep inside the maximum security penitentiary at Marion, Illinois.

Peter James Gushi, on July 2, was flown under heavy guard to an undisclosed prison in the West. There he was segregated from other prisoners for his own protection, and passed the time writing his memoirs. His wife, Mary Jane, was given a new identity and relocated by the government to a mobile home park not far from her husband's prison. While in custody Gushi was given three lie detector tests regarding his story of tossing $300,000 over his fence in the middle of the night. For the record the government said he passed all three with flying colors.

William Anthony "Tony" Marzano received an extra week to wind up his personal affairs, and on July 9 reported to the Federal penitentiary at Terre Haute, Indiana, to begin his seven-year term.

Pasquale Charles Marzano remained free on bond, pending appeal, and the government billed him his portion of the trial costs. While pressing his battle to avoid prison the convicted ringleader of the Purolator vault gang devoted two days a week on the sandlots of his native Cicero coaching Little League baseball, explaining, "I teach the kids how to swing a bat and slide into base without getting hurt."

The 7th Circuit United States Court of Appeals twice refused to overturn Marzano's conviction and finally, in July of 1976, the swarthy felon struck out for the last time. An order for his arrest was issued, and on Wednesday, July 21, he was brought before Chief Judge James B. Parsons. In the only time he had spoken in court, Marzano asked to remain free until the end of the baseball season, so he could "stay with my team into the playoffs."

The judge said no. "This is D-Day, Mr. Marzano. You are going to jail."

Charlie had remained free for one year and nine months, from the date of the massive theft. He shrugged his broad shoulders, half waved a so-long to his raven-haired wife, Deanna, standing in the rear of the courtroom, and was led away to the Metropolitan Correction Center. From there he was transported to the Federal prison at Leavenworth, Kansas.

Luigi Michael "Lou" DiFonzo, who was acquitted of the federal charges, played a tit-for-tat game with Uncle Sam, and billed the federal government for the cost of his defense. Judge Bauer turned him down flat, however, and he returned to his home in the East.

With the trial out of the way, the insurance company that made good the Purolator loss moved to recover the portion of the loot stilled banked in the Bahamas. Chicago attorney Richard Sikes, a former federal prosecutor, who sat through the trial as a representative for Commercial Union Assurance Company, took a plane to Grand Cayman Island to begin negotiations with the four banks where $1,154,200 was known to have been deposited by DiFonzo and Charlie Marzano. It was a matter now between the banks and the insurer. If DiFonzo wanted to get any of it back, he would have to prove in the courts that it was his money in the first place. He found it more profitable to cooperate with the authorities, however.

Testimony during his trial indicated his "commission" for "laundering" the $1.1 million of Purolator cash in phony accounts on Grand Cayman was to have been $50,000. The crafty DiFonzo learned he could double that amount — this time legally. By cooperating and assisting the insurance company in getting the money back, and avoiding the long and costly procedure of tracking it down through secret accounts, DiFonzo stood to collect a $100,000 "finders fee." Outrageous, perhaps, but cheap at half the price to the insurer.

A secret out-of-court agreement between the banks in George Town, the insurance company, and DiFonzo, called for DiFonzo to simply prove he was the "James Morini" who deposited $1,153,549 in the names of the four dummy corporations. He could then withdraw the money, under the watchful eyes of the insurance representative, and turn it over to the insurance company, which would give him his cut off the top.

After weeks of quiet negotiations, involving lawyers from Chicago, New York, George Town, and Jamaica, the agreement was reached during the Christmas holidays in 1976, in Miami's International Airport Hotel. Those present included Sikes, the Chicago lawyer; DiFonzo; James MacDonald, representing Commercial Union, along with Sikes; Anton Duckworth, a lawyer for the Grand Cayman banks; and O.L. Panton, a lawyer from Jamaica. The group remained closeted from noon until early evening on Sunday, December 28, sending out for sandwiches while they haggled. By mutual agreement, the results of their discussions were not made public. DiFonzo, however, was seen going through the hotel lobby with a broad smile on his face.

A news reporter who recognized him said, "Hey, Lou.

What's this I hear about Freddie Prinze, the comedian, going to play Lou DiFonzo in the movie about the big heist?"

"Ahhh," scoffed DiFonzo, with a wave of his hand. "Who's Freddie Prinze? I oughta play myself, you know? But they probably couldn't afford my fee. I gotta get paid big money for big deals...."

CHAPTER 31
Where are they now?

Like the legendary curse of the mummy's tomb, ill fortune has befallen all who had a hand in the great Purolator heist, and the same could be said of many of its fringe characters. Only the lawmen who solved the puzzle seem to have escaped the scythe of fate.

Ramon "Ray" Stratton, the extraordinary special agent in charge of the case, is now retired from the Federal Bureau of Investigation, and, with his wife Ruby, is at peace with the world, back in his native Oregon. There he is a scoutmaster again, of not one but two Boy Scout troops. His photographic mind and uncanny memory still hold more information than many FBI files, and the feds occasionally reach out to him for advice whenever a particularly tough case requires a master's touch.

Stratton's sidekick in Purolator, Michael Balgley, later headed a joint FBI — Drug Enforcement Administration task force on Crime Syndicate narcotics rackets, before moving on to Washington D.C. for a job in bureau headquarters as as supervisor in its Office of Planning and Evaluation.

Martin Pollakov, the undercover stool who blew the whistle on the Purolator gang, collected the $40,000 reward posted by the New York City insurance company, but it is unlikely he enjoyed spending it. Pollakov was given a new identity and moved out of town to spend the rest of his days looking over his shoulder and wondering whether a face from the past will recognize him.

Larry Buchman, the Chicago television reporter who gave police the tip that led to the Bahamas, and recovery of part of the loot, was killed on September 23, 1977, in a plane crash at Amman, Jordan, where he was on assignment.

Derrick Tricker, the dashing British sleuth with a propensity for scotch unmatched in the Western World, never made it to his hoped for retirement home in Miami. At last word he had accepted a lesser police post in far-flung Oman on the southeastern tip of the Arabian Peninsula.

The two top men at Purolator both found themselves in new jobs within a year after the embarrassing theft. Joseph I. Woods, the vice president at Purolator at the time, packed his Nixonian suits and resigned, taking a job as chief investigator for a private detective agency. Russell Hardt, the Purolator manager who admitted "I didn't do my job" in adhering to his own security regulations, quit to take an executive job with a rival armored truck corporation.

The first of the Purolator yeggs to throw in the towel, James "Jimmy the Greek" Maniatis, did his time at Marion and faded into a life of blissful obscurity, quietly prowling the flew markets, and collecting Social Security.

Peter James Gushi, "the Machiavellian Judas," fretted through his prison term in federal protective custody in San Diego. He then began a new life, in a new town, with a new name and surgically altered nose, still smarting over the three-hundred grand he tossed to the midnight extortionists. He missed his own Godfather's funeral, but so did a lot of people who knew "Jimmy the Bomber" Catuara.

The glib-talking Luigi DiFonzo, who beat the Purolator rap, was nailed by the federal government on another. DiFonzo, who returned to Boston, was indicted by a federal grand jury in 1978 on charges of submitting false statements to the Securities and Exchange Commission in connection with his former Chicago commodities business.

With the tough-talking Charlie Marzano no longer around to advise him that "nobody cops a plea," DiFonzo pleaded guilty to two charges of providing the SEC with false documents concerning silver and platinum futures. On Tuesday, January 30, 1979, Federal Judge Stanley J. Roszkowski in

Chicago sentenced him to six months in jail.

William Anthony "Tony" Marzano started his prison life in the federal penitentiary at Terre Haute, Indiana, and ended it in minimum security quarters on Elgin Air Force Base, Florida. His original seven-year sentence was reduced in the interim to five years. One of his cellmates along the way was Watergate figure E. Howard Hunt, who encouraged Marzano to write a book. And when he got out, that's what he did. He hired two women ghost writers and put together his own version of the grand theft.

Tony's book contained no surprises, but did fill in a few of the blank spots. For one, he disclosed that he and Charlie were armed when they pulled the heist. The carrying of pistols made Tony nervous, however, and one of the reasons he left the sunshine of Grand Cayman and hied it back home was those damn guns. They were still stashed in the trunk of his Ford at the airport in Columbus, Ohio, and he didn't want anyone to find them. Tony also confirmed that there was no elaborate compromising of the Purolator security system. Ralph Marrera simply took the combination and unlocked the vault. Then Tony and Charlie walked in and cleaned it out. Marrera had been leading up to the big night for months, befuddling the Indian board monitor at Wells Fargo. He started by banging empty money carts against the vault door, causing the noise sensor to set off the alarm at Wells Fargo. Then, when the runner inquired, Marrera blandly told him that all was well. He gradually worked his way up to actually unlocking the vault, pulling the door open a crack — just enough to set off the alarm — and then shutting it and spinning the dial. Again, when the Wells Fargo man investigated, Marrera just shrugged his shoulders.

The game of crying wolf went on until, on the very night the thieves struck the vault, the Wells Fargo man didn't even bother to check.

One day not long after his recollections appeared in print Tony Marzano sat sipping white wine at a table in the chic Tamborine Restaurant on Chicago's East Chesnut Street, his back safely against a glass wall as he chatted amiably with *Tribune* reporter John O'Brien. Only a few short years earlier the Taylor Street truck driver and ex-convict would have received the tip of the doorman's boot, but suddenly Tony was a celebrity in his black velvet jacket and stylish matching ensemble.

"After the score Charlie and me, we took the dough to a basement over on the West Side and counted it," he explained, cigaret in hand. "I thought the score would be only a few million bucks. Well, I was riding high when the count went over three and a half million."

Chicago's ace television crime reporter, John "Bulldog" Drummond, asked Tony if he knew what happened to the still missing $1.2 million. "Hey," laughed Marzano innocently. "If I had a million and a half, do you think I'd be writing a book?"

The only member of the gang still in prison seven years after it all was Tony's cousin, Pasquale Charles Marzano, who, despite Tony's story placing both men in the vault, had waged a tireless legal battle to gain his freedom, still protesting his innocence.

In July, 1977, nearly three years after the theft, Judge Bauer, without comment, reduced Charlie's sentence from 20 to 15 years, making him eligible for parole as early as 1981. Officials of the federal penitentiary at Leavenworth had described the mastermind of the biggest cash caper in America as a "model inmate."

"He's one of our best-behaved and positively motivated residents," said a spokesman for Warden Charles L. Benson. "His first parole hearing is still several years away, but given his present attitude, I wouldn't be surprised if the board gives him every consideration and he makes it." Although Leavenworth housed 1900 felons at the time, Marzano was moved up to membership of a select 200 who shared "open style living quarters" in the Honor Dormitory. There the one-time Little League coach demonstrated his competitive ability by taking on the government through the law books. In 1979 the man, who federal authorities are convinced knows the whereabouts of the missing $1.2 million, performed a daring act of chutzpah and filed a petition in federal court seeking to be declared a pauper, so the court would have to pay for transcripts and other legal costs.

By his own count, Charlie Marzano has been to court more than 40 times since being sent away for the Purolator job. While felons with lesser gumption might have accepted their fate, Marzano loosed a flood of habeas corpus petitions, rehashing old legal arguments and raising new ones, all aimed at affecting his release. By August of 1978, Marzano had appeared in court so many times the federal government transferred him from Leavenworth to the Metropolitan Correctional Center in downtown Chicago, to save the cost of transporting him back and forth.

There, from a cell overloooking the Loop, he continued his battle within the system, filing document after document after document. Opposing federal lawyers, led by Julian Solotorovsky, found it all ironic and wasted effort. Because of his penal record, initially a good one, Marzano stood every chance of being released on parole by the end of 1981, and most likely in time for Christmas. But whether it was the mummy's curse or his own rugged nature, Marzano did not fare well back in Chicago, where jailers branded him a troublesome inmate, stripped him of visitor and telephone privileges, and tossed him into isolation. Again he took legal actions, this time against everyone from the warden on down with help from a dozen other prisoners he militantly organized. The inmate with the number 01862-164 would go down fighting if need be. And with only $52.94 in his prisoner savings account.

And what of Ralph Ronald Marrera? Psychiatrists said the dapper, west suburban dandy, once so well thought of by his male friends and popular with the girls, was little more than a vegetable — a prisoner of his own fogged mind. He sits in his chair, his head tilted to one side, his chin resting on his chest, and his eyes staring blankly. For a time federal agents staked out Marrera's home, hoping to catch him play-acting, and haul him off to court. They eventually set aside the vigil, unable to refute the opinion of the experts who said the one time inside man at Purolator was now completely mad, his own inside man, inside himself. He didn't even care about sex.

In a report to Judge Bauer, Dr. John W. Hanni, who made a psychiatric evaluation at the judge's request, said Marrera showed clear cut symptoms of "impaired function of the central nervous system and a diagnosis of organic brain syndrome." Marrera, he held, was disoriented, and referred to his wife Alberta as Sylvia, which was the name of his mother.

"He is completely unable to orient himself as to time and place," the report said. "He states that his memory is poor, and this is confirmed by direct questions, most of which he is unable to answer if the event being inquired about is more than a day or so in the past. As a matter of fact, tests of memory show that both recent and remote memory are grossly impaired. He remembers very little of his past.

"He does not know the President of the United States, nor the Governor of the State, and appears to be totally unaware of any current events.... He was unable to tell what religion he was raised in.

"All intellectual functions are grossly impaired. He is unable to read. As he puts it, 'I can see the word but I don't know what it means.' He can perform simple additions if they involve totals under 5 because he can count on his fingers.... He is unable to say the alphabet.

"He doesn't know what an air conditioner or a furnace is. He doesn't know what a garage is, or what it is used for, or what one puts in it. After being asked a number of questions he stated, 'I sound stupid,' and began to cry. A little later he said, 'I'm thinking how dumb I am I can't remember nothing.'

"His wife says that he cries frequently and on a daily basis.

"The patient is unable to walk without assistance. He is grossly apathetic and withdrawn. He initiates no social interaction whatsoever. He sits where he is placed, eats when the food is served to him, and will watch the television set when it is on, but it is apparent that he does not comprehend what is going on.

"He does not ask for anything except for assistance to go to the bathroom. His wife must help him with all of his personal hygiene. His entire day is spent either in bed, sitting on a couch, or sitting at the table for his meals. At one point, when I was talking with him, he said, 'What I like best is to sleep."

And could it be that sleeping in Ralph Marrera's fried brain is the secret of the missing $1.2 million?

The strain of caring for a full-grown man with the seeming mentality of a child may have proved too much for Marrera's family, and in 1979 he was placed in a nursing home on Chicago's West Diversey Parkway. When FBI agents made a routine inquiry of him in November of 1980, however, he was not there and they were unable to determine his whereabouts.

Of the $4,374,398.96 taken from the Purolator money warehouse in the derring-do venture of October 20, 1974, the still missing $1,213,043 remains the final mystery. "It is completely unaccounted for," Stratton said, from retirement in Oregon. "My hunch is that Charlie Marzano holds the key to the puzzle. The 'Marzano keeper theory,' I'd call it."

The "Marzano keeper theory" is quite simply this: After swinging by Marrera's grandmother's home to drop $1,454,140 into the hole that had already been prepared in the basement, Charlie dropped another chunk of the loot somewhere around Harlem Avenue, on the western edge of Cicero. He is known to have many relatives and friends out there. It could be that he has a million-dollar friend out there, someone he trusts to sit on the swag until he gets out of the cooler. It can be assumed it isn't in a bank. Not all of it, anyway. There are federal bank examiners and if $1.2 million showed up suddenly in somebody's account it could attract too much interest of the wrong kind.

According to Gushi, Charlie showed up alone at the "let's have breakfast" rendezvous alongside the tollway on the morning of the theft. He was driving the van containing the remainder of the money. DiFonzo and Tony Marzano arrived later in their own cars. So Charlie was alone with the loot and had ample opportunity to drop off a hefty sack of it without anyone knowing otherwise. The most likely possibility is that a treasure hole was prepared in more than one basement.

Thus could it be that somewhere out there on the western outskirts of Frank Sinatra's "My Kind of Town," lies $1,213,043 just waiting to be claimed and spent?

If you were a modern-day pirate... where would you hide that kind of treasure?

CHAPTER 32
Epilog

On Thursday, February 26, 1981, two canvas bags containing $1.2 million in cash fell from the back of a Purolator armored truck in Philadelphia. Before the armed guards were aware of what happened, two men scooped up the money and sped off.

"The doors just swung open and the money fell out," said police Lt. James Potocnak.

The cash, all in $100 bills, had been picked up at the Federal Reserve Bank downtown, and was being taken to the offices of Purolator Armored, Inc. The van was going through South Philadelphia when it hit a pothole and the rear doors, which were not locked, flew open. A yellow aluminum container on wheels rolled out of the truck and tumbled noisily into the street. The container, which was not locked, contained two white bags full of cash. A witness told police, "After the cart rolled out, it just sat in the street for a couple of minutes. Then a maroon car pulled up with two guys inside it. One of them got out and went over to the cart and picked up the bags. Then he got back into the car and they drove away, laughing like hell."

When the Purolator guards got to the Philadelphia money warehouse they pulled into the parking lot, walked around to the rear of their truck, and discovered the open doors flapping in the wind. They money cart was gone. They retraced their route, and when they got to the corner where the money had dropped out, they found the witness, pushing the empty cart off to the side of the road.

Some things never change.